AN 01-45HD-1

PILOT'S HANDBOOK

Navy Models

F4U-5, -5N, -5NL, -5P

AIRCRAFT

Schiffer Military/Aviation History
Atglen, PA

The U.S. Navy F4U-5, -5N, -5NL, -5P pilot's handbook used to print this book is from the collection of John M. Campbell.

The information in this book is true and complete to the best of our knowledge. All recommendations are made without any guarantee on the part of the author or publisher, who also disclaim any liability incurred in connection with the use of this data or specific details.

We recognize that some words, model names and designations, for example, mentioned herein are the property of the trademark holder. We use them for identification purposes only. This is not an official publication.

Cover photography from the John M. Campbell collection.

Library of Congress Catalog Number: 95-67632

Printed in China.
ISBN: 0-88740-821-4

Published by Schiffer Publishing Ltd.
77 Lower Valley Road
Atglen, PA 19310
Please write for a free catalog.
This book may be purchased from the publisher.
Please include $2.95 postage.
Try your bookstore first.

Pilot's Handbook

for

NAVY MODELS

F4U-5, -5N, -5NL, -5P AIRCRAFT

THIS PUBLICATION SUPERSEDES AN 01-45HD-1 DATED 1 JUNE 1950 REVISED 1 APRIL 1951

PUBLISHED UNDER AUTHORITY OF THE SECRETARY OF THE AIR FORCE AND THE CHIEF OF THE BUREAU OF AERONAUTICS

15 July 1951

Revised 1 June 1952

LIST OF REVISED PAGES ISSUED

INSERT LATEST REVISED PAGES. DESTROY SUPERSEDED PAGES.

NOTE: The portion of the text affected by the current revision is indicated by a vertical line in the outer margins of the page.

Page No.	Date of Latest Revision
*ii	1 June 1952
*1	1 June 1952
*5	1 June 1952
*18	1 June 1952
19	15 February 1952
24	15 February 1952
25	15 February 1952
*29	1 June 1952
*30	1 June 1952
36	15 February 1952
37	15 February 1952
48A	15 February 1952
48B	15 February 1952
*51	1 June 1952
*52	1 June 1952
*67	1 June 1952
*70	1 June 1952
*97	1 June 1952
98	15 February 1952
*99	1 June 1952
*101	1 June 1952

* The asterisk indicates pages revised, added or deleted by the current revision.

BuAer

ADDITIONAL COPIES OF THIS PUBLICATION MAY BE OBTAINED AS FOLLOWS:

USAF ACTIVITIES.—In accordance with Technical Order No. 00-5-2.

NAVY ACTIVITIES.—Submit request to nearest supply point listed below, using form NavAer-140; NASD, Philadelphia, Pa.; NAS, Alameda, Calif.; NAS, Jacksonville, Fla.; NAS, Norfolk, Va.; NAS, San Diego, Calif.; NAS, Seattle, Wash.; ASD, NSC, Guam.

For listing of available material and details of distribution see Naval Aeronautics Publications Index NavAer 00-500.

TABLE OF CONTENTS

Section I
DESCRIPTION

Section II
NORMAL OPERATING INSTRUCTIONS

Section III
EMERGENCY OPERATING INSTRUCTIONS

Section IV
OPERATIONAL EQUIPMENT

Appendix I

OPERATING CHARTS

Appendix II

NIGHT FIGHTER EQUIPMENT

Appendix III

PHOTOGRAPHIC EQUIPMENT

Appendix IV

WINTERIZATION EQUIPMENT

ILLUSTRATIONS

Figure 1-1. Model F4U-5 Airplane

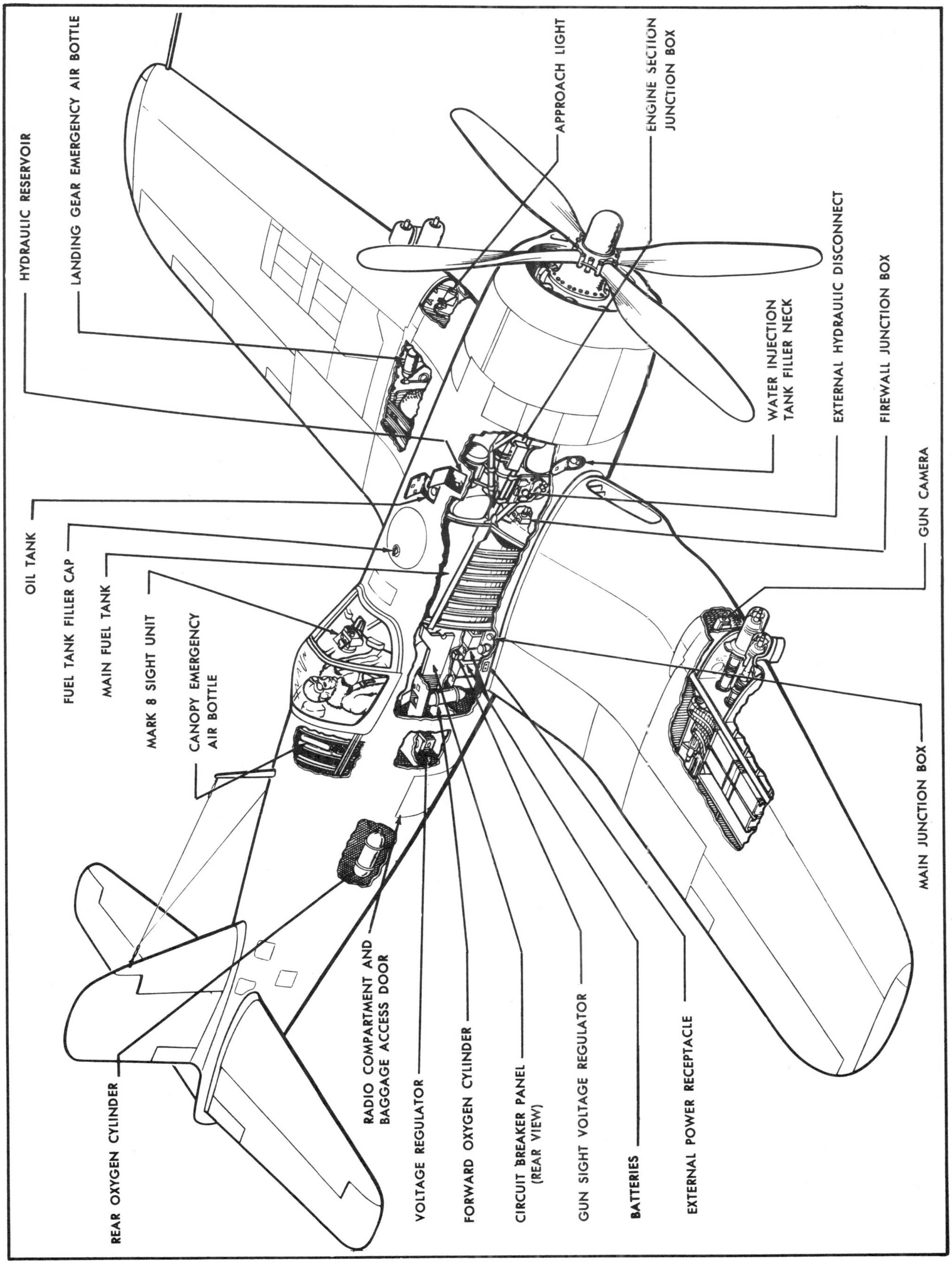

Figure 1-2. General Arrangement

Figure 1–3 Deleted

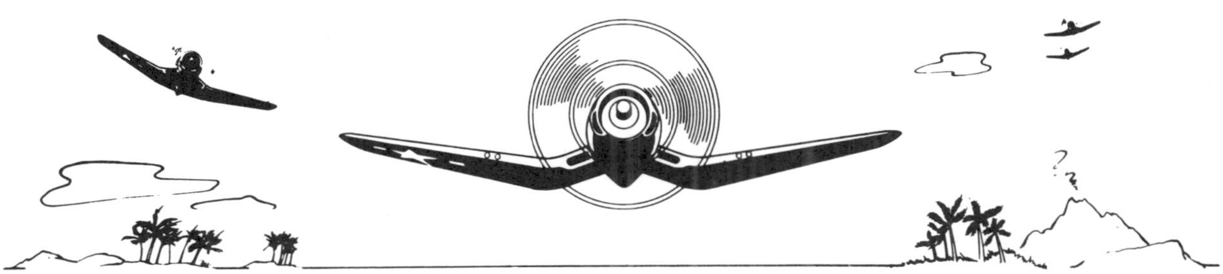

Section I

DESCRIPTION

MAIN DIFFERENCES — F4U SERIES AIRPLANES

MODEL DESIGNATION	F4U-1D, FG-1D	F4U-4	F4U-4B	F4U-5	F4U-5N, F4U-5NL	F4U-5P
EXTERNAL RECOGNITION FEATURES	 3-BLADED PROPELLER CIRCULAR ENGINE COWL TWIN PYLONS ON WING CENTER SECTION	 4-BLADED PROPELLER NON-CIRCULAR ENGINE COWL WITH AIR DUCT IN LOWER LIP TWIN PYLONS ON WING CENTER SECTION	 4-BLADED PROPELLER NON-CIRCULAR ENGINE COWL WITH AIR DUCT IN LOWER LIP TWIN PYLONS ON WING CENTER SECTION	 4-BLADED PROPELLER NON-CIRCULAR ENGINE COWL WITH AIR DUCTS ON LOWER HALF OF EACH SIDE TWIN PYLONS ON WING CENTER SECTION CENTERLINE PYLON	 F4U-5 FEATURES RADAR NACELLE ON RIGHT WING F4U-5NL CONTAINS DEICING EQUIPMENT	 F4U-5P FEATURES COMPASS TRANS. IN FIN. CAMERA DOORS IN AFT FUSELAGE
COCKPIT		REARRANGED TO CONSOLE TYPE	REARRANGED TO CONSOLE TYPE	REARRANGED IN ACCORDANCE WITH LATEST NAVY CONCEPTS	REARRANGED IN ACCORDANCE WITH LATEST NAVY CONCEPTS	REARRANGED IN ACCORDANCE WITH LATEST NAVY CONCEPTS
ENGINE MODEL	R-2800-8W	R-2800-18W OR R-2800-42W	R-2800-18W OR R-2800-42W	R-2800-32W	R-2800-32W	R-2800-32W
MAXIMUM ARMAMENT*	6—.50 CAL. MACH. GUNS 2400 ROUNDS OF AMM. 8—5-INCH ROCKETS 2—1000 LB. BOMBS	6—.50 CAL. MACH. GUNS 2400 ROUNDS OF AMM. 8—5-INCH ROCKETS 2—1000 LB. BOMBS OR 2—11. 75" ROCKETS	4—20 MM. CANNONS 924 ROUNDS OF AMM. 8—5-INCH ROCKETS 2—1000 LB. BOMBS OR 2—11. 75" ROCKETS	4—20 MM. CANNONS 924 ROUNDS OF AMM. 8—5-INCH ROCKETS 1—2000 LB. BOMB (CENTERLINE PYLON ONLY) 2—1000 LB. BOMBS 2—11. 75" ROCKETS	4—20 MM. CANNONS 924 ROUNDS OF AMM. 8—5-INCH ROCKETS 1—2000 LB. BOMB (CENTERLINE PYLON ONLY) 2—1000 LB. BOMBS 2—11. 75" ROCKETS	4—20 MM. CANNONS 924 ROUNDS OF AMM. 8—5-INCH ROCKETS 1—2000 LB. BOMB (CENTERLINE PYLON ONLY) 2—1000 LB. BOMBS 2—11. 75" ROCKETS
MAXIMUM FUEL CARRYING CAPACITY	MAIN FUEL TANK.......237 GALS. THREE DROP TANKS....510 GALS.	MAIN FUEL TANK.......233 GALS. TWO DROP TANKS.....300 GALS.	MAIN FUEL TANK.......233 GALS. TWO DROP TANKS.....300 GALS.	MAIN FUEL TANK.......234 GALS. TWO DROP TANKS.....300 GALS.	MAIN FUEL TANK.......234 GALS. TWO DROP TANKS.....300 GALS.	MAIN FUEL TANK.......234 GALS. TWO DROP TANKS.....300 GALS.
NORMAL GROSS WEIGHT	12000 LBS.	12500 LBS.	12400 LBS.	12,900 LBS.	13,800 LBS.	13000 LBS.

*NOT NECESSARILY CARRIED SIMULTANEOUSLY

1–1. THE AIRPLANE.

1–2. GENERAL. The Chance Vought F4U-5 airplane is a single-engine, single-seat, low-wing monoplane, designed as a carrier-based and land-based fighter. It will be recognized immediately as a member of the F4U Corsair fighter series by its characteristic "inverted gull wing." The main external features which differentiate it from previous modifications of the Model F4U airplane are itemized in the above table. It is equipped for operation as a long range fighter when carrying external auxiliary fuel tanks, or as a fighter-bomber when carrying bombs on the external pylons. The airplane carries four M3 (T-31) 20-mm guns, with further provision for eight 5-inch wing rockets and two 11.75-inch rockets. The approximate gross weight is 12,900 pounds with full ammunition load and full main fuel tank but no external load. The approximate over-all dimensions are:

Length	34½ ft.
Height	13 ft.
Span	41 ft.
Height (with wings folded)	16 ft.

The airplane is powered by a Pratt & Whitney Double Wasp engine (Model R-2800-32W) with an automatically controlled two-stage, variable-speed supercharger and a propeller speed to engine speed ratio of 0.450 to 1. The Hamilton Standard Hydromatic propeller has four aluminum alloy blades (6837A-0), hub (24E60-159); diameter, 13 feet 2 inches; low pitch stop 27 degrees, high pitch stop, 65 degrees.

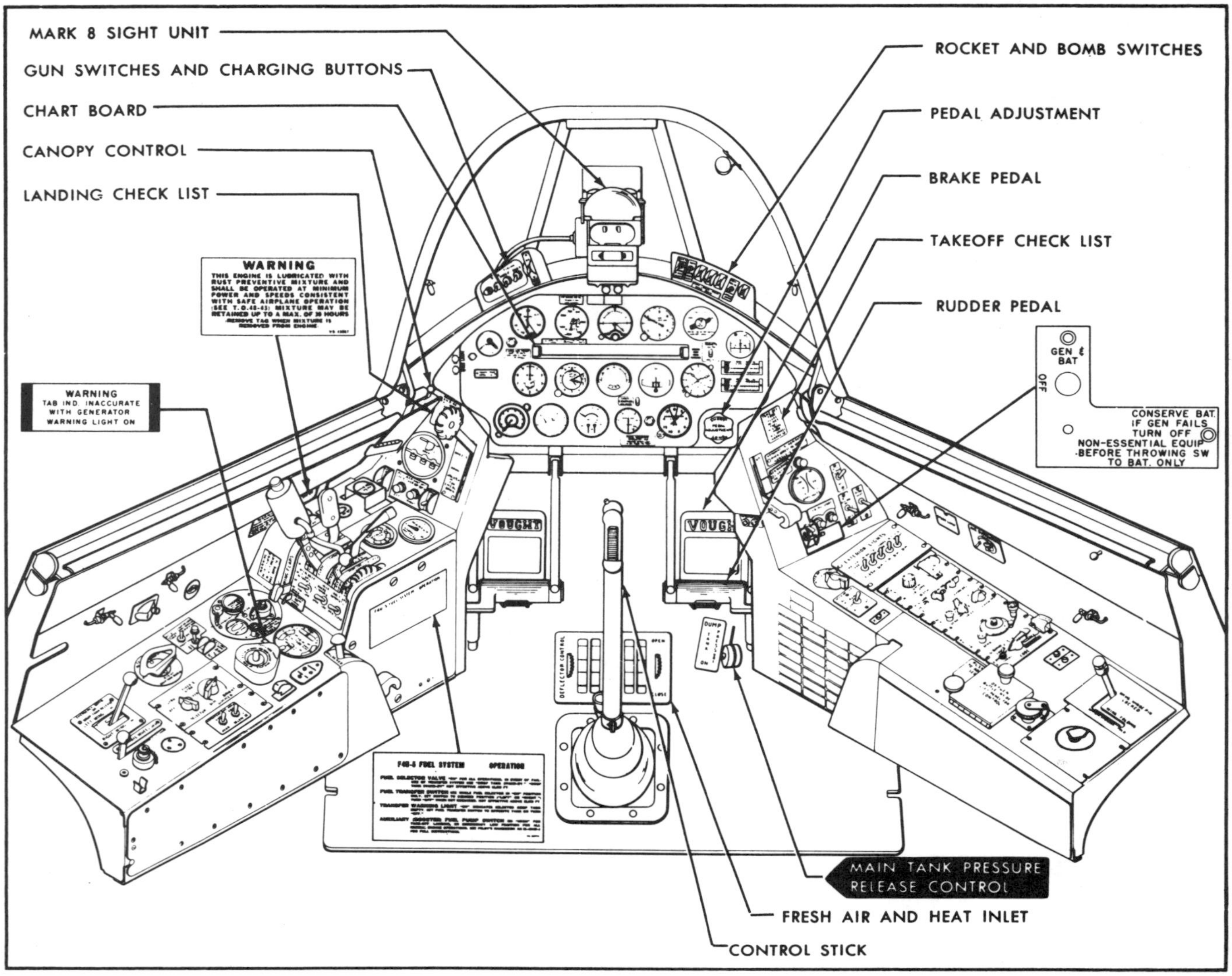

Figure 1-4. Cockpit, Forward View

1–3. FLIGHT CONTROLS.

1–4. SURFACE CONTROLS. Location and operation of ailerons, elevators and rudder are conventional with stick and pedal control. A pistol grip handle on the control stick contains three electrical switches which operate the gun, bomb release, and rocket firing circuits.

1–5. RUDDER PEDALS. The rudder pedals are of the hanging type with a 6-inch fore and aft adjustment. They can be locked in any intermediate position within the adjusting range by turning the easily reached knob on the right side of the instrument panel (see figure 1–8). Both pedals are adjusted in unison to assure their automatic alignment. When folded aft, the pedals expose a cushioned surface which affords the pilot a leg rest which he can use during long flights.

1–6. SURFACE CONTROL LOCK. The surface control lock is a welded steel tube assembly, the forward part of which secures the rudder pedals in neutral (see figure 1–9). The aft section consists of two U-shaped tubes, one above the other, which secure the control stick in neutral (see paragraph 2–100 for instructions on installing the control lock).

1–7. TABS. The tabs on the control surfaces consist of balance tabs on each aileron, a trim tab on the left aileron, and combination spring and trim tabs on the rudder and elevators. The aileron balance tabs are deflected automatically in a direction opposite to that of the ailerons when the ailerons are deflected. This reduces the stick forces required to operate the ailerons. The spring feature in the combination spring-trim tab on the rudder and elevators causes the tab to be deflected automatically when loads on those surfaces become excessive. This automatic deflection of the spring tab reduces the control forces.

1–8. The trim tabs are operated electrically and controlled by seven toggle switches (see figure 1-10). The three-position "LEFT–NOSE–RIGHT" toggle operates the rudder trim tab. The five-position "NOSE UP–LEFT WING DOWN–NOSE DOWN–RIGHT WING

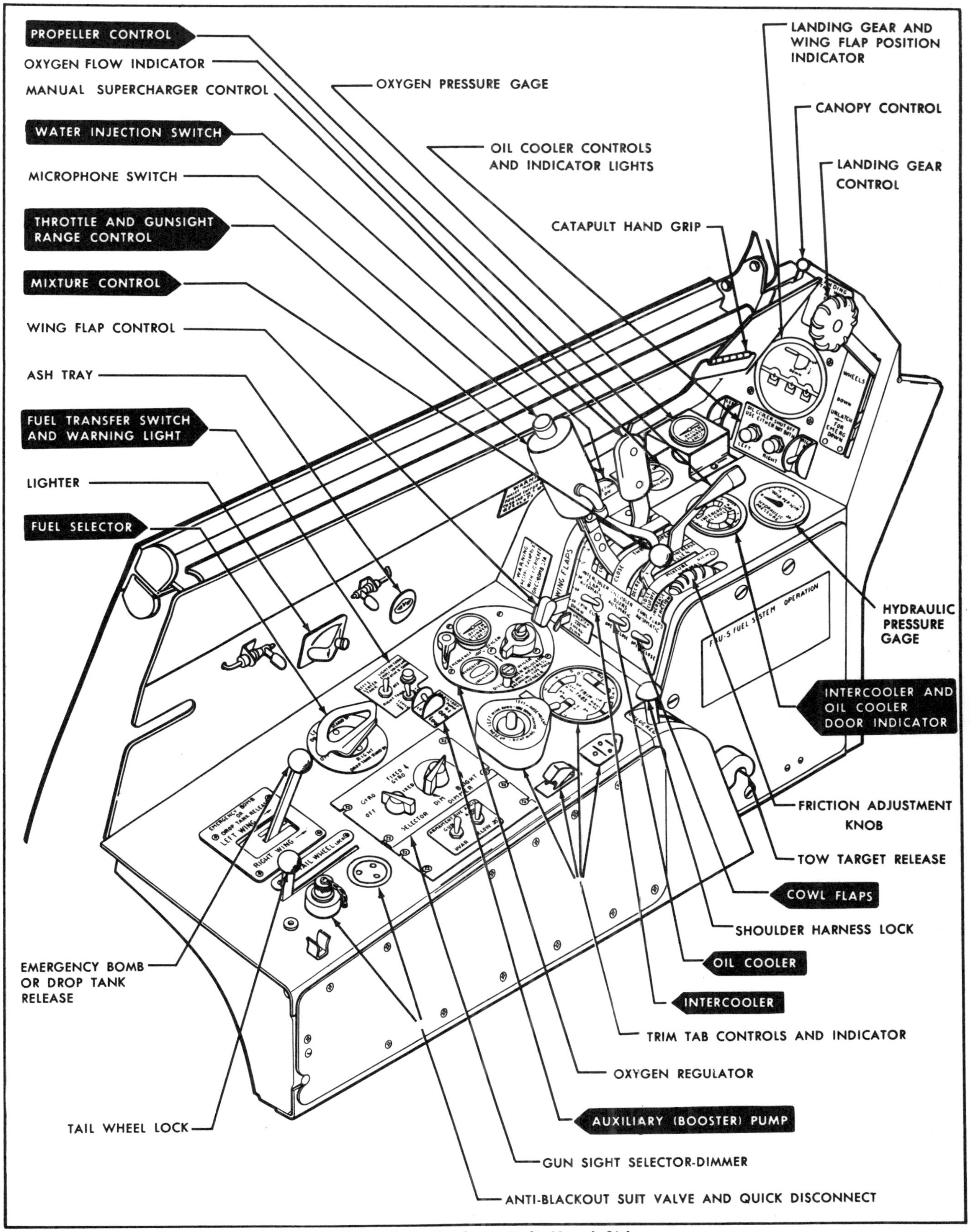

Figure 1-5. Cockpit, Left Hand Side

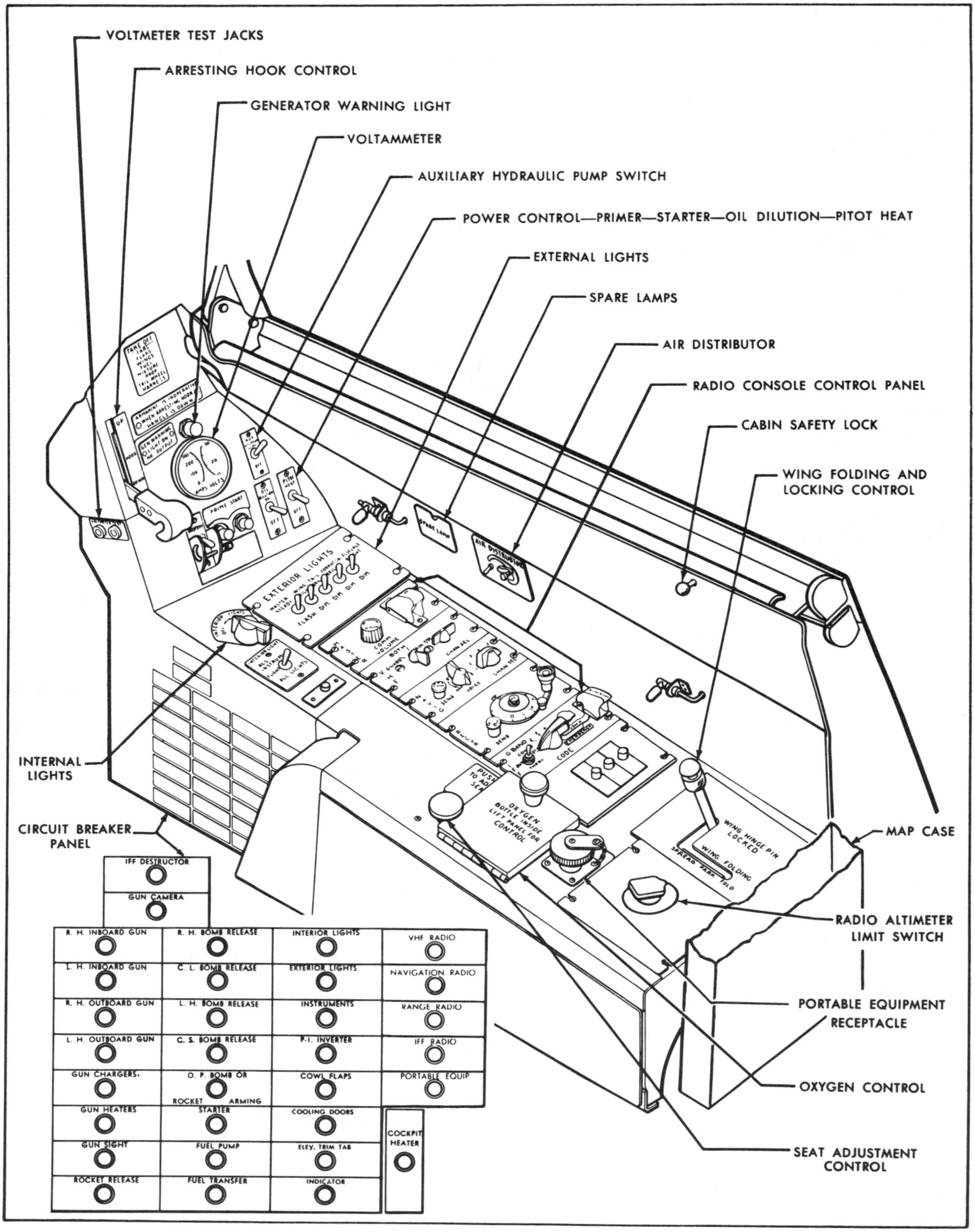

Figure 1-6. Cockpit, Right Hand Side

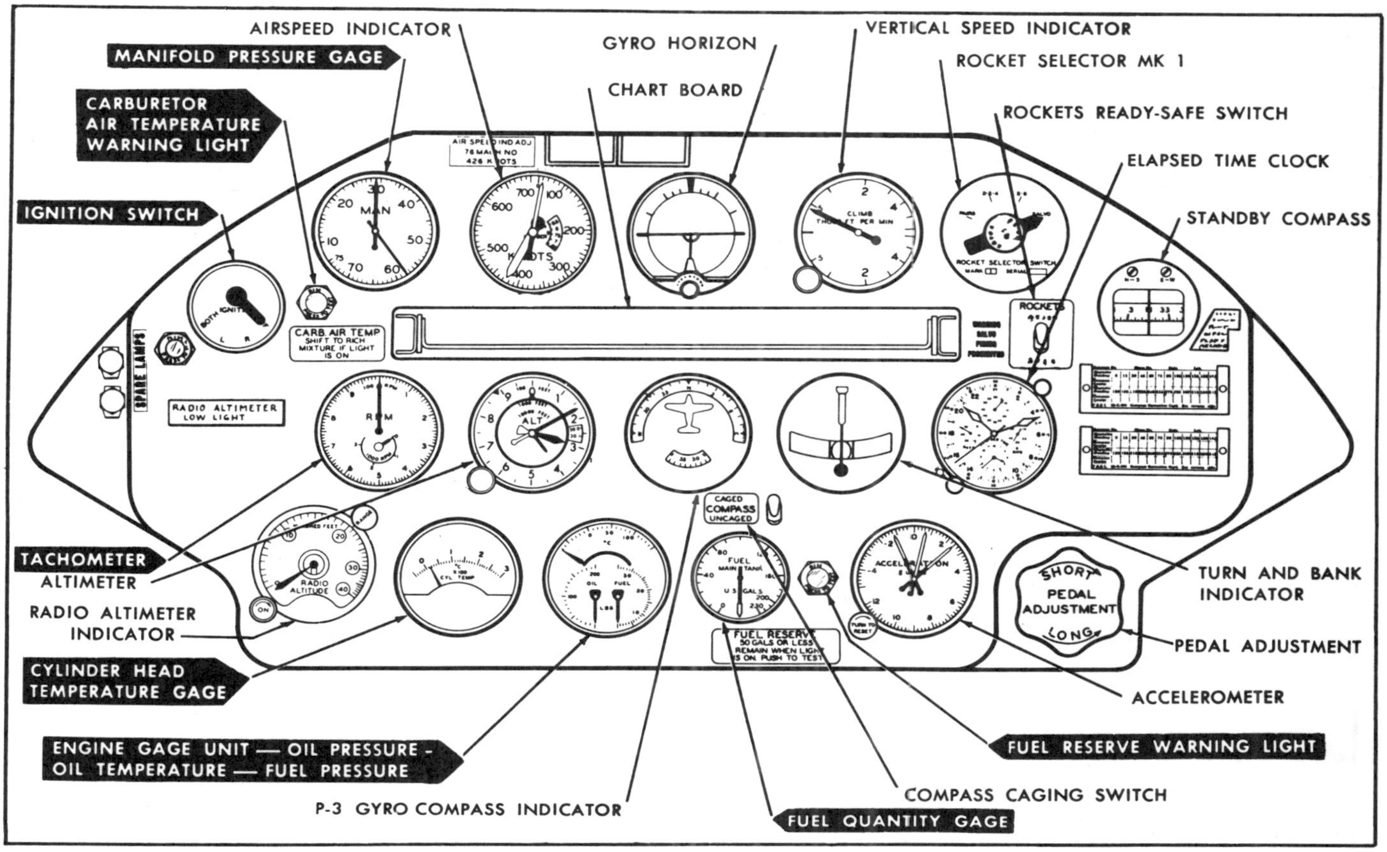

Figure 1–7. Instrument Panel

DOWN–OFF" toggle operates the aileron and elevator trim tabs. These two switches are contained in a composite control and are used for normal operation of the trim tabs. The other five switches are used for emergency override operation of the trim tabs.

WARNING

Tab indication is inaccurate if generator warning light is "ON."

1–9. WING FLAPS. The wing flap control mechanism operating the center section and outer panel flaps is designed so that the flaps can be lowered hydraulically from the full up position of zero degrees to the full down position of 50 degrees in 10-degree steps.

CAUTION

The flaps must not be extended more than 30 degrees when 11.75-inch rockets are carried on the center section pylons.

The flap control handle is located on the left-hand control panel outboard of the engine control unit (see figure 1–12). The flap position is indicated on the flap control housing as well as on the electrically actuated landing gear and flap position indicator on the inclined portion of the left-hand control shelf.

1–10. EMERGENCY WING FLAP CONTROL. Emergency extension of the flaps is effected by placing the flap control handle in its extreme down or "EMERGENCY DOWN" position. The handle cannot be placed in this position without displacing the latch which normally restricts handle movement to the normal down position. Placing the wing flap control handle in the "EMERGENCY DOWN" position throws a switch which energizes a solenoid shut-off valve isolating the flap system from the other hydraulic sub-systems. It also starts the electrically driven auxiliary hydraulic pump which provides pressure directly to the wing flap selector valve to lower the flaps. The normal hydraulic system fluid supply is taken from a standpipe in the hydraulic reservoir. The auxiliary pump which provides 1,500 (± 100) psi pressure takes fluid from the bottom of the tank. Thus in the event of hydraulic system leak and subsequent fluid loss there will be enough fluid left in the reservoir to permit one emergency operation of the flaps.

1–11. The operation of the emergency flap system should be checked before each flight as follows:

a. Power control switch on or external electric power source connected.

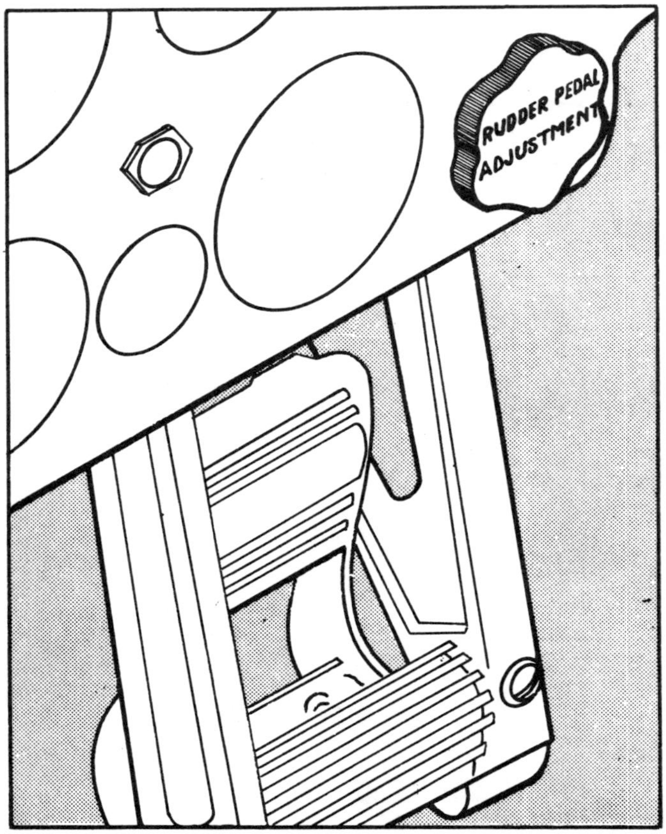

Figure 1-8. Rudder Pedal Adjustment Control

b. Relieve hydraulic system pressure by operating one of the sub-systems (such as the canopy).

c. Place the wing flap control handle in the "EMERGENCY DOWN" position. Check flap position indicator that flaps are fully extended and check hydraulic system pressure gage that main system pressure remains at zero. If the gage shows pressure in the main system, it indicates that the solenoid shut-off valve, isolating the flap system from the rest of the hydraulic system during emergency flap operation, is not functioning properly.

d. Return flap control handle to the "UP" position. The flaps will retract when the engine is started.

1–12. The wing flap system includes a mechanism which causes the flaps to "blow up" or return to the up position from the angle set by the cockpit control when excessive air loads are imposed upon the surfaces. The flaps will remain in the blown-up position until the air speed is reduced when they will return to their preset position. The mechanism is set so that with the flaps full down (50 degrees) and power on for level flight, the flaps will begin to "blow up" between 100 to 115 knots indicated air speed. At lesser flap settings, the blow-up speeds will be greater than that with the flaps full down (see figure 2–1 for flap down speed restrictions with flap blow-up mechanism inoperative).

1–13. DIVE BRAKE. The landing gear may be used as a dive brake in accordance with instructions contained in paragraph 2–82.

1–14. POWER PLANT CONTROLS.

1–15. DESCRIPTION. The power plant controls are located conveniently in two logical groups in the cockpit (see figure 1–11). The throttle, propeller, and mixture controls, master water injection switch, cowl flaps, intercooler flap, and oil cooler door switches comprise one group on the left-hand control shelf. The oil dilution, primer, and starter switches comprise the other, located at the base of the inclined section of the right-hand control shelf. The ignition switch and the carburetor air temperature warning light are located on the left side of the main instrument panel.

Note

An additional lever, located outboard of the throttle in some engine control units (airplanes Bureau Serial No. 121793 through 122066 and 122153 through 122206), is inoperative and has been locked in its foremost position. The lever will be omitted from future engine control units.

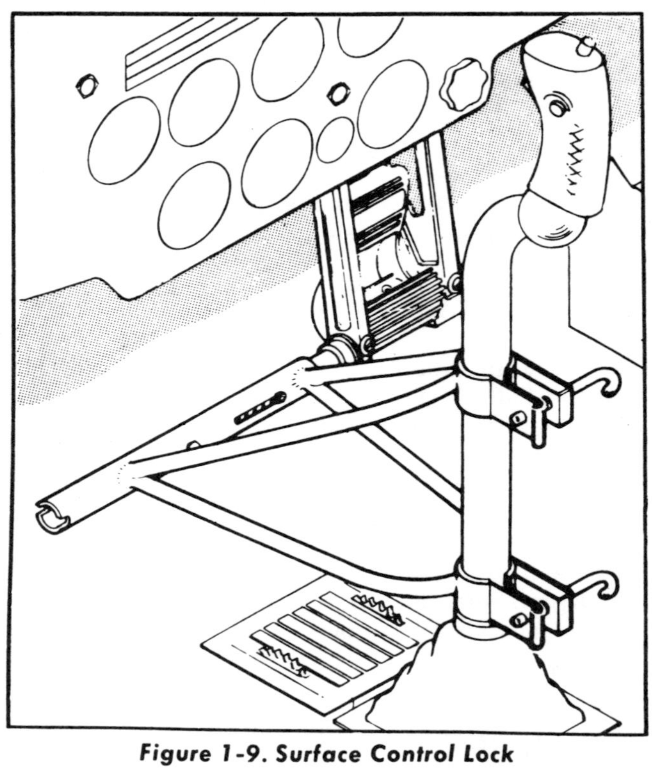

Figure 1-9. Surface Control Lock

1-16. THROTTLE CONTROL. The throttle control is part of the engine control group located on the left-hand control shelf. An automatic manifold pressure regulator is linked to the throttle, to the dual auxiliary stage blower oil selector valve, and to the carburetor. This regulator operates and correlates the carburetor throttle with the supercharger impeller drive coupling oil selector valve which is an integral part of the regulator. The regulator maintains constant manifold pressure within limitations for any position of the pilot's throttle control regardless of change in altitude or engine rpm by regulating the throttle at the carburetor and the dual auxiliary stage supercharger speed.

Note

The installation of a bleed air valve which dumps excess engine air overboard before reaching the carburetor has reduced somewhat the tendency for the engine to surge. Surge, however, will still be encountered in the cruise range at intermediate and high altitudes, the onset of surge varying widely between airplanes. The range of rpm's and manifold pressures at which surging will occur will increase as altitude is increased. At 40,000 ft. and above, it may not be possible to use less than 2,400 rpm without encountering surge. For instructions on how to eliminate surge, refer to paragraphs 2-65 and 2-66 or to the Power Plant Chart (figure A-4).

1-17. MIXTURE CONTROL. The mixture control lever has three positions "RICH," "NORMAL," and "IDLE CUT-OFF" which are marked plainly on the face of the engine control unit (see figure 1-11). The R-2800-32W engine is equipped with an updraft injection carburetor with automatic mixture control. Both the "RICH" and the "NORMAL" positions are com-

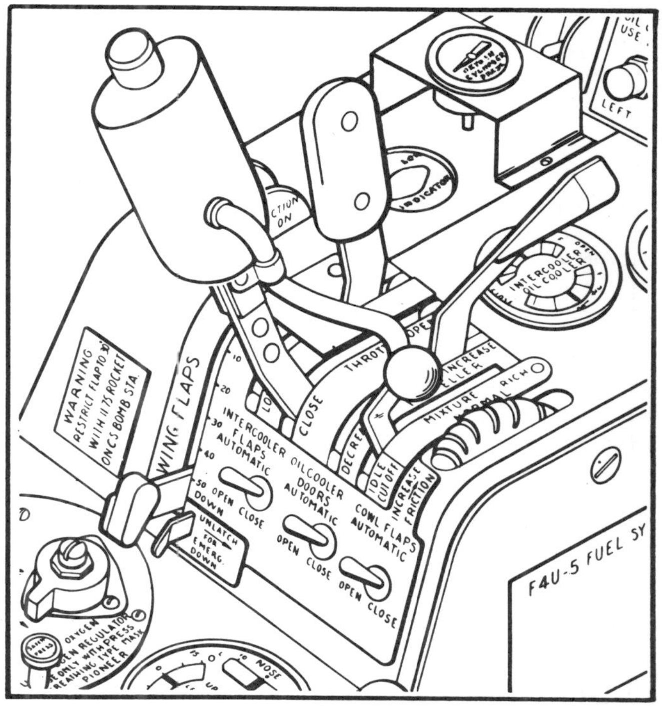

Figure 1-11. Power Plant Controls

pensated for altitude and temperature. The mixture control lever positions are to be used in operation of the carburetor as follows:

a. "RICH"—This position is to be used for taxiing, all other ground operations, take-off, and carrier approach.

b. "NORMAL"—This position may be used for all power conditions in flight, up to and including combat power, providing cooling is adequate. If cooling is not sufficient, the "RICH" position must be used.

c. "IDLE CUT-OFF"—This position will stop completely all fuel flow from the carburetor, regardless of fuel pressure, throttle position, or engine speed. Fuel will be discharged from the carburetor at any fuel pressure above 10 pounds per square inch when the mixture control is not in the "IDLE CUT-OFF" position. Therefore, THE MIXTURE CONTROL SHALL ALWAYS BE LEFT IN "IDLE CUT-OFF" WHENEVER THE ENGINE IS NOT RUNNING, TO PREVENT FLOODING OF THE ENGINE THROUGH INADVERTENT USE OF THE AUXILIARY (BOOSTER) FUEL PUMP.

Note

When adjusting the mixture control to the "NORMAL" position, make sure the control is set properly by feeling for the "notch" in the carburetor which indicates correct positioning of the carburetor lever.

1-18. PROPELLER GOVERNOR CONTROL. The propeller governor control is located next to the throttle on the engine control unit (see figure 1-11). Operation of the control is the conventional forward to "IN-

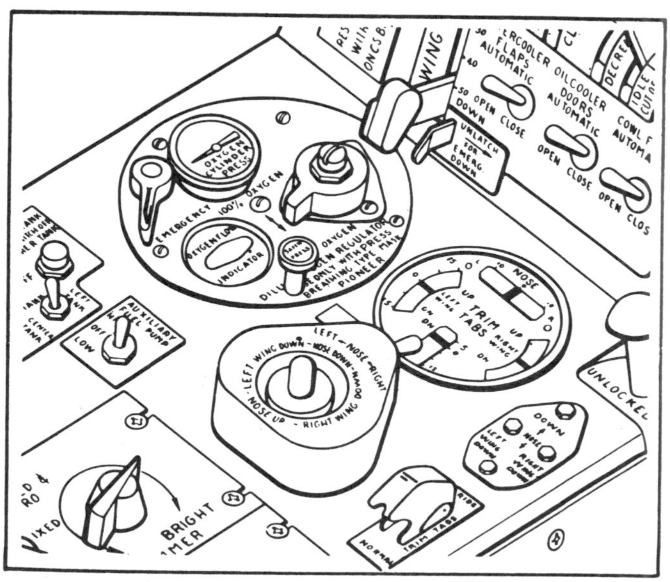

Figure 1-10. Trim Tab Controller

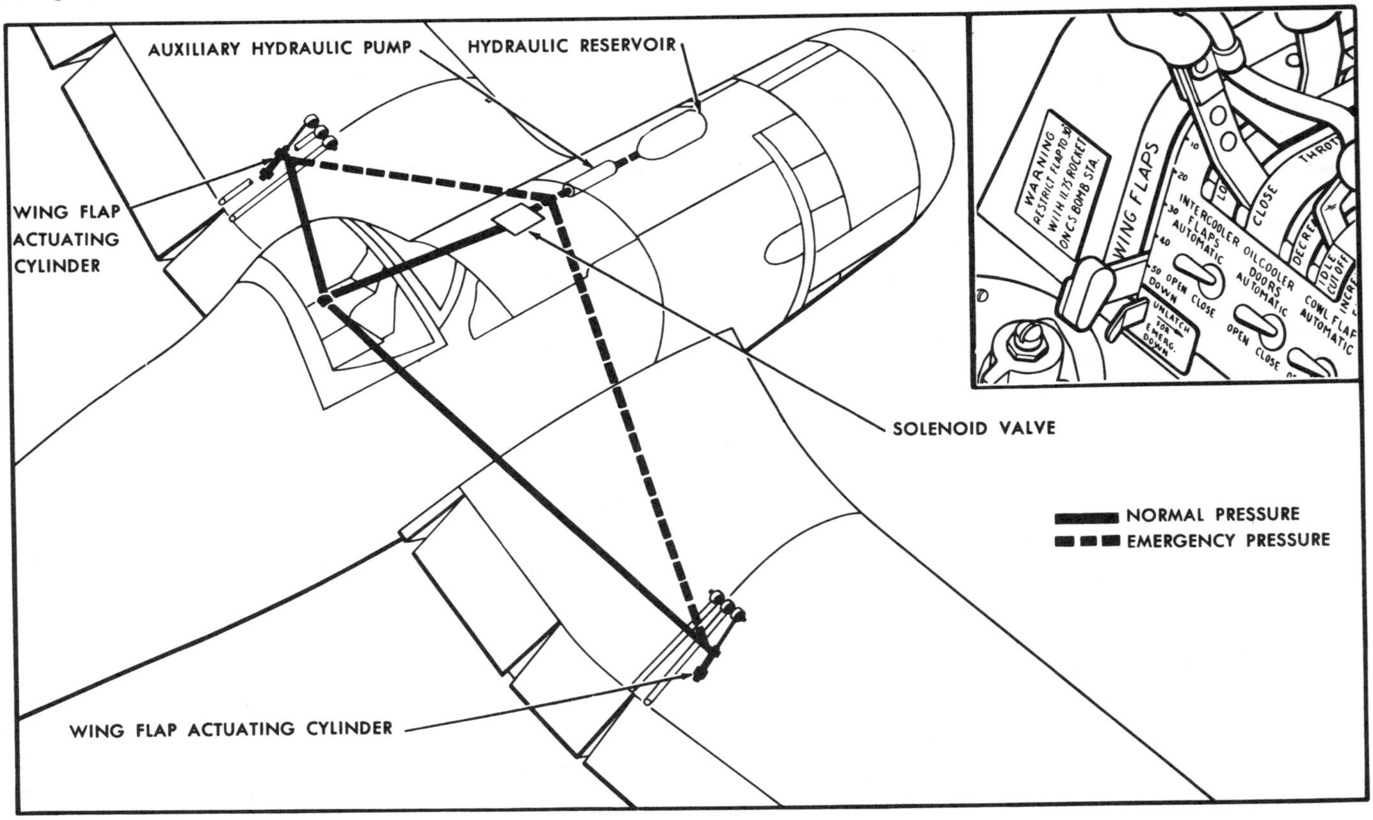

Figure 1-12. Wing Flap Control Hydraulic System Diagram

CREASE" and aft to "DECREASE" rpm. In the full forward position the governor is set at full take-off rpm (2800). In the full aft position the governor will hold engine speed to approximately 1200 rpm.

1–19. MASTER WATER INJECTION SWITCH. The master water injection switch is located on the left-hand control shelf just outboard of the throttle control (see figure 1–11). It has two positions, "ON" and "OFF." The water injection system cannot operate unless the master switch is turned to the "ON" position.

1–20. COWL FLAP CONTROL. The cowl flap switch is located on the left-hand control shelf just aft of the engine control unit. (See figure 1–5.) The cowl flap controls consist of this four-position switch, a microswitch actuated by the propeller governor control lever below 2300 rpm, an override switch on the landing gear, a controller box, an electric cowl flap motor, and a thermocouple. The cowl flap switch has fixed "AUTOMATIC" and "OFF" positions and momentary "OPEN" and "CLOSE" positions. When the switch is in "AUTOMATIC," the controller at fuselage station 230 and the propeller-governor-actuated microswitch in the engine-control unit govern the position of the cowl flaps. The controller box energizes the cowl flap motor to open and close the cowl flaps in response to cylinder head temperatures transmitted by thermocouples located in the No. 2 engine cylinder. Cylinder head temperature is maintained below an operating limit of 248°C. At 2300 rpm or less, the propeller-governor-actuated microswitch sets the controller to a lower operating range, permitting the cowl flaps to control the temperature below 232°C. A second microswitch, located on the left landing gear scissors, overides the automatic operation and causes the cowl flaps to open fully for adequate engine cooling when the airplane is on the ground. All the automatic controls (cylinder head temperature, propeller control microswitch, and landing gear microswitch) can be overridden by placing the cowl flap control switch in the "OPEN" or "CLOSE" positions, thus directly energizing the cowl flap motor to open or close the flaps.

1–21. INTERCOOLER FLAP CONTROL. The intercooler switch is located on the left-hand control shelf just aft of the engine control unit (see figure 1–5). The switch has four positions, "AUTOMATIC," "OFF," "OPEN," and "CLOSE." When the switch is set to the "AUTOMATIC" position, the position of the intercooler flap is automatically controlled by a pressure switch which is sensitive to the pressure differential across the cooling air side of the intercooler. The pressure switch is connected electrically to a solenoid valve which causes the intercooler flap hydraulic actuating cylinder to extend or retract. The automatic operation of the flap can be overridden by placing the switch in either the "OPEN" or "CLOSE" position. These positions should be used only when the automatic action fails. The switch should be left in "AUTOMATIC" for all normal operation. The intercooler flap electrical circuit is also designed so that the flap closes whenever the engine is governed below 2300 rpm. The position of the flap is shown by an indicator on the left-hand control shelf just forward of the engine control levers.

1-22. The intercooler flaps will move automatically to the following approximate settings:

a. Normal climb or normal maneuvers — one-half open.

b. Severe operating conditions and maneuvers at low speeds — full open.

c. Level flight and high speed cruise — fully closed.

The above settings are to be set manually with the control switch in the event the automatic actions fails.

Note

When the centerline pylon is installed, the intercooler flap cannot be opened fully so that there may be some reduction in available intercooling. This may necessitate a reduction in power during climbs at altitude and/or an increase in air speed.

1-23. CARBURETOR AIR TEMPERATURE WARNING LIGHT. A warning light on the left-hand side of the main instrument panel (see figure 1-7) indicates when the average carburetor air temperature exceeds the maximum allowable limit of 43°C. Carburetor air temperature warning light operation can be checked by pushing the light to test the bulb. If the airplane is on the ground, engine not running, the power control switch or the external electric power source must be on when testing the light. Operating the engine at high power with excessively high carburetor air temperatures can cause detonation and serious damage to the engine except when operating at combat power.

Note

When operating at combat power (water injection system on) the carburetor air temperature warning light may be on without danger of detonation.

1-24. The carburetor air temperature is controlled by the position of the intercooler flap. The flap has an automatic control which is designed to provide adequate cooling of the engine air for all normal operating conditions. The intercooler flap can also be set manually to the open or closed position, in the event the automatic action fails.

Note

Should the warning light come on in flight, immediately shift the mixture control handle to the "RICH" position. If at low speed, shift the mixture control to "RICH" and immediately open the intercooler flap wide by turning the intercooler flap switch to the "OPEN" position. Note also that when the centerline pylon is installed, it may be necessary to reduce power somewhat in addition to opening the intercooler flap as far as possible.

1-25. OIL COOLER DOOR CONTROL. The oil cooler door switch is located on the left-hand control shelf aft of the engine control unit (see figure 1-5). It is a toggle switch with "AUTOMATIC," "OFF," "OPEN," and "CLOSE" positions. When the switch is set to "AUTOMATIC," the position for all normal engine operation, the oil cooler doors are opened and closed by hydraulic actuating cylinders, the operation of which is controlled by a thermostat. The doors are opened when the oil being returned to the tanks reaches a temperature of 75°C. The doors reach their full open position at 95°C. The doors can be opened or closed manually by placing the control switch in the "OPEN" or "CLOSE" position. The position of the oil cooler doors is shown on an indicator on the left-hand control shelf just forward of the engine control unit.

1-26. IGNITION SWITCH. The ignition switch is located on the left-hand side of the instrument panel (see figure 1-7). It has four positions, "L," "R," "BOTH," and "OFF."

1-27. STARTING SWITCHES. The electric starter switch and the primer switch are located at the base of the inclined section of the right-hand control shelf (see figure 1-17). They are push button momentary contact switches with spring return.

1-28. OIL DILUTION SWITCH. The oil dilution switch is located next to the starter switch. It has an "OFF" and momentary "ON" position. See paragraph 2-97 for oil dilution procedure.

1-29. FUEL SYSTEM.

1-30. FUEL. Grade 115/145; grade 100/130 may be used, subject to the limitations contained in figure A-4, Power Plant Chart.

1-31. DESCRIPTION. For management of the fuel system, refer to paragraphs 2-8 through 2-19. The fuel system (see Fuel System Diagram, figure 1-13) consists of the main fuel cell, and the following pilot-operated controls: tank selector valve control, auxiliary (booster) fuel pump switch, fuel transfer pump switch, the normal and emergency external auxiliary fuel tank jettison control, and a fuel tank pressure relief control. Fuel pressure is provided by an engine-driven fuel pump

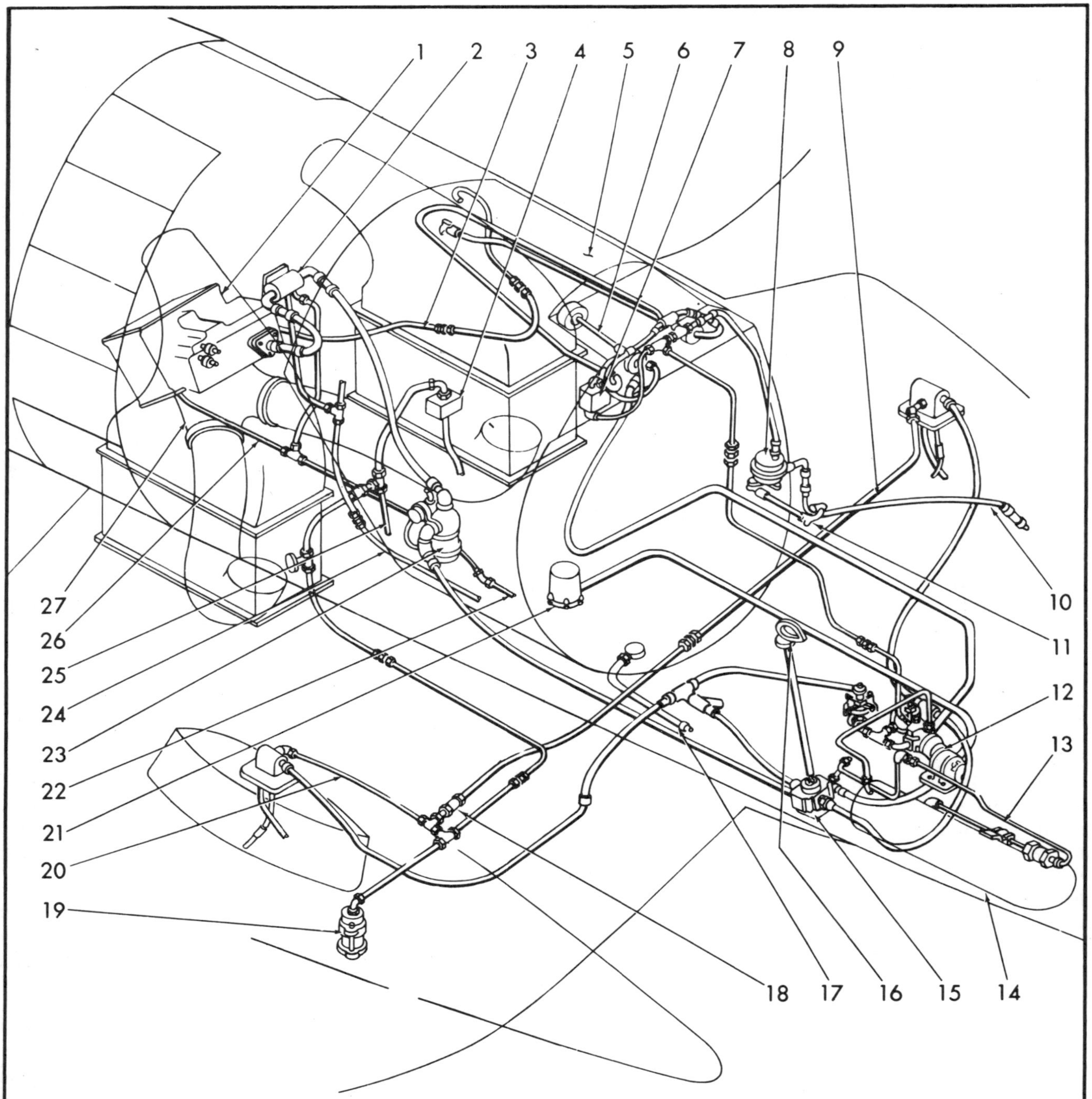

1. Carburetor
2. Engine-driven Fuel Pump
3. Vapor Return Line
4. Centerline Tank Pressure and Vacuum Relief Valve
5. Main Fuel Cell
6. Shut-off Float Valve
7. Fuel Transfer Indicator Pressure Switch
8. Relief Check Valve
9. R. H. External Tank Pressure Line
10. Main Cell Vent Line
11. Main Cell Pressure Dump Control
12. Fuel Transfer Pump
13. Heater Fuel Line
14. Cockpit Heater
15. Fuel Selector Valve
16. Fuel Selector Control Handle
17. Centerline External Tank Fuel Line
18. Check Valve
19. L. H. and R. H. Pressure and Vacuum Relief Valve
20. L. H. External Tank Pressure Line
21. Auxiliary (Booster) Fuel Pump
22. Line to Pressure Gage
23. Fuel Strainer
24. Seal Drain Line
25. Centerline External Tank Pressure Line
26. Balance Line
27. Carburetor Air Box

Figure 1-13. Fuel System Description Diagram

supplemented by an electrically driven submerged auxiliary pump. Fuel transfer pressure is provided by an electrically driven fuel transfer pump.

1–32. Fuel system gages and warning lights in the cockpit include a fuel quantity gage, a fuel pressure gage (part of the engine gage unit) and a fuel reserve warning light (which lights when 50 gallons or less remain in the main cell) on the main instrument panel. The fuel transfer warning light, which lights when the transfer switch is on and the external auxiliary tank being used is empty, is located on the left-hand control shelf adjacent to the fuel transfer switch. (See figures 1–5 and 1–7.)

1–33. FUEL TANKS.

1–34. MAIN FUEL CELL. The main fuel cell is a self-sealing cell with a capacity of 234 U. S. gallons. It is located in the fuselage between the firewall and the forward bulkhead of the cockpit. Fuel quantity in the main cell is measured by a liquidometer installation within the cell which transmits readings to the quantity gage on the instrument panel. A vapor return line from the carburetor enters the cell at the top of the forward side.

1–35. EXTERNAL AUXILIARY TANKS. Provision is made for carrying 150-gallon Mk. 5, Mod. 4, or Mk. 12 external auxiliary fuel tanks on the left and right center section pylons and the centerline pylon. Two tanks can be carried in combination on either the left- or right-hand pylons or on the centerline and right-hand pylons. Tanks cannot be carried on the left and centerline pylons simultaneously. Total fuel which can be carried in the main cell and auxiliary tanks is 534 U. S. gallons.

1–36. PRESSURIZING. Potential high altitude boiling of fuel in the main cell and resultant fuel loss are minimized by pressurizing the cell. An automatic check relief valve in the overboard line from the main fuel cell vent line remains open under 18,000 feet and closes above that altitude so that the cell pressurizes itself as the fuel vaporizes. This valve relieves at 2.5 psi maximum pressure. A vacuum relief valve on top of the main cell relieves the vacuum side which results from a rapid loss of altitude. There is a manual tank pressure release control on the cockpit floor so that the pilot can dump fuel tank pressure before going into combat. When the control is operated, the fuel system is vented to the atmosphere, minimizing the damage which might occur under gunfire. All three external auxiliary tanks can be pressurized to approximately 4 psi. The pressurizing line is tapped into the auxiliary stage of the engine supercharger. Tank pressure is regulated by two check relief valves which allow transfer of fuel up to altitudes of 35,000 feet.

1–37. CONTROLS.

1–38. FUEL SELECTOR VALVE. The fuel selector valve, located on the left-hand control shelf, has four operating positions, "ON," "OFF," "RIGHT DROP TANK STAND-BY," and "LEFT OR CENTER DROP TANK STAND-BY" (see figure 2–3). *The "STAND-BY" positions are emergency positions only.*

1–39. AUXILIARY (BOOSTER) FUEL PUMP SWITCH. The auxiliary fuel pump, submerged in the main fuel cell, is operated by a 3-position switch located on the left-hand shelf (see figure 1–5). The positions of the switch are, "HIGH," "LOW," and "OFF."

1–40. FUEL TRANSFER SWITCH. A 3-position toggle switch, located on the left-hand control shelf, controls the transfer pump and the solenoid valves in the transfer lines. The positions of the switch are "LEFT TANK," "RIGHT TANK," and "OFF" (see figure 1–5).

1–41. MAIN TANK PRESSURE RELEASE CONTROL. The manual control for operating the main tank pressure release is located on the floor of the cockpit. It has two positions, "ON," and "DUMP" (see figure 1–4).

1–42. EXTERNAL AUXILIARY FUEL TANK JETTISON CONTROLS. The electrical external auxiliary fuel tank release controls consist of the bomb release switches located on the left and right armament switch boxes and the bomb release thumb button on the control stick. The manual emergency control for releasing the auxiliary tanks is located on the aft end of the left-hand control shelf. Moving the knobbed handle forward into the left, center or right-hand slot releases the corresponding auxiliary tank.

1–43. WATER INJECTION SYSTEM.

1–44. The water-alcohol supply for the water injection system is contained in two interconnected tanks with a total capacity of 28 gallons. The tanks are suspended from the engine mount tubes in the accessory compartment. The filler cap is accessible through a door in the right-hand upper wing gap cover panel (see figure 1–2). A water strainer, an electric water pump, water regulator, and the necessary tubing, wiring, and switches comprise the rest of the system.

1–45. Water flow to the engine is provided by the water pump and controlled by the water regulator. The system is actuated by closing the master water injection switch and the throttle-actuated microswitch. When the water injection system is operated, the manifold pressure regulator is reset, making available higher manifold pressures below critical altitude. These higher manifold pressures between Military and full Combat Power can be controlled by the throttle. When the water supply is exhausted there will be a drop in manifold pressure and the throttle should be adjusted so as not to exceed Military Power. Further, when the water supply is exhausted, the carburetor air temperature warning light should be watched. If it comes on, the intercooler flap should be opened or power reduced (refer to paragraph 1–24).

1–46. LANDING GEAR CONTROLS.

1–47. NORMAL CONTROL. The hydraulic control to retract and extend the landing gear is on the forward inclined section of the left-hand control shelf. It is tire-shaped for ready identification (see figure 1–14). The

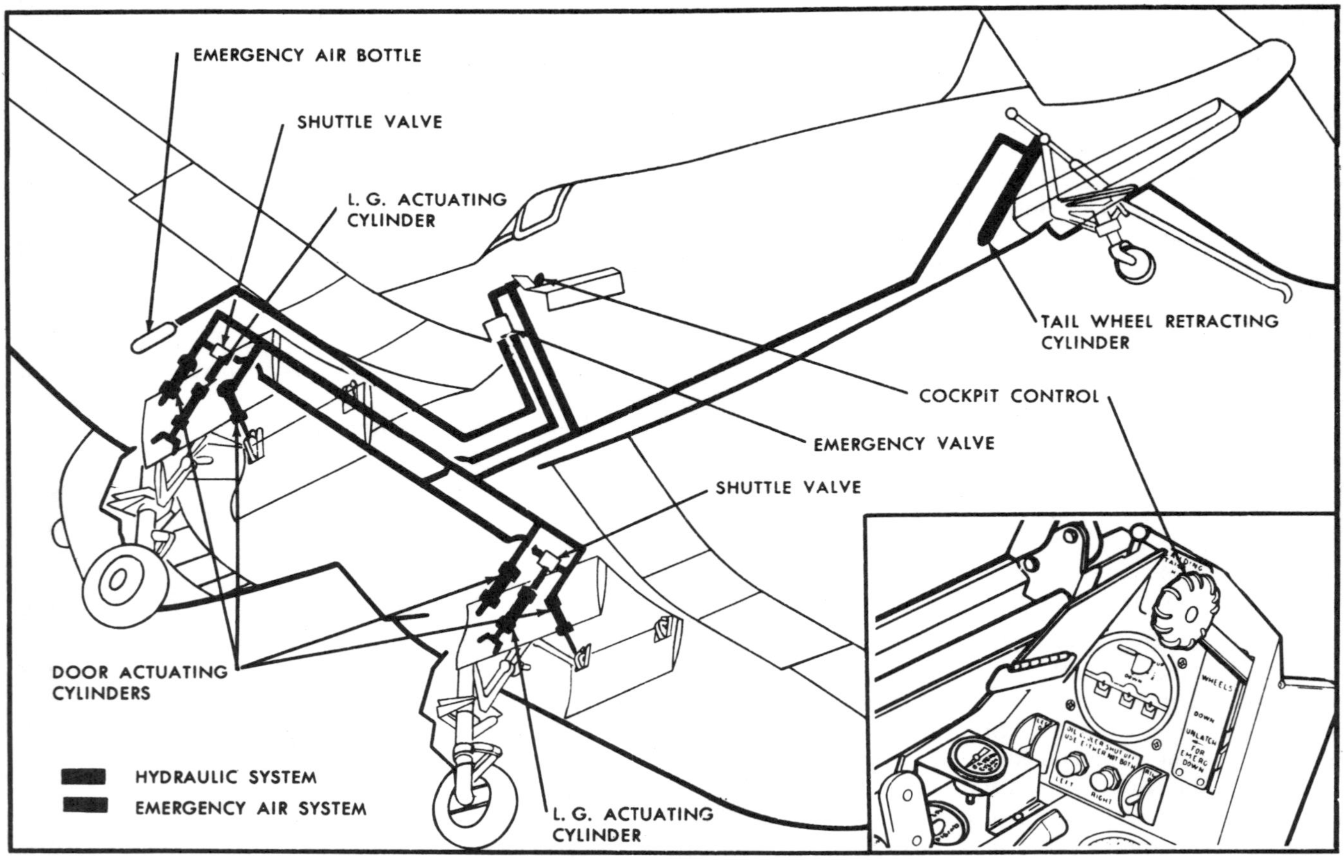

Figure 1–14. Landing Gear Control Hydraulic System Diagram

placed in the "WHEELS DOWN" position. The landing gear "up and locked" and "down and locked" positions are shown on the gear and flap position indicator on the inclined section of the left-hand control shelf. No intermediate gear positions are shown.

CAUTION

Do not attempt to retract the landing gear after use of the air system as damage to the hydraulic reservoir will result.

1–48. The main landing gear and the tail wheel can be retracted only when each main oleo strut is nearly fully extended (airplane airborne or on jacks) although the control handle can be placed in the "UP" position while the airplane is on the ground. The positive mechanical down locks on the main gear are so designed as to prevent gear retraction on the ground should the control lever be tripped accidentally. The tail wheel is retracted through the same sequence valve which closes the main gear doors so that the tail wheel cannot retract until the main gear has retracted.

1–49. A cowl flap override switch located on the lower scissors of the left-hand landing gear overrides the automatic cowl flap control and opens the cowl flaps automatically whenever the airplane is on the ground. In aircraft Bureau Serial No. 124666 and subsequent, a LANDING GEAR WARNING light is located below the landing gear control handle. When the control handle is moved, the light goes on and stays on until the landing gear is locked in the position selected by the control handle.

1–50. EMERGENCY CONTROL. Emergency operation of the landing gear is effected by placing the landing gear control handle to the extreme down or "EMERGENCY DOWN" position (red slot). The landing gear is then extended by an 1800 psi charge of compressed air operating through a shuttle valve in the landing gear down line. When the control handle is placed in the "EMERGENCY DOWN" position, the hydraulic pressure holding the tail wheel up is released and the tail wheel is spring-extended. A latch on the inboard side of the control restricts movement of the handle to the normal "WHEELS DOWN" position. This latch must be released before the handle can be placed in the "EMERGENCY DOWN" position. The emergency system will extend the landing gear at speeds up to approximately 110 knots. However, the handle may be placed in the "EMERGENCY DOWN" position at any speed; then, as soon as the airplane has slowed down sufficiently to permit extension, the landing gear will lower.

1–51. The compressed air bottle and pressure gage are mounted on the left-hand side in the left-hand wheel well. Pressure in the bottle can be read by depressing the plunger on the gage. The bottle should be checked by the pilot before each flight that it is charged to 1800 psi.

1—52. BRAKES. The brakes of the airplane are actuated by two independent hydraulic systems, right and left. Hydraulic pressure from the master cylinders, located outboard and forward of the brake pedals, is transmitted to the brake units on the wheels when the brake pedals are depressed.

1—53. ARRESTING HOOK CONTROL. The arresting hook control handle is on the right hand inclined panel. It is hook shaped for ready identification and has two positions, "UP" and "DOWN" (see figure 1—6). The arresting hook control handle is connected directly to a latch which locks the hook in the up position when the control handle is placed in the "UP" position. When the control handle is placed in the "DOWN" position, the unlocked arresting hook will move up and down with respective retraction and extension of the landing gear, since the arresting hook is mechanically linked to the tail gear. The arresting hook control handle should be moved "DOWN" *before* lowering the landing gear to prevent the excessive jarring which occurs when the hook is lowered after the landing gear. Then, since the arresting hook is mechanically linked to the tail gear, the hook will come down when the tail gear extends. After landing aboard carrier, the arresting hook control handle should be placed in the "UP" position. This will permit the deck crew, after disengaging the wire, to lift the hook manually to its "PARKED" position, about 12 inches above the deck. After the next carrier take-off, retraction of the tail gear will complete retraction of the hook and automatically lock it in the "UP" position.

1—54. TAIL WHEEL LOCK CONTROL. The tail wheel lock control is located on the aft end of the left hand control shelf (see figure 1—16). It has two positions, a forward "LOCKED" position and an aft "UNLOCKED" position. The tail wheel is locked or unlocked by moving the knob-topped handle to the desired position.

1—55. WING FOLD AND LOCKING CONTROLS.

1—56. WING FOLD AND LOCKING CONTROLS. The wings can be folded and spread and the wing hinge pin locked by the operation of one control on the aft end of the right hand control shelf. The control which is a knobbed lever operating in a right angled slot, has four positions, "WING HINGE PIN LOCKED," "SPREAD," "PARK," and "FOLD" (see figures 1—15 and 2—5). A visual check that the wings are fully spread and the wing hinge pins are "home" is provided by observing the gap cover doors at the wing joint. These doors will not close until the outer panels are completely spread and the wing hinge pins are "home." A red warning flag at each wing folding joint, raised when the wing hinge pin is not in position, drops flush with the wing surface only when the locking pins are actually in the locked position.

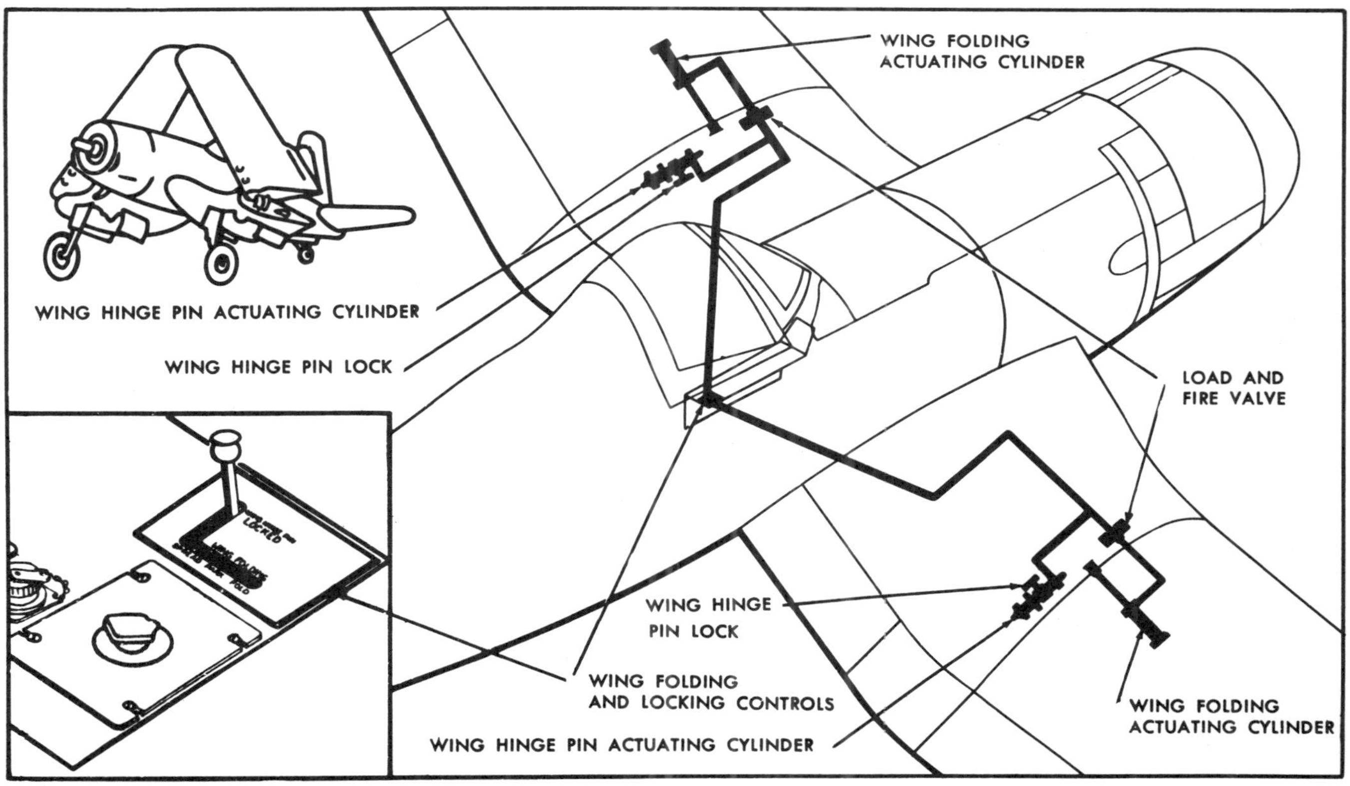

Figure 1—15. Wing Fold Control Hydraulic System Diagram

Figure 1-16. Tail Wheel Lock

1–57. HYDRAULIC SYSTEM.

1–58. HYDRAULIC OIL. Specification MIL-O-5606 (red fluid).

1–59. DESCRIPTION. The hydraulic system consists of a reservoir, an engine-driven variable displacement pump, an electrically driven auxiliary pump, a system relief valve, check valves, hydraulic fuses, thermal expansion valves, and actuating cylinders. The system raises and lowers wing flaps, operates the intercooler flap and oil cooler doors, raises and lowers landing gear, opens and closes canopy, spreads and folds wings, and charges the guns. The system operates at a normal pressure of 1500 psi. The auxiliary pump provides 1500 (± 100) psi system pressure when engine is not running or in the event of main hydraulic pump failure. The operation of the auxiliary pump is controlled by a toggle switch located on the slanting section of the right-hand control shelf (figure 1–17). The switch has an "OFF" and "ON" position.

CAUTION

The electrically driven auxiliary hydraulic pump should be turned "ON" only when it is needed to operate a system, or systems, and turned "OFF" immediately thereafter.

1–60. HYDRAULIC RESERVOIR. The 8¾-quart reservoir is located at the top of the engine accessory compartment on the right-hand side of the airplane forward of the oil tank (figure 1-2). A glass window with "FULL" and "LOW" indications located adjacent to the filler neck on the aft end of the tank provides a visual check of the fluid level in the tank. The tank is pressurized to 12 psi above atmospheric pressure through a line which delivers air pressure from the intercooler air duct to a pressurization valve and from there to the vent port on the top forward end of the reservoir. The pressurization valve also relieves excessive pressures within the reservoir.

1–61. EMERGENCY FACILITIES. In the event of main hydraulic system failure, the landing gear and canopy are operated by separate air pressure bottle systems (paragraphs 3–18 and 3–22). In addition the canopy can be operated manually. The wing flap emergency system utilizes pressure from the auxiliary hydraulic pump and fluid from below the standpipe level of the reservoir (paragraphs 1–10 and 3–22). The brakes are independent, self-contained hydraulic units and so are unaffected by main hydraulic system failure.

1–62. ELECTRICAL SYSTEM.

1–63. DESCRIPTION. *(Refer to paragraph 3–28 for emergency operation.)* Electric power is supplied by a direct-current 28-volt one-wire system in which the negative side of the current is carried through the electrically bonded structure of the airplane. Electric power is provided by: a 28-volt 200-ampere generator, a 24-volt 17-ampere-hour battery, or from an outside source through the external power receptacle. A voltage regulator regulates the generator output at a steady level (approximately 27.5 volts). A differential-type reverse current relay connects the generator to the electric system when the generator voltage exceeds that in the battery by a given amount, and disconnects the generator from the electric system at a reverse current of 15 to 25 amperes flowing from the battery to the generator. Thus, the battery is kept free from feeding power to the generator and running it as a motor. Circuits are protected by thermal-type circuit breakers. Provision is made for carrying two batteries, one for emergency conditions. Only one will normally be carried in the airplane.

1–64. CONTROLS. Most of the electrical system controls and all the radio controls are at finger-tip convenience as noted below.

1–65. ELECTRICAL AND RADIO CONTROLS. The following electrical system components are on the right-hand control shelf (figure 1–17): the power control, primer, starter, oil dilution, pitot heat, and auxiliary hydraulic pump switches, voltammeter and generator warning light on the inclined section; the exterior lights console containing five toggle switches, and the interior lights rheostat and switch on the horizontal section. Radio controls are on five radio console panels on the right-hand control shelf. (Refer to paragraph 4–29.) The heater switch is on the air distribution box mounted on the right side of the cockpit.

1–66. The following electrical controls are on the left-hand side of the cockpit (figure 1–5): selector-dimmer, the fuel transfer switch and warning light, the auxiliary (booster) fuel pump switch, the electric trim tab controller, the intercooler, oil cooler, and cowl flap switches, and the water injection control switch on the horizontal section; right and left oil cooler shut-off switches and warning lights (inoperative on this installation), and a landing gear and flap indicator on an inclined section of the shelf; a microphone button on the throttle.

1–67. VOLTAMMETER. The voltammeter is located on the slanting section of the right-hand control shelf (figure 1–17). The voltmeter indicates the voltage at the plus bus in the main junction box and the ammeter indicates the output of the generator. When the generator warning light adjacent to the voltammeter is on, the ammeter is showing battery current. When the light is off, generator current is shown. Voltammeter test jacks are located on the inboard vertical side of the right-hand control panel. The test jacks are used to check the airplane's voltmeter against a test standard.

1–68. POWER CONTROL SWITCH. The power control shelf has three positions: "GEN & BAT," "BAT ONLY," and "OFF." During normal operation the switch should always be in the "GEN & BAT" position. In the event of a generator failure the generator cut-out will isolate the generator and all busses but the primary bus from the circuit. A red warning light located above the voltammeter will indicate that the battery is then being used as the source of power supply. When items other than the instruments, intercooler flaps, or cowl flaps are needed the power control switch may be tripped to the "BAT ONLY" position.

CAUTION

Battery is discharging excessively when the power control switch is in the "BAT ONLY" position. Turn off all unnecessary load.

WARNING

Do not turn the power control switch on while the engine is not running unless the mixture control is in "IDLE CUT-OFF." Should the auxiliary (booster) fuel pump switch be turned to "HIGH" or "LOW" while the mixture control is in any position but "IDLE CUT-OFF" with the power control switch on, the lower cylinders may become flooded resulting in damage to the engine when it is started.

1–69. EXTERNAL POWER RECEPTACLE. The external power receptacle is located on the right-hand side of the fuselage, forward and above the trailing edge of the wing (see figure 1–2).

1–70. EXTERIOR LIGHTS SWITCHES. *(See figure 1-17.)* The exterior lights switches are located on the forward end of the right-hand control shelf. In airplanes Bureau Serial No. 121793 through 124560, five toggle switches are mounted on the exterior lights control panel. These switches are the MASTER, WING, TAIL, FORMATION, and FUSELAGE switches. The MASTER switch has three positions, "STEADY," "OFF," and "FLASH," and it controls the flow of current to the three-position "DIM–OFF–BRIGHT" individual light control switches. In airplanes Bureau Serial No. 124666 and subsequent, the exterior lights control panel contains a rotary selector-type MASTER switch with four positions: "OFF," "STEADY," "FLASH," and "CODE." The operation of the exterior lights is the same on these airplanes as on earlier models except that the fuselage lights may be coded either manually or automatically as selected by the CODE toggle switch. With the CODE toggle switch in "MANUAL" and the MASTER switch on "STEADY" or "FLASH," the code KEY button can be used to manually code the fuselage lights. With the MASTER switch on "CODE" and the CODE toggle switch on "AUTOMATIC," the fuselage lights will flash any preset code selected by the CODE SELECTOR switch. The code indicator light will flash in unison with the code KEY button when the CODE toggle switch is in "MANUAL."

1–71. INTERIOR LIGHTS. Cockpit lighting is provided by the instrument panel and check list lights and by three lights on each side of the cockpit. In airplanes Bureau Serial No. 124666 and subsequent, two portable cockpit flood lamps are provided. Clips are mounted on each side of the windshield for storing these lamps when they are not in use. Airplanes Bureau Serial No. 124666 and subsequent have edge-lighted control panels.

1–72. The interior lights controls are located on the forward portion of the right-hand control panel. In airplanes Bureau Serial No. 121793 through 122206, a rheostat which controls the intensity of the interior lights also serves as a master on-off switch. Power flows through the rheostat to the interior lights toggle switch. This switch has three positions: "ALL LIGHTS," "ALL INSTRUMENTS," and "FLIGHT." When this switch is placed in the "FLIGHT" position, only the flight instruments will be lighted and they can be turned on or off, or their intensity can be varied, by operating the rheostat. The cockpit lights turn on when the toggle switch is in the "ALL LIGHTS" position and can be controlled by the rheostat and individual switches contained in each light. In airplanes Bureau Serial No. 123144 through 124560 two rheostats are provided: one for instrument lights and one for cockpit lights. The instrument lights rheostat controls the flow of power to the instrument light two-position "FLIGHT–ALL INSTRUMENTS" toggle switch. The COCKPIT LIGHTS rheostat controls the flow of power to the six cockpit lights, each of which contains an individual switch. In air-

Figure 1-17. Electrical Controls

planes Bureau Serial No. 124666 and subsequent, the instrument lights are controlled by the two rotary switches: one for FLIGHT instrument lights, and one for NON-FLIGHT instrument lights. The CONSOLE lights rotary switch controls cockpit and console lights. These three switches operate on a-c power from the MAIN inverter or from the STAND-BY inverter in case of main inverter failure. The cockpit flood lamps operate on d-c power and are controlled by the COCKPIT FLOOD LAMPS circuit breaker.

1–73. APPROACH LIGHT. The approach light is mounted in the leading edge of the left-hand wing outer panel. In airplanes Bureau Serial No. 121793 through 124560, the approach light is connected to the EXTERIOR LIGHTS circuit breaker and operates when the arresting hook is extended. A practice landing APPROACH LIGHT toggle switch is mounted on the underside of the lower radio deck in the radio compartment. In airplanes Bureau Serial No. 124666 and subsequent, the approach light is connected to the exterior lights MASTER switch. With the MASTER switch in any "on" position, the approach light flashes when the landing gear is extended and is steady when the arresting hook is locked down. A practice landing APPROACH LIGHT toggle switch is mounted on the underside of the lower radio deck in the radio compartment. After this switch has been momentarily closed, the approach light is steady when the landing gear is extended. The system is restored to normal operation by either extending the arresting hook or opening the EXTERIOR LIGHTS circuit breaker.

1–74. CIRCUIT-BREAKER PANEL. All of the electrical circuits in the airplane are protected by circuit breakers located on the vertical face of the right-hand control shelf (see figure 1–6). When pushed in (normal position), a breaker maintains a closed circuit up to the rated current of a circuit. If an electrical overload of sufficient magnitude and duration occurs in a circuit, the breaker pops out, breaking the circuit. The circuit may be closed again by resetting the circuit breaker button. If an overload is due to a short circuit or other similarly serious cause which will make the overload permanent, the breaker will pop out again, and it should be left out.

1–75. COCKPIT HEATER SWITCH. The cockpit heater switch is located on the air distributor box on the right-hand side of the cockpit (see figure 4–8).

1–76. ELECTRICALLY HEATED FLYING SUIT RECEPTACLE. The electrically heated flying suit receptacle is located on the aft end of the right-hand control shelf (see figure 1–6).

1–77. MARK 8 GUNSIGHT UNIT SWITCHES. The MK 8 gunsight unit switches are located on the left-hand control shelf (see figure 1–5, also paragraph 4–11).

1–78. ARMAMENT SWITCH BOXES. Two armament switch boxes are mounted on the left and right windshield cowl (see figure 4–5). The left-hand box contains the master armament switch, two gun selector switches for the inboard and outboard pairs of guns, a gun safety switch, and the gun charging button. The right-hand armament switch box contains bomb and rocket arming and selector switches. The control stick hand grip contains three trigger switches, one each for guns, rockets, and bombs (see figure 4–4).

1–79. ELECTRICALLY DRIVEN INSTRUMENTS. The following electrically driven instruments, warning lights and switches are mounted on the pilot's instrument panel (see figure 1–7): tachometer indicator, engine gage unit (oil temperature, oil pressure, and fuel pressure), fuel quantity gage, fuel quantity warning light, carburetor air temperature warning light, rocket selector, gyro horizon, P-3 gyro flux gate compass indicator (see note below), the compass caging switch (in F4U-5 and F4U-5P airplanes only), and the single-pulse-ripple-pulse switch.

Note

On the north heading a compass deviation of 10 degrees results from extension of the chartboard, therefore, USE STAND-BY ONLY WITH CHARTBOARD STOWED AND INTERIOR LIGHTS DIMMED.

1–79A. AN/APN-1 RADIO ALTIMETER. *(See figures 1–6 and 1–7.)* The radio altimeter provides direct measurement of "absolute altitude" during flight (refer to paragraph 4–41A). The altitude limit switch is located on the right-hand control panel, directly inboard of the wing folding and locking control in F4U-5 and F4U-5P airplanes and on the instrument board in F4U-5N airplanes (see figure B-4). A red warning light located above and to the left of the radio altitude indicator in F4U-5 and F4U-5P airplanes and on the left side of the radar indicator in F4U-5N airplanes will go on when the aircraft descends below the altitude set on the altitude limit switch.

1–80. MISCELLANEOUS CONTROLS AND EQUIPMENT.

1–81. CANOPY CONTROL.

1–82. DESCRIPTION. From inside the cockpit, the fully transparent, clear vision canopy enclosure is normally opened and closed hydraulically. There is a hydraulic pressure release inside and outside the airplane so that the canopy can be pushed open or shut manually when there is no hydraulic pressure. Under emergency conditions the canopy can be opened rapidly by using a compressed air system. The canopy is locked in the fully open and closed positions by hydraulic pressure, and in intermediate positions by hydraulic fluid locked in the actuating cylinder. Should the hydraulic system fail, a

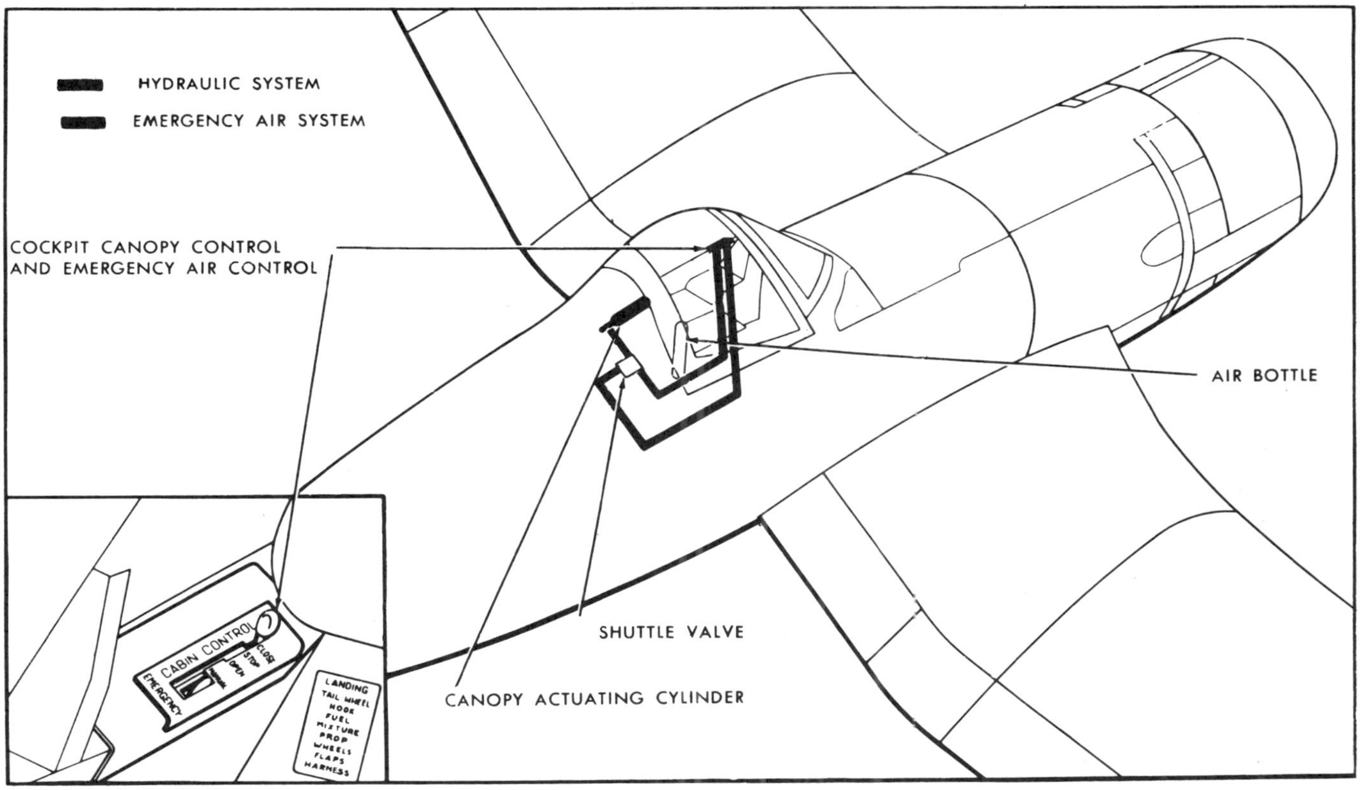

Figure 1-18. Canopy Control Hydraulic System Diagram

check valve in the pressure line prevents the loss of hydraulic fluid. This forms an emergency hydraulic lock which holds the canopy closed until the cabin control handle is moved to the "EMERGENCY" or to the "MANUAL" position.

1-83. A safety lock engages at all times when the canopy is in full open position. The lock is released automatically when the canopy is closed hydraulically. It must be released manually, however, when the canopy is pushed closed by hand.

1-84. COCKPIT CANOPY CONTROL. The canopy control handle is located at the forward end of the left-hand side of the cockpit (figure 1-18). The knobbed handle has five positions reading from front to rear, "CLOSE," "STOP," "OPEN," "MANUAL," and "EMERGENCY." The canopy is moved hydraulically to its full open or closed position by placing the control handle in either "OPEN" or "CLOSE" positions and leaving it there. The canopy is then held in the selected position by hydraulic pressure. The canopy is moved to intermediate openings by placing the handle in the "OPEN" or "CLOSE" position until the canopy reaches the desired position and then returning the handle to the "STOP" position and leaving it there. The canopy will then be held in place by hydraulic fluid in the actuating cylinder. With the handle in the "MANUAL" position the canopy can be opened by merely pushing it.

1-85. CABIN SAFETY LOCK. Before the cabin can be closed manually the safety lock must be released by operating the safety lock handle on the right side of the cockpit (figure 1-6). Lock handle positions are "CLEAR" and "BLOCKED." The control must be held at "CLEAR" before the cabin can be closed manually. The handle returns automatically to "BLOCKED" when the cabin is opened.

1-86. EXTERNAL MANUAL RELEASE HANDLE. The external manual release is a pull ring stowed behind a small door on the right-hand side of the fuselage. This control is necessary only in the case of a crash landing when the cockpit handle has been left in the "CLOSE" position. Normally when the sliding section has been closed from the outside, the control system is left in "MANUAL" and the canopy can be opened by pushing aft on the external actuating handle.

1-87. CANOPY EMERGENCY CONTROL. The full aft position of the canopy control handle is painted red. This is the "EMERGENCY" position. A spring latch must be operated before the handle can be placed in this position. Placing the handle in "EMERGENCY" releases a charge of compressed air which moves the canopy from the full closed to the full open position in 3 seconds. The air bottle pressure gage is located within the fuselage just above the radio compartment access door on the right side of the airplane (figure 1-2). The bottle should be checked by the pilot before each flight to be sure that it is charged to 1,800 psi. The emergency system may be used at any flight speed.

1-88. PILOT'S SEAT. The pilot's seat is bucket-shaped to hold a Navy-type seat parachute, a PK-2 Parakit, and an SP-1 seat pad. The seat back is designed so as to support the entire length of a BP-1 back pad. The seat is adjustable through a vertical seat movement of 7 inches, 3½ inches up and down from the neutral position. As the seat is raised through its full vertical adjustment of 7 inches, it moves forward 1 inch. The 101-degree angle between the bucket and the seat back does not change as the seat height is varied. The seat is free for adjustment when the knob on the right-hand control shelf is depressed (see figure 1–6). The seat is equipped with two arm rests which can be rotated into or out of position. The right one is toed slightly inboard to more nearly fit the arm when holding the control stick.

1–89. EYE-LEVEL MIRROR. A small, round mirror is rigidly fixed to the upper right-hand edge of the windshield. (See figure 1–4.) The mirror is aligned upon installation to reflect the pilot's eye when he is at the proper seat height for gunnery. This permits pilots of varying heights to determine the optimum seat adjustment. Do not disturb the mirror setting.

1–90. SAFETY BELT. An adjustable safety belt with a quick-release safety buckle is attached to the seat. The loose ends of the shoulder straps fit into the buckle, and both the shoulder straps and the safety belt are released when the buckle is opened.

1–91. SHOULDER HARNESS INERTIA REEL. Shoulder straps extend over the shoulders and are attached to an inertia reel behind the seat. The reel, controlled by a handle on the left-hand control shelf (see figure 1–5), permits the pilot to lock the shoulder straps at any adjusted length, or to release them, allowing him to lean forward in the cockpit. In either the "LOCKED" or "UNLOCKED" position, spring tension keeps the straps snug against the pilot. The control handle is "UNLOCKED" by pushing down on it and then aft. It is "LOCKED" when it is pushed down and forward. When "LOCKED," the reel prevents the shoulder straps from extending. Even when the reel is "UNLOCKED," the pilot is still protected during sudden maneuvers or a crash landing, as the reel, suspended by two light springs in a floating position within the housing, is locked automatically by inertia loading which prevents further strap extension.

1–92. PILOT'S HEADREST. The pilot's headrest is of the fixed type covered with an 8 x 10 inch piece of sponge rubber.

1–93. CATAPULT HANDGRIP. The catapult handgrip is located within the sheathing on the left-hand side of the airplane just forward of the engine control unit. When not in use, the handle folds flush with the side of the cockpit behind a small door (see figure 1–5).

1–94. CHARTBOARD. In F4U-5 and F4U-5P airplanes, the chartboard slides in and out of a slot in the center of the instrument panel (see figure 1–7). It is equipped with locks for the "in" position which must be engaged before catapulting or landing. A spring behind the board ejects it approximately 1 inch when the latch is removed. In F4U-5N airplanes, the chartboard is stowed in the map and data case when not in use.

1–95. MAP AND DATA CASE. An aluminum map and data case forms the aft end of the right-hand control shelf (see figure 1–6).

1–96. RELIEF TUBE. The horn of the relief tube is located on the forward side of the control stick.

1–97. PILOT'S CHECK LISTS. A take-off check list is mounted on the right-hand inclined panel and a landing check list is mounted on the left-hand inclined panel. Both lists are edge-lighted for night flying. In aircraft Bureau Serial No. 121793 through 122206, the lights are in the cockpit lighting circuit, and in aircraft Bureau Serial No. 123144 and subsequent, the lights are in the non-flight instrument lighting circuit.

1–98. DELETED.

1–99. REAR VISION MIRRORS. Three rear vision mirrors are located on the aft side of the front sliding section frame.

1–100. CIGARETTE LIGHTER AND ASH TRAY. The cigarette lighter and ash tray are located on the left-hand side of the cockpit (see figure 1–5). The lighter is the conventional push-in type which pops out when hot. To remove the ash tray for cleaning, pull out the inner half of the assembly. To replace, snap it back into place.

1–101. TOW TARGET CONTROL. The tow target control handle is located on the inboard face of the left-hand control shelf (see figure 1–5). Instructions for releasing the target when towed are printed on the control nameplate. The instructions read: "PULL TO RELEASE TOW TARGET."

1–102. BAGGAGE COMPARTMENT. A maximum of 100 pounds of non-magnetic gear can be stowed in the baggage compartment located in the rear fuselage. The compartment is located just aft of and is accessible through the radio compartment access door on the right-hand side of the fuselage. The compartment consists of a plywood floor with a canvas body equipped with zipper fasteners and straps. The following instructions are stenciled on the face of the compartment: "Lock wire zippers together after packing bag. Maximum baggage 100 pounds. Warning, do not stow any magnetic material in this baggage compartment due to the close proximity of the remote compass transmitter. Caution, secure loose ends of straps."

1–103. OPERATIONAL EQUIPMENT. Operational equipment is described in Section IV as follows:

1–104. ARMAMENT. Paragraph 4–1.

1–105. OXYGEN. Paragraph 4–52.

1–106. RADIO COMMUNICATION, NAVIGATION AND IFF EQUIPMENT. Paragraph 4–29.

1–107. HEATING AND VENTILATION. Paragraph 4–43.

1–108. ANTI-BLACKOUT EQUIPMENT. Paragraph 4–48.

Section II

NORMAL OPERATING INSTRUCTIONS

2—1. BEFORE ENTERING THE COCKPIT.

Flight Limitations

ITEM	OPERATION or CONDITION	RESTRICTION
Airplane	Spins	No intentional spinning permitted
Airplane	Inverted Flight	Ten seconds duration
Airplane	Diving	Dependent on altitude (See paragraphs 2—84 through 2—86)
Airplane	With external useful load items installed	The following maneuvers are prohibited: loop, snap roll, chandelle, Immelmann turn
Landing Gear (including use as a dive brake)	Retracting or extending	270 knots IAS
	Flying with landing gear down and locked (See Paragraph 2-82)	350 knots IAS
Wing Flaps:		
Blow-up operative	Deflected 0-50°	200 knots
Blow-up inoperative	Deflected 50°	130 knots
	Deflected 40°	145 knots
	Deflected 30°	170 knots
	Deflected 20° or less	200 knots
Cabin	Open	260 knots
Ailerons	Full throw	300 knots
Ailerons	One-half full throw	350 knots
Cooling flaps and doors (cowl, *intercooler,*oil cooler)	Open	No restrictions*(protected by relief system)
Twin Pylon:		
11.75″ rocket	Diving	No restrictions
Mk. 5, Mod. 4 External Auxiliary Fuel Tank (150 gal.)	Diving	5.0 g (see paragraph 2—83)
Mk. 12 External Auxiliary Fuel Tank	Diving	5.0 g (see paragraph 2—83)
1,000 lb. bomb	Diving	(See paragraph 2—83)
Centerline Pylon:		
11.75″ rocket	Diving	5.0 g (see paragraph 2—83)
Mk. 5, Mod. 4 External Auxiliary Fuel Tank (150 gal.)	Diving	5.0 g (see paragraph 2—83)
Mk. 12 External Auxiliary Fuel Tank	Diving	5.0 g (see paragraph 2—83)
1,000 lb. bomb	Diving	(See paragraph 2—83)
2,000 lb. bomb	Diving	(See paragraph 2—83)

THESE LIMITATIONS AND RESTRICTIONS ARE SUBJECT TO CHANGE AND LATEST SERVICE DIRECTIVES AND TECHNICAL ORDERS MUST BE CONSULTED.

Figure 2—1. Flight Limitations

2–2. INITIAL GROSS WEIGHT AND LOADING DATA. Check gross weight and center of gravity location for take-off, and check anticipated loading for landing. Loading data is furnished in Handbook of Weight and Balance Data, AN 01-1B-40.

2–3. AIRPLANE PRE-FLIGHT CHECK. Before entering the airplane, make certain that it is ready for flight. Observe where it stands and note whether there are any puddles of fuel, oil, or hydraulic fluid beneath it indicating a possible leak in one of these systems. Then, make the following pre-flight check:

a. Pitot tube cover removed.

b. Check that all removable cowling and access doors are fastened securely.

c. Check that prescribed armament and/or fuel load is carried and is secure.

d. Check personally—or have checked by a reliable service crew member—that proper fuel, and lubricating and hydraulic oil quantities are aboard and that all tank caps are secure. Fuel quantity should be checked with a suitable dip stick calibrated to record accurately when the airplane is in a three-point position.

e. Check charges in emergency air bottles (landing gear and canopy).

f. Control lock and battens removed.

g. Wheel chocks in place.

2–4. ENTRANCE TO CLOSED AIRPLANE. Entrance to the cockpit is gained from the right hand side of the airplane by means of the upper and lower cockpit access steps, the cockpit manual release handle, the handhole in the instrument panel access door, and the handgrip in the sliding section frame. The access steps are linked mechanically with the tail wheel so that they retract and extend along with the landing gear. On the ground the bottom step can be pushed manually to its stowed position from outside the cockpit. This automatically closes the top step Furthermore, it is possible to operate the top step by hand or foot which automatically drops the bottom step. A step on the left hand side of the airplane permits the mechanic to leave the airplane while the pilot enters from the right. The step, which is spring-loaded in the closed position, is pushed open with the toe. The use of the external manual release handle is necessary only in case of a crash landing when the cockpit control handle has been left in the "CLOSE" position. Normally when the sliding section has been closed from the outside, the control system is left in "MANUAL" and the canopy can be pushed aft with the external handgrip.

2–5. ON ENTERING COCKPIT.

Note

Take-off and landing check lists are installed on the inclined sections of the right and left hand control shelves respectively as check-off reminders.

2–6. STANDARD CHECK FOR ALL FLIGHTS. Upon entering the cockpit check that the ignition switch is "OFF," the mixture control is in "IDLE CUT-OFF," and the external power source, when available, is connected and the power control switch is "OFF." Then make a complete cockpit check. The following sequence is suggested:

a. Adjust rudder pedals and seat height.

b. Adjust safety belt and shoulder harness. After adjustment, the harness can be "UNLOCKED" to facilitate movement in the cockpit.

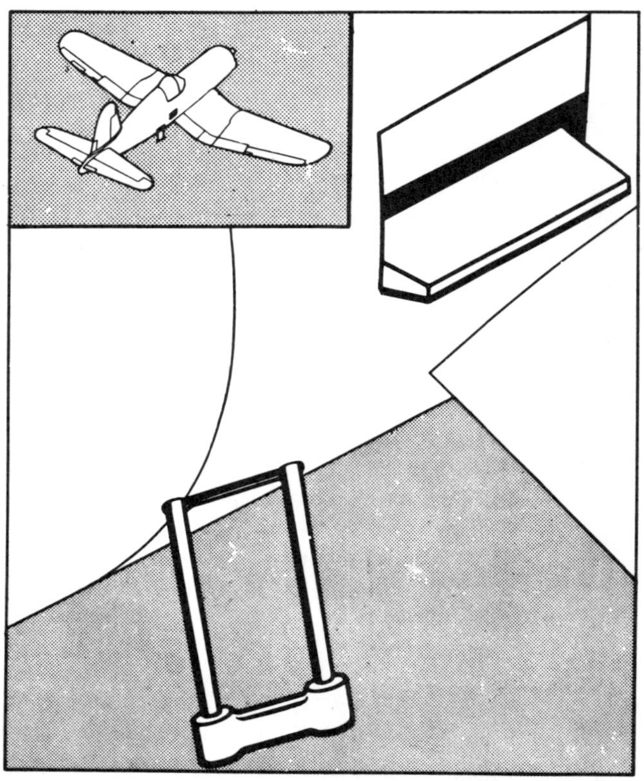

Figure 2–2. Cockpit Entrance Facilities

c. Check controls for freedom and direction.

d. Emergency bomb release handle—aft.

e. Fuel system controls—"OFF." (Fuel selector, fuel transfer, and auxiliary pump switches.)

f. Gun sight selector—"OFF." (Refer to paragraph 4–15 for MK 6 fire control system check.)

g. Check control tab operation.

h. Check oxygen system (paragraph 4–59).

i. Intercooler door—closed. (Switch "CLOSE," then "OFF.")

j. Oil cooler switch—"AUTOMATIC."

k. Cowl flaps—open. Switch "OPEN" then "AUTOMATIC.")

l. Wing flaps—"UP" after checking emergency operation (paragraph 1–11).

m. Master water injection switch—"OFF."

n. Engine controls—throttle closed; propeller control —full "INCREASE."

o. Landing gear handle — "DOWN" (paragraph 3–19).

p. Canopy—"OPEN."

q. Instrument panel—check altimeter setting, clock, and fuel quantity gage; uncage compass if necessary.

r. Check armament switches (paragraph 4–7).

s. Chart board—locked in. (F4U-5 and F4U-5P airplanes only.)

t. Arresting hook—"UP."

u. Engine starting switches—"OFF."

v. Exterior and interior lights switches—"OFF."

w. Radios switches—"OFF."

x. Cockpit heater—"OFF."

2–7. NIGHT FLIGHT CHECK LIST. In addition to the standard check, before night flights the light switches should be checked on entering the cockpit. (Refer to paragraphs 1–70 through 1–72.)

Note

> When operating in combat areas, the exterior lights to be used in flight can be selected before take-off, and turned on with the MASTER exterior light switch after take-off.

2–8. FUEL SYSTEM MANAGEMENT.

2–9. GENERAL. For a description of the fuel system, refer to paragraph 1–29. For emergency fuel system management instructions, refer to paragraph 3–13. For a diagram of fuel flow to accompany this section, see figure 2–4, Fuel System Management Diagram.

2–10. FUEL TANK SELECTION. Fuel flow from the tanks to the engine-driven pump is controlled by the fuel selector valve. The control for this valve, located on the left-hand control shelf, has four positions, "ON," "OFF," "LEFT OR CENTER DROP TANK STAND BY," and "RIGHT DROP TANK STAND BY."

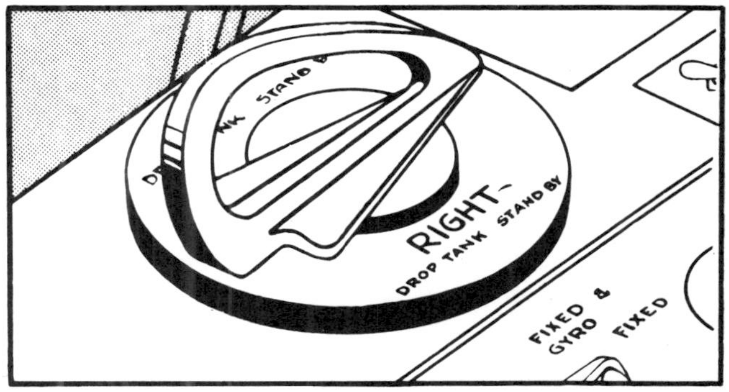

Figure 2-3. Fuel Selector

2–11. NORMAL FUEL FLOW. When the selector is turned to its normal "ON" position, all fuel is supplied to the engine from the main fuel cell. With the selector in this position and the fuel transfer switch in a transfer position, the external auxiliary fuel tank being used is emptied first by transferring its contents to the main cell which is kept full automatically during transfer until the auxiliary tank is empty. The fuel transfer warning light will warn when the auxiliary tank is empty. An auxiliary fuel (booster) pump is submerged in the main cell and discharges devaporized fuel into the main fuel line, through a fuel strainer and thence to the engine-driven pump which forces the fuel under proper pressure to the carburetor.

2–12. DROP TANK STAND BY. The "RIGHT DROP TANK STAND BY" and "LEFT OR CENTER DROP TANK STAND BY" position are EMERGENCY positions of the fuel selector valve which route auxiliary tank fuel directly to the engine without first transferring it to the main cell. The STAND BY settings are used in the event of failure of the fuel transfer system.

Note

> When operating with the fuel selector valve in either of the STAND BY positions, operation will probably be unsatisfactory above 12,000 feet. Do not operate in STAND BY for take-off.

2–13. AUXILIARY (BOOSTER) FUEL PUMP. The auxiliary (booster) fuel pump switch is located on the left-hand control shelf. The pump has the following four functions:

a. It provides a steady flow of vapor-free fuel to the carburetor during high altitude operation. The switch should be set to the "LOW" position for all normal flight operations.

b. The auxiliary pump also serves as an emergency fuel pump in the event of failure of the engine-driven pump. In this event the pump switch should be in the "HIGH" position.

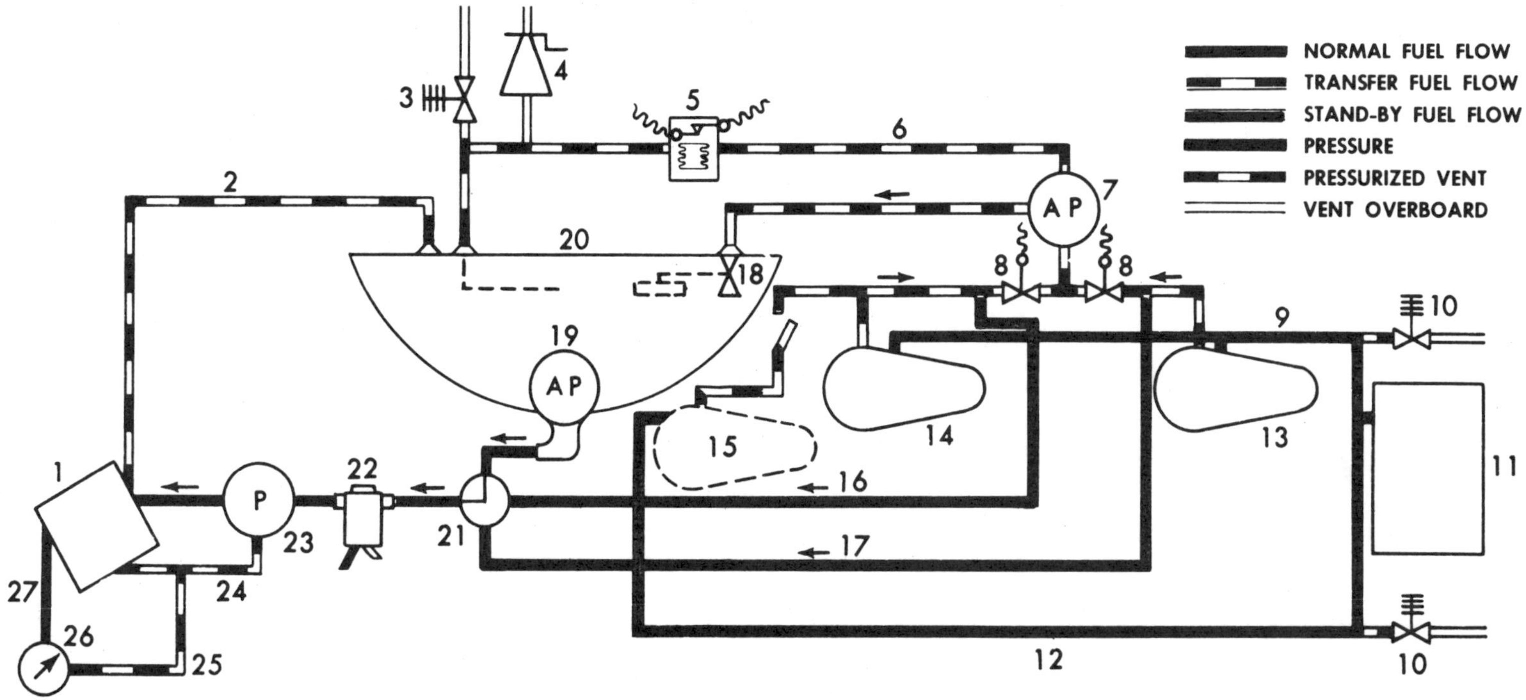

PILOT'S INSTRUMENT PANEL

FUEL PRESSURE GAGE

FUEL QUANTITY GAGE

FUEL RESERVE WARNING LIGHT

L. H. CONTROL PANEL

FUEL TRANSFER WARNING LIGHT

AUXILIARY (BOOSTER) FUEL PUMP SWITCH
"HIGH"—"OFF"—"LOW"

FUEL TRANSFER SWITCH
"LEFT TANK"—"OFF"—"RIGHT TANK"

SELECTOR VALVE CONTROL HANDLE
"OFF"—"LEFT or CENTER DROP TANK STAND-BY"
"ON"—"RIGHT DROP TANK STAND-BY"

1. Carburetor
2. Vapor Return Line
3. Vacuum Relief Valve
4. Main Fuel Cell Vent (Pressure Dump) Valve
5. Transfer Warning Pressure Switch
6. Pump Vent Line
7. Fuel Transfer Pump
8. Fuel Transfer Solenoid Shut-off Valves
9. L. H. and R. H. External Tank Pressurization Line
10. External Tank Pressure and Vacuum Relief Valves
11. Intercooler Exit Duct
12. Centerline External Tank Pressurization Line
13. R. H. External Tank
14. L. H. External Tank
15. Centerline External Tank
16. L. H. or Centerline External Tank Stand-by Line
17. R. H. External Tank Stand-by Line
18. Shut-off Float Valve
19. Submerged Fuel Pump
20. Main Fuel Cell
21. Fuel Selector Valve
22. Fuel Strainer
23. Engine-driven Fuel Pump
24. Pump Vent Line
25. Gage Vent Line
26. Fuel Pressure Gage
27. Gage Pressure Line

Figure 2-4. Fuel System Management Diagram

c. The pump furnishes fuel pressure for starting the engine. The switch is set on "LOW" for this purpose.

d. The pump is set at "HIGH" as a precaution during all take-offs and landings.

2–14. FUEL TRANSFER. The fuel transfer switch is a 3-way toggle switch with "RIGHT," "LEFT OR CENTER," and "OFF" positions. When it is turned to either one of the two transfer positions a solenoid shut-off valve in the line from the corresponding external auxiliary fuel tank is opened and the fuel transfer pump is started. During transfer fuel flows from the auxiliary tank until the float valve in the main tank closes the intake port. Flow is stopped even though the transfer pump continues to run. Flow is resumed when the fuel level in the main fuel cell drops enough for the float valve to open again. This process will continue until the auxiliary tank is empty at which time a warning light on the left-hand control shelf adjacent to the tank selector valve will light. When the auxiliary tank is empty, the transfer switch should be turned to the other drop tank position or to the "OFF" position. The fuel transfer warning light will not indicate an empty auxiliary tank when operating with the fuel selector valve in the "STAND-BY" position.

2–15. The operation of the fuel transfer warning light can be checked by pushing the light to test the bulb. If the airplane is on the ground, engine not running, the battery and fuel transfer switch must be on when testing the light.

2–16. The transfer pump may cease to transfer fuel above approximately 35,000 feet due to vapor formation. If this occurs, the transfer light will come on even though the auxiliary tank is not empty and it will be necessary to descend to a lower altitude before the remaining fuel can be transferred.

Note

The transfer switch should be off whenever the "STAND-BY" positions are being used. If the transfer switch is turned on while operating with the selector in the "STAND-BY" position, engine operation will probably be unsatisfactory above 6,000 feet.

2–17. SWITCHING FUEL TANKS. To switch from one external auxiliary fuel tank to the other under normal transfer conditions, it is necessary only to throw the fuel transfer switch to the other tank transfer position. If only one auxiliary tank is being carried and it has been emptied, turn the fuel transfer switch to the "OFF" position. The fuel transfer switch shall be in the "OFF" position during the take-off and landing, when fuel from the main tank only shall be used.

WARNING

While operating with the fuel selector in the "STAND-BY" position, never run the tank dry at low altitude. The fuel pressure should be watched closely and the shift to the full tank should be made at the first fluctuation. It should be noted that the transfer warning light will NOT indicate an empty auxiliary tank when operating with the fuel selector valve in the "STAND-BY" position. Three thousand feet is considered the minimum safe altitude at which a tank should be allowed to run dry. Refer to paragraph 3–16 for procedure in the event an auxiliary tank is run dry and fuel suction is lost.

2–18. VAPOR ELIMINATION. The vapor return line running from the carburetor to the top of the main fuel cell returns approximately two quarts of fuel to the main cell in an hour of normal engine operation.

2–19. MAIN TANK PRESSURIZING. The main cell pressure release control should be left "ON" (aft) at all times except in combat or in the event of a forced landing. To release the pressure in the main cell, push the handle forward to its "DUMP" position.

2–20. OIL SYSTEM MANAGEMENT.

2–21. OIL PRESSURES AND TEMPERATURES. The minimum oil pressures for safe flight for the various operating ranges are given in the table below:

RPM	OIL PRESSURE (Min.)
2600-2800	100 psi
2250	90 psi
1600	90 psi

The normal and maximum oil pressures and the oil temperatures are given on the Power Plant Chart, figure A–4. Oil temperatures can best be kept from exceeding the allowable limit by:

a. Opening the oil cooler doors. The automatic flap control is set so that the doors will be fully closed at 75°C and fully open at 95°C. The electric override positions of the oil cooler door switch just aft of the engine control unit permit manual opening and closing of the doors.

b. Reducing engine speed.

c. Increasing air speed.

Note

The oil cooler shut-off switches and warning lights on inclined section of left-hand control panel are not operative on airplanes Bureau Serial No. 121793 through 124551 and 124553 through 124694. The oil cooler shut-off switches are operative and the indicator lights are removed on airplanes Bureau Serial No. 124552 and 124695 and subsequent. This switch should be used for emergency only and is not to be used to shut off the oil coolers for quick engine warm-up. Refer to paragraph 3–17A for operating instructions.

2-22. STARTING ENGINE.

2-23. PROCEDURE. The following is the recommended procedure and check list to be used for engine starting:

a. Ignition switch—"OFF."

b. Cowl flap switch—"AUTOMATIC" (flap full open).

c. Oil cooler door switch—"AUTOMATIC."

d. Intercooler flap switch—"AUTOMATIC."

e. Master water injection switch—"OFF."

f. Mixture control—"IDLE CUT-OFF."

g. Throttle—Set to give 800-1000 rpm after engine start.

h. Propeller control—full "INCREASE."

i. Auxiliary (booster) fuel pump switch—"OFF."

j. Transfer pump switch—"OFF."

k. Oil dilution switch—"OFF."

l. Power control switch—"OFF." Connect external power source and turn propeller through four revolutions (16 blades) with starter to clear out engine.

m. Fuel selector—"ON."

n. Auxiliary (booster) fuel pump switch—"LOW" (check that fuel pressure is approximately 10 psi).

o. Ignition switch—"BOTH."

p. Engage starter and prime engine.

q. When engine begins to fire regularly on prime, move mixture control *SLOWLY* to "RICH." *Do not pump or move throttle abruptly.* There will be a lapse of time after moving the mixture control into the rich position until fuel feeds from the discharge nozzle. Therefore, it is IMPORTANT to keep the engine firing regularly (at least 350-400 rpm) by continuing to use the priming switch until normal carburetion is established. If for any reason the engine stops firing, move the mixture control to "IDLE CUT-OFF" immediately, and continue cranking and priming until engine starts.

Note

Normally it should not be necessary to operate the starter any more than 30 seconds in order to start the engine. If the starter switch is held on for one minute and the engine does not start, allow the starter to cool for one minute before making another attempt. After the second and succeeding cranking cycles, allow five minutes for cooling.

r. Idle the engine at 600 to 800 rpm until normal oil pressure is built up (100 psi minimum). If oil pressure does not register on the gage almost immediately, STOP engine and investigate.

2-24. FAILURE TO START ON FIRST ATTEMPT. If the engine does not start, wait a few minutes to allow excess fuel to drain out of the blower drain and the carburetor air box drain. Ground crew standing by with fire extinguisher should check for fire in induction system through carburetor air box drain and for fire in exhaust pipe outlets.

2-25. IMPROPER PRIMING. Inspection of the exhaust pipe outlets of the upper cylinders should indicate whether the engine has been over- or under-primed.

2-26. UNDER-PRIMING. No trace of smoke from the exhaust pipe outlets indicates under-priming. The use of the primer switch should be governed accordingly.

2-27. OVER-PRIMING. Excessive black smoke from the exhaust pipe outlets indicates over-priming. If the engine is over-primed, clear the cylinders and induction system of excess fuel as follows:

a. Mixture-"IDLE CUT-OFF."

b. Auxiliary (booster) fuel pump switch-"OFF."

c. Ignition switch-"OFF."

d. External power supply-disconnected.

e. Throttle-full open.

f. Clear engine by turning propeller over four revolutions (16 blades) with starter.

WARNING

NEVER TURN OVER A HOT ENGINE BY HAND.

2-28. ENGINE FIRE DURING STARTING. Refer to Section III, paragraph 3-2 for the recommended procedure to follow should fire break out in the engine during starting.

2-29. WARM-UP AND GROUND TEST.

CAUTION

Do not run up engine past 1500 rpm with wings folded and jury struts removed.

2-30. WARM-UP CHECK LIST.

a. Mixture-"RICH."

b. Propeller control-full "INCREASE."

c. Cowl flaps switch-"AUTOMATIC" (check "OPEN" and "CLOSE" override positions).

d. Oil cooler door switch-"AUTOMATIC."

e. Intercooler flap switch–"AUTOMATIC."

f. Throttle–1200 rpm.

g. Auxiliary (booster) fuel pump switch–"OFF" after engine is running satisfactorily.

h. Oil dilution switch–"OFF."

Warm-up engine until oil temperature reaches a minimum of 30°C.

2–31. GROUND TEST.

2–32. IGNITION SAFETY CHECK. The ignition safety check may be performed during warm-up with engine idling at 1000 rpm.

a. Switch ignition from "BOTH" to "RIGHT" and back to "BOTH."

b. Switch ignition from "BOTH" to "LEFT" and back to "BOTH."

c. Switch ignition to "OFF" (momentarily) and back to "BOTH."

A slight drop in rpm when operating on each separate magneto and complete cutting out of the engine at the "OFF" position indicates proper connection of the ignition leads.

2–33. ENGINE CHECK. Increase manifold pressure until manifold pressure is the same as the local barometer reading. The rpm should be approximately 2050. The engine instruments should give the following readings:

a. Fuel pressure–25½ to 26½ psi.

b. Auxiliary (booster) fuel pump–check pump pressure with switch in "HIGH" position. Pressure should increase but not exceed 29½ psi. Main fuel cell must be full.

c. Oil pressure–120 ± 5 psi.

d. Oil temperature–30° to 80°C.

2–34. MAGNETO CHECK. The magneto check should always be made prior to the idle mixture check to be sure that the plugs are not fouled.

a. Engine speed–30 inches Hg, manifold pressure.

b. Propeller control–full "INCREASE."

c. Switch ignition from "BOTH" to "RIGHT" and back to "BOTH."

d. Switch ignition from "BOTH" to "LEFT" and back to "BOTH."

Normal drop-off in either the "RIGHT" or "LEFT" position is 50 to 75 rpm and should not exceed 100 rpm. Difference in drop between "LEFT" and "RIGHT" should not exceed 30 to 40 rpm.

Note

Permit engine to stabilize on "BOTH" after operation on one set of plugs before checking the other set.

2–35. PROPELLER GOVERNOR CHECK.

a. Place propeller governor control in the full "INCREASE" position.

b. Engine speed—2000 rpm.

c. Move the propeller control from full "INCREASE" to full "DECREASE." The engine speed should drop to about 1200 rpm.

d. Return the propeller control to full "INCREASE." RPM should return to 2000 rpm.

2–36. IDLE MIXTURE CHECK.

a. Engine speed–600 plus or minus 25 rpm.

b. Auxiliary (booster) fuel pump switch–"ON."

c. While observing tachometer, place mixture control handle in "IDLE CUT-OFF" position.

d. Return mixture control to "RICH" position before engine dies.

If a momentary rise of not more than 10 rpm is observed before normal drop-off, mixture strength is correct. If a greater rise in rpm is noted, the mixture is too rich. If there is no rise in rpm, the mixture is too lean.

Note

A momentary drop in manifold pressure of ¼ inch Hg. will indicate a momentary rise of 10 rpm.

2–37. ELECTRICAL CHECK WITH ENGINE RUNNING.

a. Disconnect external power source, if used.

b. Power control switch on.

c. Turn on some electrical equipment such as cockpit or instrument lights.

d. Run the engine up past approximately 1400 rpm to close the reverse current cutout; the generator warning light should go out.

e. Increase engine rpm and check the voltage. The voltage should increase to approximately 27.5 volts and stay there regardless of any further increase in engine rpm.

f. In F4U-5N, check inverters by turning on instrument lights. Switch to stand-by inverter. Lights should stay on with switch in either position. If lights go out, inverter is not operating.

Note

Main inverter requires a minimum of 30 seconds warm-up with engine operating at engine speeds above generator cut-in level.

2–38. HYDRAULIC CHECK. The following functional check of the hydraulic system should be made:

a. Check normal operation of wing flaps in all positions from "UP" to normal "DOWN," noting positions on combination flap and landing gear indicator. Return to full "UP" position.

b. Check operation of oil cooler door and intercooler flap switches by placing them in all positions and noting positions on the indicator just forward of the throttle. The intercooler door should be closed manually and the switch left in its "OFF" position. The oil cooler door switch should be left in the "AUTOMATIC" position.

c. Check power and manual operation of the canopy. Normal hydraulic system gage pressure is 1500 (plus or minus 50) psi when no units are operating. Pressure will fluctuate and then stabilize at this value as individual systems are actuated. After the operation of the last sub-system, allow pressure to stabilize before checking to see that it remains constant. Oscillation or noticeable change in gage reading when no unit is in operation indicates malfunctioning of the system.

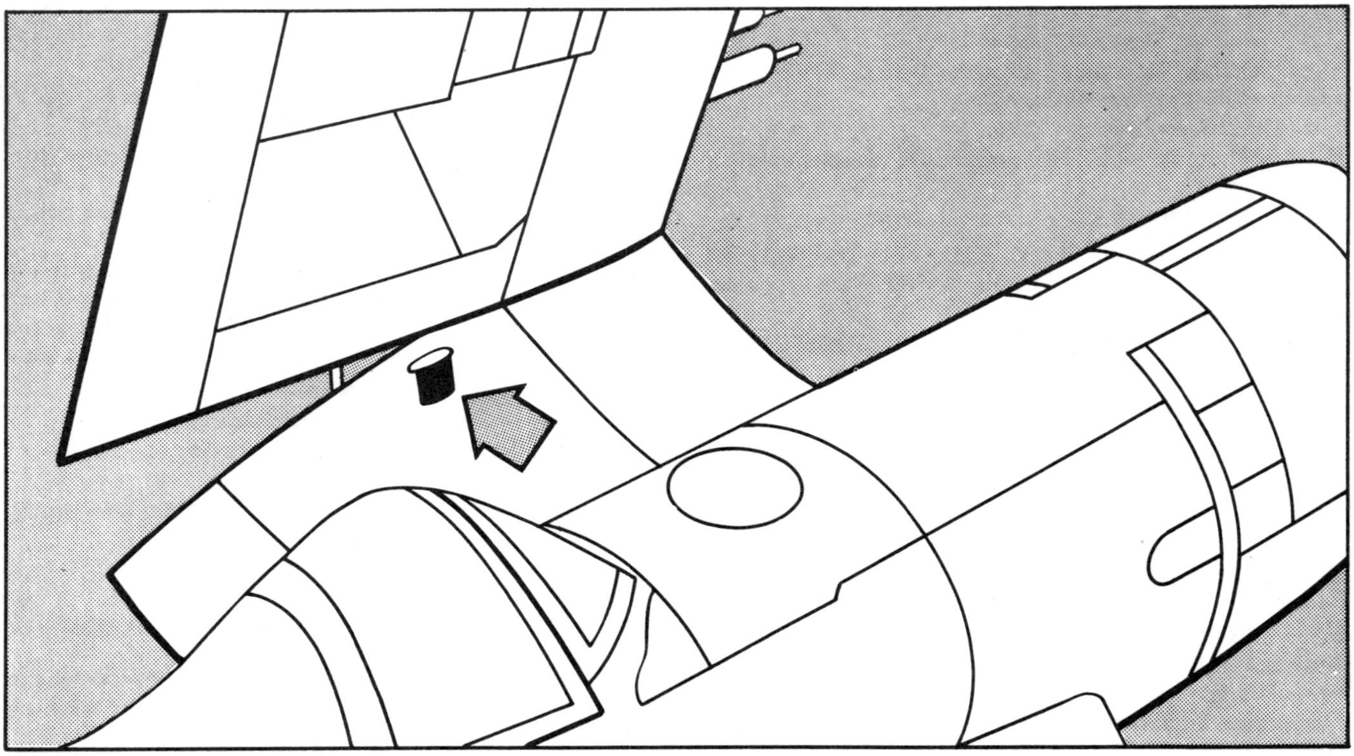

Figure 2-5. Wing Hinge Pin Lock Indicator

2–39. RADIO CHECK. Test radio operation according to instructions in paragraph 4–42.

2–40. WING SPREADING. To spread the wings, move the control handle to the "SPREAD" position. This unfolds the wings and inserts the pins through the hinges in proper sequence. When the wings are completely spread, move the control lever to the "WING HINGE PIN LOCKED" position. This locks the hinge pins in place.

2–41. WING FOLDING. To fold the wings, move the control hinge pins and fold the wings in the proper sequence. When the operation is complete, the handle should be moved forward to the "PARK" position.

WARNING

The wing-fold control shall be in the "WING HINGE PIN LOCKED" position for all flight operations.

2–42. No provision is made in the wing-folding hydraulic system to keep the outer panels "in step." That is, there is no flow equalizer installed. The wings must not be left free in any intermediate position between fully spread and fully folded, as air loads will cause them to shift position, blowing one down and the other up. When fully folded, the wings should be locked with jury struts. The wings may be moved to vertical by temporarily unlocking the jury struts and spreading the wings to the vertical position with the wing-fold control (with hydraulic system pressure up). The jury struts are telescopic with a limit stop at the vertical position. To fold one wing, hold the opposite wing down (two or three men at the tip). By locking the up wing with a jury strut, the wings will remain in this position as long as the wing-fold control is in the "PARK" position.

2–43. EMERGENCY TAKE-OFF.

2–44. It is possible to make an emergency take-off provided the oil temperature is above 20°C prior to take-off.

2–45. TAXIING INSTRUCTIONS. Remember the following when taxiing:

a. Use the S-turn procedure for best forward vision.

b. Let the airplane roll free where possible, using the brakes as sparingly as is practicable.

c. Use the tail wheel lock in extended crosswind taxiing to alleviate the need for riding the downwind brake.

d. Use low power, bearing in mind that badly overheated brakes are not fully effective. Overheating the brakes can score the brake disks, causing the brakes to seize, requiring replacement.

e. Keep electrical loads at a minimum to minimize battery discharge.

2-46. TAKE-OFF.

2–47. CHECK PRIOR TO TAKE OFF. The following should be checked prior to take-off.

a. Shoulder harness and safety belt—secure and "LOCKED."

b. Canopy—"OPEN."

c. Tail wheel—"LOCK."

d. Fuel selector—"ON."

e. Fuel transfer switch—"OFF."

f. Auxiliary (booster) fuel pump switch—"HIGH." Check fuel pressure.

g. Rudder tab—six degrees "NOSE RIGHT."

h. Elevator tab—one degree "NOSE UP."

i. Aileron tab—Neutral.

Note

To obtain accurate readings on tab indicator, the generator warning light must be off.

j. Intercooler flap—closed and switch in "AUTO MATIC."

k. Oil cooler door switch—"AUTOMATIC."

l. Cowl flaps—switch in "AUTOMATIC."

m. Master water injection switch—"OFF."

n. Wing flaps—set as required.

o. Propeller—full "INCREASE."

p. Mixture control—"RICH."

q. Throttle friction lock—tight enough to prevent throttle creeping back.

r. Check magnetos, cylinder head and oil temperatures, and oil pressure.

s. Chart board—"LOCKED IN." (F4U-5 and F4U-5P airplanes only.)

t. Compass caging switch—"CAGE" and then "UNCAGE." (F4U-5 and F4U-5P airplanes only.)

u. Arresting hook—"UP."

v. Power control switch on.

w. Wing fold—"WING HINGE PIN LOCKED."

Note

On F4U-5NL airplanes Bureau Serial No. 124504 and subsequent, the Deicer Boots switch must be in the "OFF" position.

2-48. FLAP SETTINGS. Any flap deflection from zero to 50 degrees (full down) may be used for take-off, the higher settings giving shorter ground runs. Take-offs with flaps up are easily accomplished with small increase in run, dispensing with the need for retracting flaps after take-off. In addition, the rate of climb immediately after take-off with flaps "UP" exceeds that with flaps deflected. Take-off at high flap settings should be made only when it is necessary to obtain the shortest possible deck run, and only after experience with settings increased gradually from the recommended settings of 20 degrees. When a high flap setting is used, the elevator tab should be set slightly more tail-heavy (about one degree).

2-49. At manifold pressures greater than 44 inches Hg with the flaps down, the tail cannot be held on the ground, even with the stick full back. Also, when operating from a wooden deck, the wheels will start slipping at approximately the same manifold pressure. As a result, when making a carrier take-off it is necessary to advance the throttle through the final portion of its travel as the airplane starts to roll. This operation should cause no difficulty.

CAUTION

When carrying 11.75″ rockets the maximum allowable flap deflection is 30 degrees.

2-50. TAB SETTINGS. The rudder force required to maintain a straight run will be high unless the rudder tab has been set at approximately six degrees "NOSE RIGHT" prior to the take-off run. Use of the proper tab settings is particularly important when high flap settings and maximum power are used. Individual airplanes will require slightly different tab settings from those given above.

2-51. MINIMUM RUN TAKE-OFF.

a. Wing flaps—full "DOWN" (50 degrees).

b. Propeller governor—full "INCREASE."

c. Elevator tabs—three to four degrees "NOSE UP."

d. Hold brakes slightly until tail starts to rise.

e. Release brakes and allow tail to rise to near normal take-off position.

f. Take off when minimum flying speed is attained (approximately 75 knots indicated airspeed). The nose will be slightly heavy. If take-off is made from unpaved or muddy runway, take off with tail slightly lower than directed above.

Note

If an obstacle is to be cleared during take-off, the wing flap setting should be reduced to approximately 30 degrees.

2-52. CATAPULT TAKE-OFF.

a. Shoulder harness and safety belt—tight and "LOCKED."

b. Cabin fully open—check safety latch.

c. Tighten engine control friction adjustment knob.

d. Check that chartboard is locked in. (F4U-5 and F4U-5P airplanes only.)

e. Place back and head firmly against seat and head rest.

f. Brace right arm.

g. Push throttle full forward and grasp catapult throttle hold.

2-53. AFTER TAKE-OFF.

2-54. After the airplane is airborne and insufficient runway remains to make an emergency landing possible:

Note

Before retracting the landing gear, the rotation of the wheels should be stopped by braking to avoid damaging the scuff plate in the wheel well.

a. Retract the landing gear.

b. When all obstacles have been cleared, reduce power to rated power (see Power Plant Chart, figure A-4).

c. When sufficient speed and altitude have been attained, retract flaps.

CAUTION

It should be noted that the best rate of climb is attained with the wing flaps up. It is therefore desirable that the flaps be retracted as soon as practicable after take-off. However DO NOT RETRACT FLAPS TOO SOON AFTER TAKE-OFF OR AT TOO LOW A SPEED. THIS MAY CAUSE DANGEROUS SETTLING OF THE AIRPLANE DUE TO LOSS OF LIFT.

d. Trim airplane for 150 knots indicated airspeed for best climb at sea level with linear reduction to 125 knots at 40,000 feet (figure A-5).

e. Check that cylinder head temperature does not exceed 248°C.

f. Set transfer switch to desired external auxiliary fuel tank.

g. Auxiliary (booster) fuel pump switch—"LOW."

h. Mixture control—"NORMAL."

i. Close canopy.

j. If anti-blackout suit is worn, plug suit hose into quick-disconnect fitting (refer to paragraph 4-48).

2-55. CLIMB AND LEVEL FLIGHT.

2-56. RATED POWER. The maximum continuous operation of the aircraft is 2600 rpm with cylinder head temperature of 232°C. A cylinder head temperature of 248°C is permissible for a period of 30 minutes. Operate in accordance with the Power Plant Chart, figure A-4, and the fuel consumption data given in figure A-3.

2-57. MILITARY POWER. Use of military power (2800 rpm) is prohibited for periods longer than 30 minutes. Operate in accordance with the Power Plant Chart, figure A-4. Do not exceed 248°C cylinder head temperature at any time.

WARNING

Do not exceed 56 inches Hg. Military Power or 50 inches Rated Power when using 100/130 grade fuel.

2-58. COMBAT POWER. The R-2800-32W engine is cleared for combat power. The manifold pressure regulator limits the maximum obtainable manifold pressure to 70 in. Hg. Manifold pressures between military and full combat powers can be controlled by the throttle. Water-alcohol consumption is approximately 2 gallons per minute.

WARNING

To prevent inadvertent use of water injection, the master switch must be "OFF" at all times except immediately preceding use of the water injection system.

2-59. To obtain combat power:

a. Mixture control—"RICH" or "NORMAL."

b. Propeller control—full "INCREASE" (2800 rpm).

c. Master water injection switch—"ON."

d. Throttle—move to range forward of throttle stop.

2-60. GENERAL FLYING CHARACTERISTICS.

2-61. Refer to the Flight Operation Instruction Charts, figure A-6, for the effects of changes in gross weight or external resistance, and to the Power Plant Chart, figure A-4, for engine operating data.

2-62. STABILITY. The airplane possesses satisfactory longitudinal stability with the center of gravity in the specified range. The longitudinal stability characteristics of the F4U-5 have been improved over those of the F4U-4 due to a forward shift in the center of gravity and the incorporation of a downward tilted thrustline.

2-63. TRIM CHANGES. Extension of the landing gear and of the wing and cooling flaps changes the trim of the airplane only slightly. The direction of trim changes are listed as follows:

a. Extend landing gear—tail-heavy as gear begins to extend, but nose-heavy when the gear is fully down.

b. Extend wing flaps—tail-heavy at small flap angles, and nose-heavy at large flap angles.

c. Open cowl flaps—nose-heavy.

d. Open oil cooler doors—tail-heavy.

e. Open intercooler flap—tail-heavy.

2-64. The airplane exhibits no unusual flying characteristics at low speeds. There is some change of both lateral and directional trim due to the application of power at low airspeeds. However, the effectiveness of the aileron and rudder trim tabs is sufficient to offset these changes of trim. All the trim tabs on this airplane are effective and sensitive.

2-65. CRUISING. The engine should be operated with "NORMAL" mixture for cruising power operation. A cylinder head temperature limit of 232°C (450°F) is not to be exceeded for continuous operation. While cruising operations may be conducted at any engine power below normal rated power, if minimum fuel consumption is important and it is tactically feasible to do so, cruising operation should be conducted at power considerably below maximum cruising. It may not be possible to operate at as low a manifold pressure and rpm for cruising as desired while flying at intermediate and high altitudes without encountering engine surge. If surge occurs, increase rpm and then advance throttle until surging ceases. Increased fuel consumption will of course result, but this is a limitation that cannot be avoided. For specific details refer to Flight Operation Instruction Charts, figure A-6.

Note

After take-off, cage and uncage P-3 compass with airplane in level flight to obtain correct heading (F4U-5 and F4U-5P airplanes only).

2-66. RECOMMENDED CRUISING. Sea level operation at approximately 165 knots indicated air speed at 1500 rpm will result in near best range operation (approximately 48 U. S. gallons per hour). Refer to figure A-6, Flight Operation Instruction Charts, for more precise flight planning, since miles per gallon of fuel consumed (under no-wind conditions) is a function of the aerodynamic characteristics of the airplane and the propeller efficiency as well as engine power output.

2-66A. It may not be possible to operate the engine at as low an rpm and manifold pressure for cruising as desired when flying at intermediate and high altitudes because of engine surge. The necessity of increasing rpm and manifold pressure to eliminate this condition will of course result in higher fuel consumption. This is a limitation that cannot be avoided and is characteristic of all highly supercharged engines. It is not possible to include fuel consumption data to cover this contingency because of the widely varying surge characteristics exhibited by different airplanes. Reliable fuel consumption data can be obtained only through experience with a particular airplane.

2-67. MANEUVERS.

CAUTION

Cage P-3 compass 15 seconds prior to exceeding 70° pitch or 110° bank, or compass may be damaged (F4U-5 and F4U-5P airplanes only).

2-68. MANEUVER FLAPS. The wing flaps have been designed for possible use in maneuvering. The flaps may be used to increase the lift to allow lower airspeed and thereby decrease the radius of turns at low speeds. The flaps are also useful in increasing the drag of the airplane so that it may be quickly decelerated to the optimum speed for a short radius turn. In general, flap deflections of 20 degrees or less will be most helpful in improving maneuverability. Therefore, a setting of 20 degrees has been established as the "maneuver flap condition."

CAUTION

Flaps are not to be used at speeds greater than 200 knots. As stated above, the flaps have also been designed for use in maneuvering the airplane in combat. With typical maneuvering flap deflection of 20 degrees or less, the airplane may be maneuvered at equivalent "flaps up" accelerations up to 200 knots.

2-69. AILERONS. The use of full lateral stick throw of the ailerons is restricted to a maximum speed of 300 knots. At higher speeds the use of ailerons shall be limited to the same stick force as is required for full throw at 300 knots, but not exceeding one half throw at 350 knots, or one quarter throw at 400 knots.

2-70. STALLS. The stalling characteristics of this airplane are consistent with those experienced on earlier model F4U-type airplanes and are not considered abnormal. Significant differences in stalling characteristics for the model F4U-5N airplane should be anticipated; however, those are discussed in Appendix II. Stall warning as indicated by slight airframe buffeting occurs at speeds very close to the actual stall and therefore will not provide a positive and early indication to the pilot. With power-on, the variation of elevator control force and/or position in approaching the stall is very slight and therefore does not provide a large degree of "feel" of a change in angle of attack or airspeed. For these reasons, FLIGHT IN CLOSE PROXIMITY TO THE STALL AT LOW ALTITUDES SHOULD BE AVOIDED OR APPROACHED WITH CAUTION.

CAUTION

Pilots should at a safe altitude thoroughly familiarize themselves with the stall characteristics of this aircraft in both "clean" and "landing" configurations. This familiarization should include stalls in both straight and level flight and in turns of various banks in the "clean" configuration as well as stalls in the "landing" configuration, using various flap positions and power settings while simulating approach and landing conditions. The above recommendation is not applicable in its entirety to the F4U-5N airplane in which accelerated power-on stalls should not be attempted.

2-71. At the stall with power-off, the airplane exhibits a moderate nose down pitch and roll-off in either direction. With POWER-ON, FLAPS DOWN, a roll-off to the left at the stall is violent and is accompanied by a 600-to-900 foot loss in altitude.

2-72. The indicated stalling speeds for a 11,600-pound fighter are given in the following table (see figure A-1).

CONDITION	FLAPS	POWER	INDICATED STALL SPEED KNOTS
Landing	50°	Closed Throttle	78
Landing	30°	Closed Throttle	79
Landing	20°	Closed Throttle	81
Landing	50°	Power on (level flight) 23 in. Hg., 2400 rpm	67
Clean	Up	Closed Throttle	88
Clean	Up	Power on (level flight) 18 in. Hg., 2400 rpm	85

2-73. SPINS.

WARNING

NO INTENTIONAL SPINNING OF THE MODEL F4U-5 AIRPLANE IS PERMITTED.

2–74. GENERAL. The spinning and spin recovery characteristics of this airplane are somewhat more severe than those of the earlier F4U-type airplanes. Satisfactory recovery from spins of five turns in each direction in the clean condition and from one turn in the landing condition has been adequately demonstrated for all presently required spin entry conditions. The number of turns required for recovery from five-turn spins in each direction varied between 1½ and 3½ turns in the clean condition, depending upon the type of entry and number of turns in the spin. In the landing condition from a one-turn spin, in both directions, the average recovery requires ¼ turn. Spins in either direction were, in general, oscillatory in character. A lateral-directional oscillation combines with the initial longitudinal oscillation if the airplane is held in the spin for more than two turns. However, the oscillation should not be interpreted to mean that a flat spin is developing. Recovery should be normal with forces within the capabilities of the average pilot. Tabs, especially the elevator tab, should be used if the recovery forces are too high.

2–75. NORMAL SPIN RECOVERY TECHNIQUE. Following is the recommended method of recovering from an inadvertent normal spin:

a. Close the throttle COMPLETELY and apply opposite controls sharply, leading with FULL opposite rudder, followed ½ turn later by FULL forward movement of the control stick. An increase in the rudder pedal force will be noted when the stick is moved forward but full rudder pedal throw should be reapplied and held if any movement has occurred. Prior to the application of full forward stick, pull rpm control full aft to prevent the engine from overspeeding during recovery. The aileron position during recovery is not considered critical and, in general, should be retained in neutral.

b. The rate of rotation will increase significantly upon application of controls for recovery, which is a good sign that recovery is starting. Hold full reversed controls until rotating stops and the airplane is thrown to an inverted attitude with considerable negative "g." This recovery condition is very positive and should not be confused with an inverted spin. At this point, the controls should be neutralized and the airplane pulled out in a symmetrical pull-out. The airplane must be eased out of the ensuing dive. Avoid a rapid aft stick movement as a high-speed stall may result with an accompanying spin re-entry requiring more altitude for recovery.

c. If unable to hold full opposite controls and the stick walks back, return controls with the spin for a brief interval, and repeat full recovery control motion.

Note

Full forward stick (against the stop) must be applied and held for spin recovery. It is further recommended that the airplane in a well-developed spin should be abandoned only if the recovery controls cannot be applied and held, and/or the airplane reaches an altitude below 5,000 feet.

2–76. INVERTED SPIN RECOVERY TECHNIQUE. If an inverted spin should occur, the following steps for recovery should be initiated immediately:

a. Close the throttle and pull the propeller control full aft.

b. Apply full opposite controls and hold until rotation stops.

c. Neutralize controls immediately after rotation has stopped; otherwise a normal spin may result.

d. In recovering from the ensuing dive, ease the airplane out carefully to avoid the danger of a high-speed stall.

CAUTION

There is a possibility of engine overspeeding, in an inverted spin. Therefore, the throttle and propeller control should be pulled full aft while attempting recovery.

Note

If an attempted maneuver should result in an inverted nose-high attitude with insufficient speed and high power setting, close the throttle and pull the propeller control full aft before an inverted stall and spin occur. Allow the airplane to fall out of the maneuver rather than attempting to salvage it. Also avoid excessive use of the controls. Recovery can be made from a well-developed, inverted spin using approximately one-half of the force required to recover from a normal spin. Recovery to normal flight can then be made from this attitude without encountering either a normal or inverted spin.

2–77. PERMISSIBLE ACROBATICS.

2–78. All normal acrobatics are permissible when not carrying bombs or similar loads, if the following precautionary measures are observed:

a. Do not exceed allowable speeds and accelerations.

b. If inexperienced, do not enter loops or Immelmanns at less than 280 knots indicated airspeed. This speed may be lessened slightly as more experience is gained in these maneuvers.

c. If inexperienced, do not enter slow rolls at less than 180 knots indicated airspeed.

d. Auxiliary fuel pump on "LOW."

2–79. DIVING.

2–79A. CONTROL FORCES. The rudder and elevator control forces developed in a dive, from level trimmed flight, and in recovery from dive will be lower in the F4U-5 than in the F4U-4. The reduced control forces are due to the incorporation of spring tabs in the rudder and elevator control systems of the F4U-5.

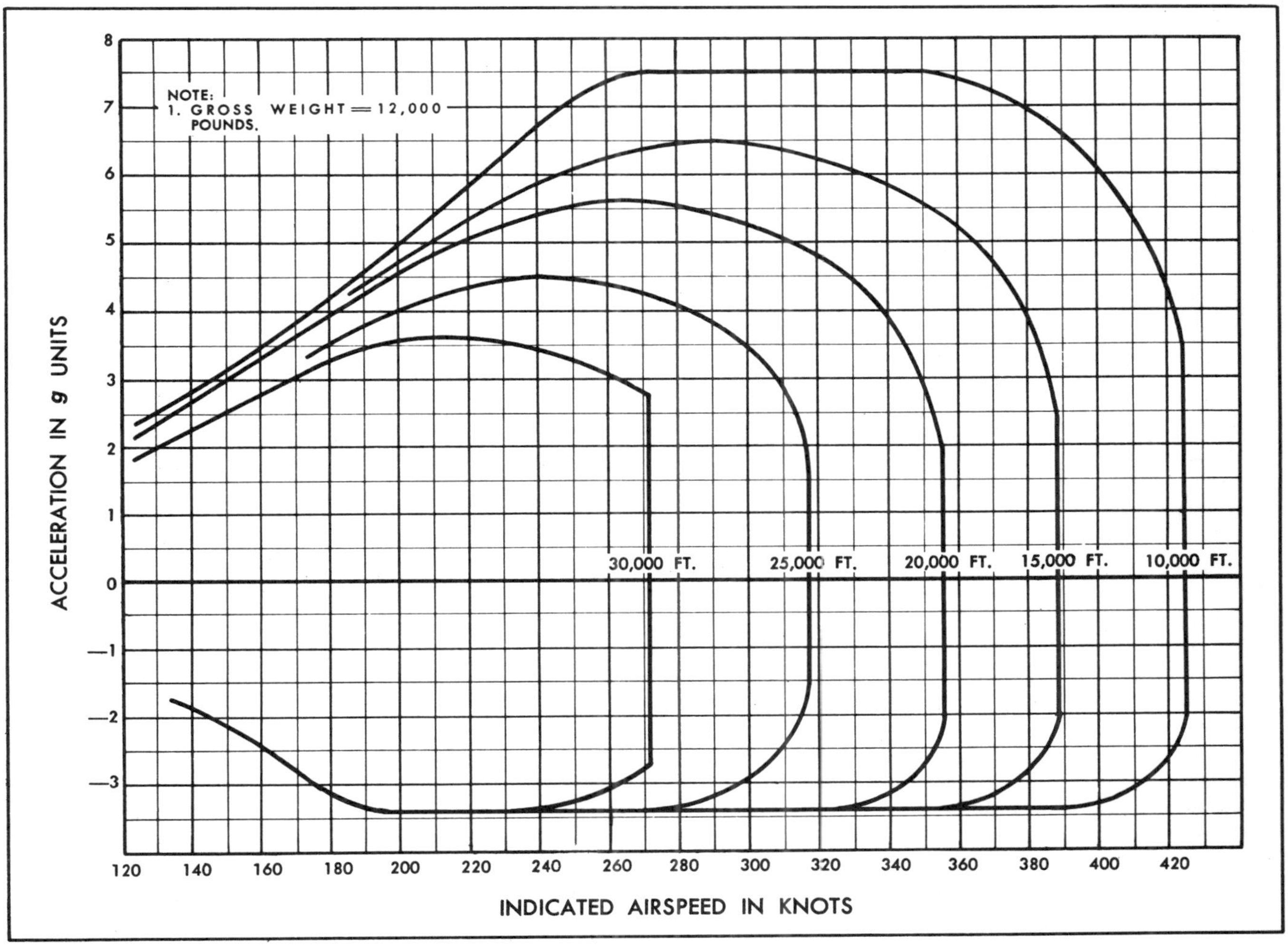

Figure 2–6. Operating Flight Strength Diagram

Note

The caging switch for the P-3 gyro flux gate compass should be caged before engaging in maneuvers which will exceed 100 degrees bank and/or 70 degrees pitch. (F4U-5 and F4U-5P airplanes only.)

2–80. CHECK LIST.

a. Windshield defroster–"ON."

b. Canopy–closed.

c. Landing gear control–"UP" or as dive brake (see paragraph 2–82).

d. Wing flap control–"UP."

e. Propeller control–Set as desired up to 2600 rpm.

f. Mixture control–"RICH."

g. Throttle–Slightly "OPEN."

Note

Approximately twenty inches manifold pressure is recommended during prolonged dives. Manifold pressures much below twenty inches, if held in a prolonged dive, will foul up the engine in the same manner as do prolonged glides with closed throttle. The throttle should be opened slowly at the completion of the dive so that the partly cooled engine will not cut out.

h. Fuel tank selector–"ON."

i. Cowl flaps–"AUTOMATIC."

j. Oil cooler doors–"AUTOMATIC."

k. Intercooler flap–"AUTOMATIC."

l. Maximum rpm limit 3120 rpm (not over 30 seconds duration).

2–81. COCKPIT CANOPY. The canopy must be closed before entering high speed dives as it is not designed to withstand speeds over 260 knots in the open position.

2–82. LANDING GEAR AND DIVE BRAKE CONTROL. .To minimize the possibility of malfunctioning of the main landing gear during retraction or extension, use of the landing gear as a dive brake is permitted only in full down and locked position except in an emergency. The maximum speed at which the landing gear extends fully and locks is 270 knots IAS. The maximum permissible speed with the landing gear down and locked is 350 knots IAS.

2—83. BUFFETING WITH EXTERNAL AUXILIARY TANKS OR BOMBS INSTALLED. No buffeting is likely to occur at speeds and altitudes shown in figure 2—6 with:

a. External stores on the twin pylon. Two universal droppable fuel tanks mounted on the twin pylons will slightly reduce the buffet limit speeds.

b. With external stores on the centerline pylon but not on either of the twin pylons. Buffeting, however, is probable within the speed range of 300 to 350 knots when all three pylons, twin and centerline, have external stores at one time. When the airplane is dived with dive brakes down, the buffeting tendency is somewhat reduced. If buffeting is encountered, the speed should be reduced since the continued vibration will damage the wing flap.

2—84. MAXIMUM PERMISSIBLE INDICATED AIR SPEEDS AND ACCELERATIONS. The maximum permissible speeds and accelerations at various altitudes are shown on figure 2—6 for a gross weight of 12,000 pounds. At other weights the permissible accelerations are such as to maintain a constant product of gross weight and acceleration except that 7.5 g positive and 3.4 g negative should not be exceeded. The limit of the actual accelerations and speeds that can be withstood with safety is indicated by a general buffeting or shaking. It is dangerous to continue increasing acceleration or speed once the buffet begins because the shaking and vibration increase the loads on the tail structure and may cause damage to the stabilizer and elevator. Therefore, when buffeting is encountered, reduce speed or acceleration IMMEDIATELY. In general, this phenomenom occurs at lower airspeeds at the higher altitudes as seen on figure 2—6.

2—85. The airplane, if permitted will attain much higher than the limit speeds. At high altitudes in particular, the limit speeds may easily be exceeded in a dive, especially if care is not taken to avoid steep dive angles. Become familiar with the diving charactertistics of the airplane gradually, while maintaining absolute control over the diving speed. The speed limits should be first approached only after such familiarization, and in dives at moderate angles. Familiarity with the limitations imposed by the shake disturbance on pullout should also be acquired gradually.

2—86. LIMIT SPEEDS FOR VARIOUS DIVE ANGLES. In order that pilots may avoid picking up airspeeds in dives, which exceed airplane restrictions, there are shown in figure 2—7 the values of airspeeds at various altitudes and dive angles which should not be exceeded. If these speeds are attained at the altitudes and dive angles listed, immediately begin and sustain a relatively severe pull-out in order to avoid exceeding the airspeed restrictions of the airplane at lower altitude. Such a pull-out can be accomplished without exceeding the acceleration restrictions of the airplane, or the pilot's limit of tolerance for sustained pull-outs at fairly high accelerations, whichever is less.

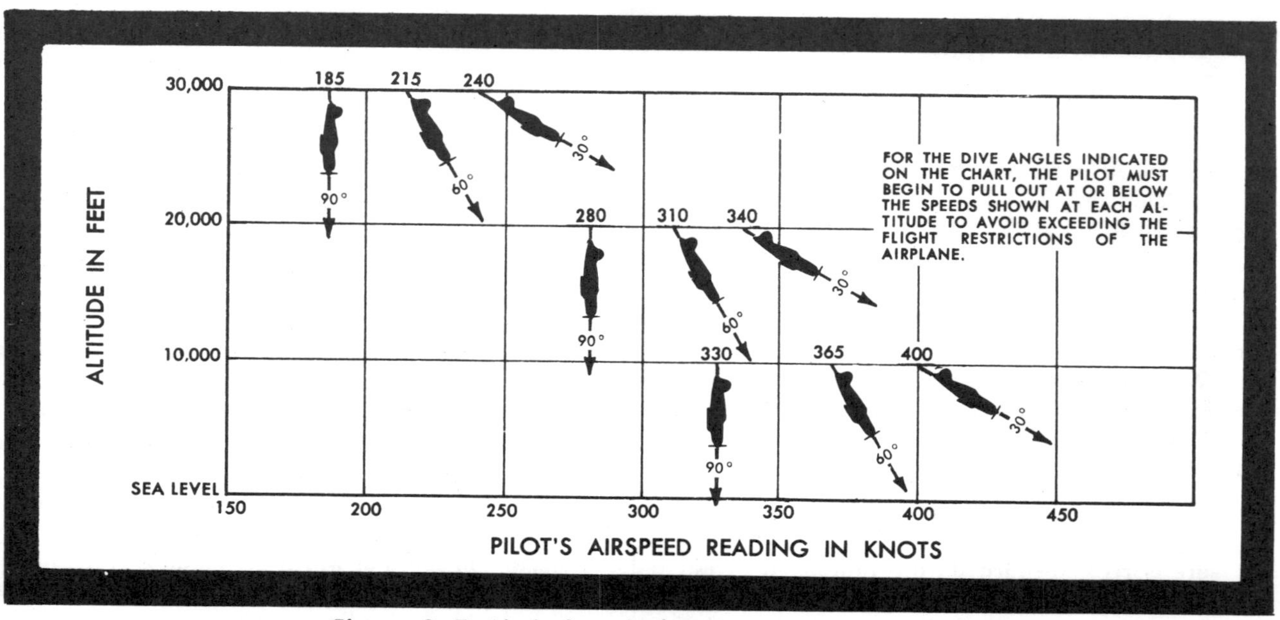

Figure 2—7. Limit Speeds for Various Dive Angles

2-87. APPROACH AND LANDING.

2-88. CHECK LIST.

a. Shoulder harness—"LOCKED."

b. Tailwheel—locked for field, unlocked for carrier landing.

c. Fuel tank selector—"ON."

d. Fuel transfer switch—"OFF."

e. Auxiliary (booster) fuel pump switch—"HIGH."

f. Tabs—as required.

g. Intercooler flap—"AUTOMATIC."

h. Oil cooler switch—"AUTOMATIC."

i. Cowl flap switch—"AUTOMATIC."

j. Wing flaps—as required (see figure 2-1, flight limitations with flaps extended).

k. Master water injection switch—"OFF."

l. Propeller control—full "INCREASE."

m. Mixture—"RICH."

n. Landing gear—"DOWN."

o. Canopy—"OPEN."

p. Master armament switch—"OFF."

q. Armament safety switch—"SAFE."

r. Gun selector switches—"OFF."

s. Chart board—locked in. (F4U-5 and F4U-5P airplanes only.)

t. Arresting hook control—"UP" for field. "DOWN" for carrier landing.

2-89. The following operating sequence is recommended.

a. Observe items on the above check list.

b. Open canopy fully.

c. Airspeed in approach—approximately 90 knots.

Note

The Deicer Boot switch must be in "OFF" position on F4U-5NL airplanes Bureau Serial No. 124504 and subsequent.

2-90. NIGHT LANDING CHECK LIST. In addition to the above, check the following interior and exterior lights as follows:

a. Master switch—"ON."

b. "WING," "TAIL," and "FUSELAGE" lights "BRIGHT."

c. Interior light selector switch — "ALL INSTRUMENTS," and dimmed down to a minimum useful illumination.

Note

Arrested landings with full or partially full external auxiliary fuel tanks shall NOT be made except during emergencies when the fuel cannot be consumed or the tanks cannot be jettisoned.

2-91. CROSS WIND LANDING. For a cross wind landing it is recommended that a wheel landing be made using slightly less than normal amount of flap (about 30 degrees), all other normal landing conditions being about the same. Use the conventional methods for correcting for cross wind. During the landing run the weather cocking tendency will be off-set somewhat by the locked tail wheel. More severe cases of weather cocking will have to be counteracted by prompt use of rudder and or brake. The brakes should be used cautiously until the tail wheel is on the ground. It should be noted that the brakes are completely independent of the main hydraulic system so that failure of the main hydraulic system does not affect this operation.

2-92. MINIMUM RUN LANDING. To make a minimum run landing, use full flap in a rather flat, nose high power approach at an indicated airspeed of 90 knots. Bring the airplane over the end of the runway at a minimum safe altitude, close throttle and land airplane. Use brakes as necessary.

2-93. WAVE-OFF. In the event of a wave-off, open the throttle smoothly. Retract the landing gear immediately. The oil cooler doors, intercooler flap, and cowl flaps will operate automatically. The flaps should be raised as soon as safe speed and altitude are attained to avoid overheating the power plant, which would result if extended operations were undertaken in the landing condition. Retrim airplane as necessary. The rudder and elevator control forces in the F4U-5 in a wave-off will be lower than those in previous F4U models. This reduction in control forces is due to the incorporation of spring tabs in the rudder and elevator control systems of the F4U-5.

2-94. STOPPING OF ENGINE.

2-95. ENGINE COOLING. Before shutting down the engine, check the following:

a. Cowl flaps—open (switch in "AUTOMATIC").

b. Intercooler flap—open to cool accessory compartment (switch "OPEN," then "AUTOMATIC").

c. Oil cooler doors—open (switch "OPEN," then "AUTOMATIC").

d. Propeller control—full "INCREASE."

2-96. TO STOP ENGINE.

a. Auxiliary (booster) fuel pump switch—"OFF."

b. Dilute oil, if necessary (see paragraph 2-97).

c. Mixture control—"IDLE CUT-OFF."

d. Ignition switch—"OFF" when the propeller stops turning.

e. Power control switch—"OFF."

f. Fuel selector—"OFF."

g. Turn off all switches used for flight such as radio lights, etc.

Note

Cowl flaps, oil cooler doors, intercooler flap, and cockpit canopy should be closed as soon as engine is cool.

2-97. OIL DILUTION. In the event of low temperature forecast, i.e., below +2°C (+35°F), engine oil should be diluted in the following manner:

a. Open the manual shut-off valve in the oil dilution line. This valve is located on the forward side of the fuel strainer and is accessible through the intercooler flap.

b. Engine speed constant–1000 rpm.

c. Oil dilution switch—"ON." In some instances, it may be necessary to dilute the engine oil in two or more periods. Dividing the oil dilution procedure into several periods has no detrimental effect on the general dilution period provided the total time does not exceed that required for the anticipated temperature.

Note

It is recommended that the oil dilution period be divided into two periods when it is necessary to service the oil tank, so that some dilution is accomplished before servicing, and the remainder is accomplished after the oil tank is serviced.

d. During the last minute of dilution, dilute the oil in the propeller dome as follows: Set the propeller control to 1600 rpm. Open the throttle until the engine speed reaches 1600 rpm. Then without moving the throttle, operate the propeller control so that the engine speed drops to 1200 rpm and then increases to 1600 rpm. Perform this operation twice. Set throttle to engine speed of 1000 rpm. Return propeller control to full low pitch (increase rpm).

e. Stop engine by moving the mixture control to "IDLE CUT-OFF" position, then turn ignition switch to "OFF." Hold dilution switch "ON" until engine stops turning.

f. Close the manual shut-off valve and safety wire before next take-off.

2–98. PRECAUTIONS. Several precautions should be observed when diluting the oil.

a. Dilution will increase considerably the inflammability of the vapors issuing from the crankcase breather. The oil itself will burn at a dilution of 20 percent or more (at an ambient temperature of 60° F). Therefore, all possible precautions against fire shall be taken during the dilution operation and during subsequent starting and warm-up. It is recommended that personnel with fire extinguishers always be maintained in the vicinity of the engine during dilution.

2–99. BEFORE LEAVING COCKPIT. Before leaving the cockpit, check the following:

a. Tail wheel–"LOCK."
b. Gun sight switches–"OFF."
c. Fuel tank selector–"OFF."
d. Fuel transfer switch–"OFF."
e. Auxiliary (booster) fuel pump switch–"OFF."
f. Wing flaps–"UP."
g. Water injection master switch–"OFF."
h. Throttle–closed.
i. Mixture control–"IDLE CUT-OFF."
j. Ignition switch–"OFF."
k. Armament switches–"OFF."
l. Auxiliary hydraulic pump switch–"OFF."
m. Engine starting switches–"OFF."
n. All light switches–"OFF."
o. All radio switches–"OFF."

2–100. INSTALLING SURFACE CONTROL LOCK. Move the rudder pedal slide full aft and insert forward tubes of the lock into the tubes of the lower end of the rudder pedals. This is done by telescoping the spring-loaded tube of the lock into the tube housing the spring. Release when aligned with rudder pedal tubes. Position control stick in the two retaining clamps of the lock and secure by inserting spring-loaded pins into locking position.

CAUTION

Check that the surface controls are locked whenever the airplane is parked for any extended period.

2–101. If the airplane is to remain parked for any length of time, before leaving it check the following:

a. Cowl flaps–closed.
b. Intercooler flap–closed.
c. Oil cooler doors–closed.
d. Canopy–closed.

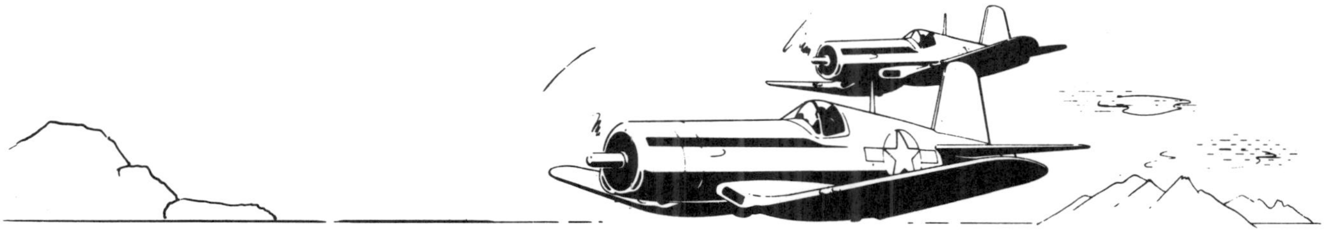

Section III

EMERGENCY OPERATING INSTRUCTIONS

3–1. FIRE.

3–2. FIRE DURING STARTING. If an induction system fire should break out while starting the engine, keep the engine running. In many cases this will draw the flames back up into the cylinders. If this, and the application of CO_2 by ground crew, is not effective in extinguishing the flames, while the ground crew continues to apply CO_2:

a. Pull mixture control to "IDLE CUT-OFF."

b. Auxiliary (booster) fuel pump switch—"OFF."

c. Throttle—open.

d. Ignition—"OFF."

3–3. ELECTRICAL FIRE. In the event of electrical system fire:

a. Turn off power control switch.

b. Turn off all other electrical switches.

3–3A. ENGINE FIRE IN FLIGHT. In the case of an engine fire in flight, if altitude and other factors permit, the procedure outlined below should be followed. Obviously, no recommended procedure can cover all cases of a fire over water and land areas, particularly when a single engine airplane such as the F4U-5 is involved, or when bail out is necessary.

a. Propeller control—full "DECREASE."

b. Throttle—closed (simultaneously with propeller control).

c. Fuel selector valve—"OFF."

d. Cowl flaps—open.

e. Mixture control—"IDLE CUT-OFF."

f. Ignition—"OFF."

g. Electrical switches—"OFF."

The decision to stay with the airplane or to bail out, after all other factors are considered, will depend upon whether the fire appears to be increasing or diminishing. If the fire goes out DO NOT ATTEMPT TO RESTART THE ENGINE.

3–4. ENGINE FAILURE.

3–5. ENGINE FAILURE DURING TAKE-OFF. If th engine should fail before leaving the ground close the throttle immediately and use the brakes as required. In the event of engine failure immediately after leaving the ground close the throttle and land straight ahead. As many as possible of the operations listed below should be performed in the order given:

a. Release auxiliary tanks or bombs.

b. Landing gear—"UP," unless sufficient runway is available straight ahead for landing with wheels down.

c. Wing flaps—full down.

d. Lower seat.

e. Switches (power control and ignition)—"OFF." It should be noted that the power control switch turns off the auxiliary (booster) fuel pump and the fuel transfer pump.

f. Fuel selector—"OFF."

3–6. ENGINE FAILURE DURING FLIGHT. Engine failure may be indicated by either freezing of the engine or by drop in altitude and loss of speed. If the engine fails but does not freeze, no absence of engine noise is apparent since the windmilling propeller simulates normal engine operation. Also, in this condition, manifold pressure can be increased and decreased normally, and the propeller blade angle can be changed within certain limits. If the engine operation is rough, decrease engine speed by placing the propeller control in the full "DECREASE" position and throttling back. While the propeller is windmilling, the hydraulic system can be operated normally. If the engine has frozen, the hydraulically activated units must be operated by the auxiliary hydraulic pump.

3–7. If altitude permits attempt to find the cause of engine failure as follows:

a. Check fuel supply immediately, and fuel tank selector setting. Should the selector be on "STAND BY," the engine will quit when the drop tank is empty. If the fuel pressure drops when the fuel selector is in the "ON" position, and the drop tanks contain fuel, it is possible that pressure may be regained by switching to the "STAND BY" position.

Note

The gliding ratio of this airplane in the clean condition at 140 knots indicated airspeed (best gliding speed) is 14:1. The gliding ratio in the landing condition at 85 knots is 5:1. Therefore the flaps and landing gear should not be extended until the pilot is certain he can make his point of intended landing.

3–8. BAIL-OUT. If the decision to bail out is made:

a. Reduce airspeed as much as possible.

b. Disconnect radio, oxygen, anti-blackout suit and/or electric flying suit connections.

CAUTION

Before bailing out at altitude, turn air valve on oxygen regulator to "100 PERCENT OXYGEN" and inhale as much oxygen as possible.

c. Unfasten safety belt and shoulder harness.

d. The canopy can be opened quickly prior to bailing-out by placing the canopy control handle full aft in the "EMERGENCY" position. This releases an air pressure bottle charge which forces the canopy from the full closed to the full open position within three seconds.

e. Raise the seat to its topmost position.

f. Abandon airplane.

3–9. FORCED LANDINGS.

3–10. In the event of a forced landing with auxiliary tanks or bombs attached, release in accordance with instructions contained in paragraph 3–25.

3–11. BELLY LANDINGS. Prepare for a belly landing as follows :

a. Release auxiliary tanks or bombs.

b. Landing gear—"UP."

c. Landing flaps—down as needed.

d. Shoulder harness and safety belt—locked tight.

e. Open canopy.

f. Fuel tank pressure release—"DUMP."

g. Prior to ground contact drop the pilot's seat to its low position.

h. Switches (power control and ignition)—"OFF."

i. Fuel selector—"OFF."

3–12. DITCHING. The same procedure as outlined above for belly landings is applicable to ditching. The airplane has excellent water landing characteristics due to the inverted gull wing which causes it to plane on contact with the water. Because of the planing feature, a full stall landing is not necessary.

3–13. EMERGENCY FUEL SYSTEM MANAGEMENT.

3–14. FUEL TRANSFER PUMP FAILURE. If there should be a failure of the electrical system or of the transfer pump while the transfer system is being used, proceed as follows:

a. Turn fuel transfer switch "OFF."

b. Turn the fuel selector to the desired stand-by position ("LEFT OR CENTER DROP TANK STAND-BY" or "RIGHT DROP TANK STAND-BY"). Gasoline will then flow directly from the selected auxiliary tank to the carburetor. Note that when operating with the fuel selector in either of the "STAND-BY" positions, operation will probably be unsatisfactory above 12,000 feet. Do not operate in either "STAND-BY" position for take-off.

CAUTION

Keep an accurate mental check on fuel consumption. Do not shift from one fuel tank to another until all the fuel in the first tank is exhausted (down to where the fuel pressure needle starts to fluctuate). It is better to know which tank is empty and which is full rather than be uncertain of how much fuel remains in either. However, flights should not be made at low altitude on a near-empty drop tank.

3–15. LOSS OF FUEL PRESSURE. In the event that fuel pressure drops considerably as indicated on the fuel pressure gage, check the following possible causes.

3–16. LOSS OF FUEL SUCTION. Should an auxiliary tank run dry while the system is being operated on a "STAND-BY" setting, fuel suction should be regained as follows:

a. Shift to main tank with positive visual check of selector valve position.

b. Auxiliary fuel pump—"HIGH."

c. Retard throttle to 1/4 position.

d. Mixture control to "IDLE CUT-OFF" until adequate pressure is built up (approximately 6 psi).

e. Nose over into steep glide.

f. Use primer if necessary.

Note

This procedure for regaining fuel suction should be understood and memorized. The first three steps are usually sufficient to recover from partial loss of suction not accompanied by complete engine cut-out.

3–17. FAILURE OF ENGINE-DRIVEN PUMP. Failure of the engine-driven pump will be indicated by a drop in fuel pressure. In the event of fuel pump failure:

a. Auxiliary fuel pump—"HIGH."

b. Check fuel selector—"ON."

c. Reduce power.

3–17A. EMERGENCY OIL COOLER BY-PASS OPERATION. In case of damage to one or both oil coolers, proceed as follows:

a. Determine which oil cooler is damaged.

b. Shut off the affected oil cooler.

c. Open oil cooler doors.

d. If both oil coolers have been by-passed, do not exceed 2,400 rpm. A lower rpm is recommended.

e. Oil temperature shall not be allowed to exceed 150°C, and it is recommended that the temperature be limited to 120°C. Reducing rpm will tend to lower the oil temperature.

3–18. LANDING GEAR.

3–19. RETRACTION. Mechanical downlocks on the main landing gear scissors prevent retraction of the landing gear as long as the weight of the airplane is on it even though the control handle may be placed inadvertently in the "UP" position. Should the control handle be in the "UP" position when the take-off is made, the landing gear will not retract when the airplane becomes airborne. In this event place the handle in the "DOWN" position and then back to the "UP" position to retract the landing gear.

3–20. EXTENSION. For emergency extension of the landing gear:

a. Reduce speed to approximately 110 knots.

b. Release the emergency latch on the landing gear control lever and place the handle in the "EMERGENCY DOWN" position.

c. Check the landing gear position indicator to see that the landing gear is down and locked.

3–21. If the landing gear is not binding, and if the pressure bottle is charged to 1800 psi, the landing gear will extend and lock. However, if it does not, the auxiliary hydraulic pump may be used in an attempt to completely extend the landing gear. The landing gear control handle must be reset to the normal operating position desired, and the emergency hydraulic pump switch turned "ON" for this operation.

Note

The primary use of the emergency hydraulic system is to operate the wing flaps in case of a main hydraulic system failure. If the main system failure is due to loss of fluid, there will be enough fluid available for one emergency operation only; therefore, if the emergency hydraulic system is used to extend the landing gear, there will be no fluid left to lower the wing flaps.

CAUTION

Do not attempt to retract the landing gear after use of the air system, as damage to the airplane hydraulic reservoir will result.

3–22. WING FLAPS.

3–23. For emergency extension of the flaps:

Figure 3–1. Emergency Bomb and External Auxiliary Fuel Tank Release

Note

If the failure in the main hydraulic system is due to loss of fluid, there will be only enough fluid available for one emergency extension of the wing flaps.

a. Reduce airspeed to approximately 100 knots.

b. Release the emergency latch on the flap control and place the handle in the full or "EMERGENCY DOWN" position. This will deflect the flaps a full 50 degrees.

Note

Note that the wing flaps are designed to start to blow up between 100-115 knots indicated airspeed. If the "blow-up" feature is inoperative the airspeed should be restricted below 130 knots with flaps fully deflected.

3–24. ARMAMENT.

3–25. EMERGENCY BOMB OR EXTERNAL AUXILIARY TANK RELEASE. The manual bomb or auxiliary fuel tank release control is located on the aft end of the left-hand control shelf and is spring-loaded outboard to prevent inadvertent release when the tail wheel lock is actuated. For electrical release, refer to paragraph 4–20. In case of electrical system failure, bombs, auxiliary tanks or 11.75-inch rockets are released manually by:

a. Placing the release control handle in the appropriate slot ("LEFT," "CENTER," or "RIGHT") and pushing the handle forward. If the arming circuits are intact, the bombs may be armed before dropping them manually.

3–26. BOMB SALVO. Salvo bombs, 11.75-inch rockets, or external auxiliary tanks as follows:

a. Master armament switch—"ON."

b. "LEFT," "CENTER," and "RIGHT" bomb rack selector switches—"ON."

c. Press bomb release button on control stick.

WARNING

Instantaneous salvo firing of outer panel rockets is prohibited.

3–27. RUNAWAY GUNS. Should the trigger switch stick resulting in uncontrolled, automatic firing, turn the master armament switch "OFF" and use it as a trigger switch. To stop a "runaway" gun, place the safety switch to "SAFE."

3–28. ELECTRICAL.

3–29. GENERATOR SYSTEM FAILURE. *(See figure 3–2.)* Low voltage may permit the reverse current cut-out to open and allow the electrical equipment to drain the battery. Loss of generator power and operation on battery power will be indicated by the generator warning light coming on. In this event, the generator cut-out will isolate the generator and all busses but the primary bus from the circuit. (Refer to paragraph 1–68.) Refer to paragraph 3–25 for manual release of bombs or auxiliary tanks in the event of electrical system failure.

3–30. IFF DESTRUCTOR.

3–31. The destruction of the RT-22/APX-1 Transpondor (F4U-5 and F4U-5P airplanes) or the RT-82/APX-6 Transpondor (F4U-5N airplanes) is accomplished manually by operating the destruct switch located on the IFF panel on the radio control shelf. In the event of a crash landing, destruction will be accomplished automatically by release of an impact switch located adjacent to the transpondor in the radio compartment.

3–32. IFF EMERGENCY SIGNAL.

3–33. The "EMERGENCY" position of the six-position IFF switch, located on the IFF panel on the radio control shelf, should be used when it is desired to transmit extremely wide SOS pulses.

3–34. OXYGEN.

3–35. Should symptoms occur at altitude which suggests the onset of anoxia, immediately depress the "SAFETY PRESS" button located on the face of the regulator. If for any reason the regulator should become inoperative and a constant flow of oxygen is not obtained by use of the safety pressure, activate the oxygen bailout equipment and descend below 10,000 feet. Whenever excessive carbon monoxide or other noxious or irritating gas is present or suspected, regardless of altitude, turn the air valve to the "100 PERCENT OXYGEN" position. This will keep the noxious gas out of the mask. The undiluted oxygen shall be used until the danger is past or the flight is completed.

3–36. EMERGENCY EQUIPMENT.

3–37. A standard quick-fit, seat-type parachute and a Pararaft kit (Model PK-1) are accommodated by the bucket-shaped pilot's seat.

NORMAL OPERATION (Generator Operative)		EMERGENCY OPERATION (Generator Inoperative)	
Power Control Switch Position	Condition of Circuits	Power Control Switch Position	Condition of Circuits
"OFF"	IFF destructor circuit and power control switch *energized.* All other circuits *inoperative.*	"OFF"	IFF destructor circuit and power control switch *energized.* All other circuits *inoperative.*
"GEN & BAT"	All circuits *energized.*	"GEN & BAT"	Starter, exterior lights, P-1 inverter, motor alternator, radio (except IFF), autopilot, radar (on F4U-5N airplanes), portable equipment, gun camera, cockpit heater, and gun heater circuits *inoperative.* All other circuits *operative.*
"BAT ONLY"	Portable equipment, gun camera, cockpit heater, and gun heater *inoperative.* All other circuits *operative.*	"BAT ONLY"	Portable equipment, gun camera, cockpit heater, and gun heater *inoperative.* All other circuits *operative.*

Figure 3-2. Power Control System Operation Chart

Section IV

OPERATIONAL EQUIPMENT

4–1. ARMAMENT.

4–2. GUNNERY SYSTEM.

4–3. DESCRIPTION. *(See figure 4–1).* The gunnery system consists of four M3 (T-31) 20-mm guns, two in each outer wing panel. Access to them is through the front and rear gun bay doors on the upper surfaces of the outer panels. The guns are supplied a total of 840 rounds from eight ammunition boxes installed in the wings outboard of the guns. Each gun is supplied a total of 210 rounds. The guns are hydraulically charged and electrically operated (figure 4–3). A gun camera mounted in the leading edge of the right outer panel operates whenever the guns are fired. Heating elements attached to the camera and the guns automatically turn on when the air temperature drops below 70°F. The gunnery system also includes a Mk. 6 fire control installation consisting primarily of a lead computing Mk. 8 sight unit located on the cockpit cowling and controlled by a switch panel located on the left-hand control panel (figure 4–2). A gunnery switch box located on the left-hand side of the cockpit cowling (figure 4–5) contains five switches; the master armament switch, the inboard and outboard gun selector switches, the gun safety switch, and the charging push button. A gun trigger switch is located on the handle grip of the control stick (figure 4–4). Two armament switches actuated by the arresting hook control handle prevent operation of the armament system whenever the arresting hook is extended.

4–4. OPERATION.

WARNING

The Deicer Boot switch must be in "COMBAT OFF" position before entering combat on F4U-5NL airplanes Bureau Serial No. 124504 and subsequent.

4–5. MASTER ARMAMENT SWITCH. The master armament switch must be placed in the "ON" position before the guns can be fired or the gun sight can be operated. However, the master armament switch does not have to be on in order to charge the guns with the charging button.

4–6. GUN CHARGING. The guns can be charged in either one of two ways. The recommended procedure is as follows:

a. Master armament switch—"ON" or "OFF."
b. Safety switch—"READY."
c. Charging button—Depress momentarily.

The guns can also be charged as follows:

a. Master armament switch—"ON" or "OFF."
b. Safety switch—"SAFE" then "READY."

Note

By charging the guns in flight some jams may be cleared.

4–7. TO SAFETY GUNS. Safety the guns as follows:

a. Master armament switch—"OFF."
b. Safety switch—"SAFE."
c. Selector switches—"OFF."

It is not necessary that the electrical or the hydraulic systems be operating after the guns have been safetied to maintain them in this condition.

CAUTION

Always safety the guns before landing.

4–8. GUN FIRING. After the guns have been charged, the armament switch must be set as follows before the guns can be fired:

a. Master armament switch—"ON."

b. Safety switch—"READY." (The trigger switch circuit is dead when the safety switch is "OFF" or in the "SAFE" position even though the master armament switch is "ON.")

c. Selector switch—"INB'D," "OUTB'D," or both as desired.

d. Trigger switch—depressed. The selected guns will fire as long as the trigger switch is closed and a supply of ammunition remains.

Note

Should the trigger switch stick, resulting in uncontrolled automatic firing, turn the master armament switch "OFF" and use it as a trigger switch. To stop a "runaway" gun, place the safety switch to "SAFE."

4–9. FIRE CONTROL SYSTEM. The Mk. 6 fire control system incorporates a Mk. 8 gyroscopic lead-computing sight unit. The sight is operated by a ranging control installation and four switches mounted on the gun sight control panel located on the left-hand control shelf.

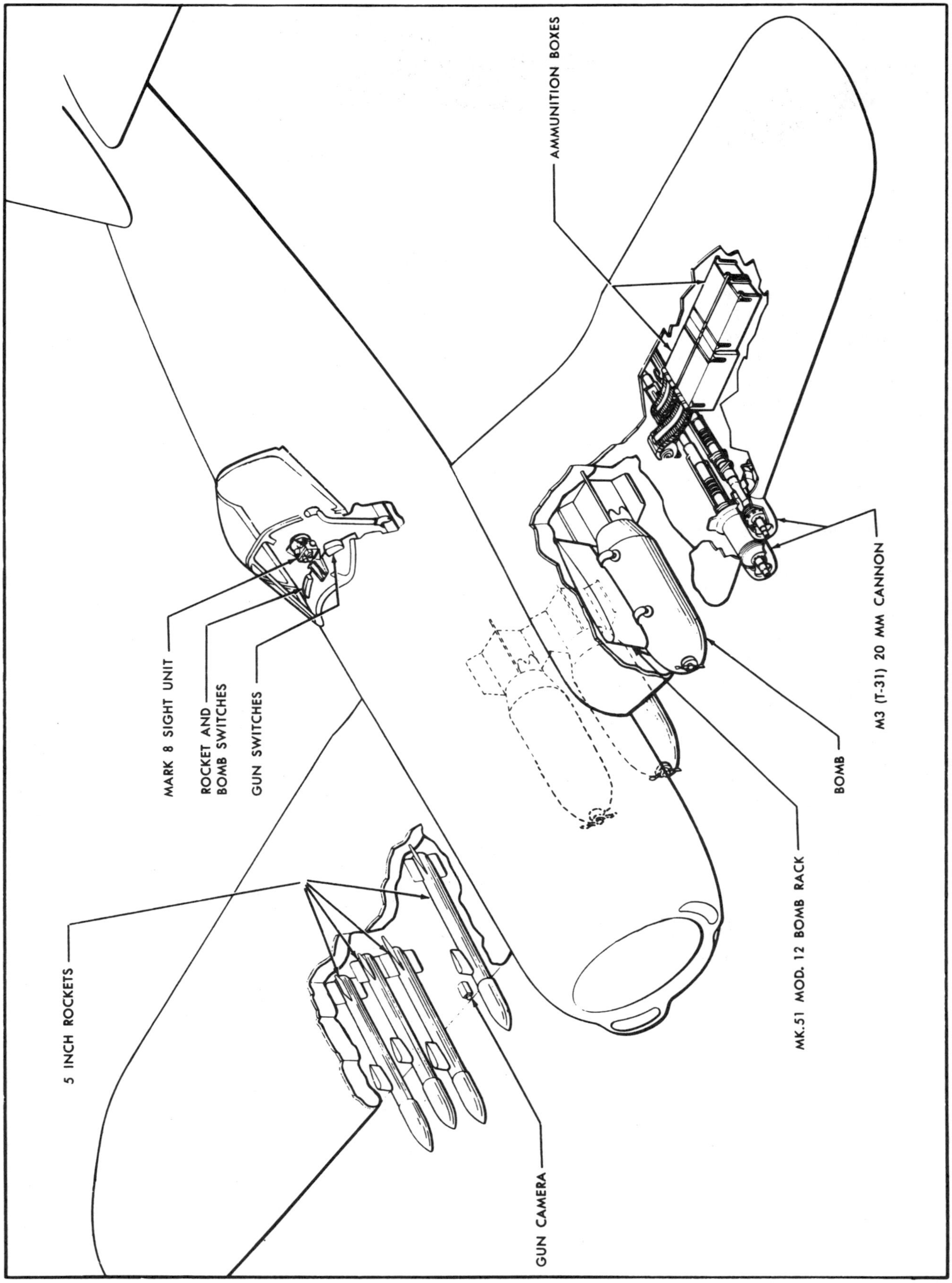

Figure 4-1. Armament Arrangement

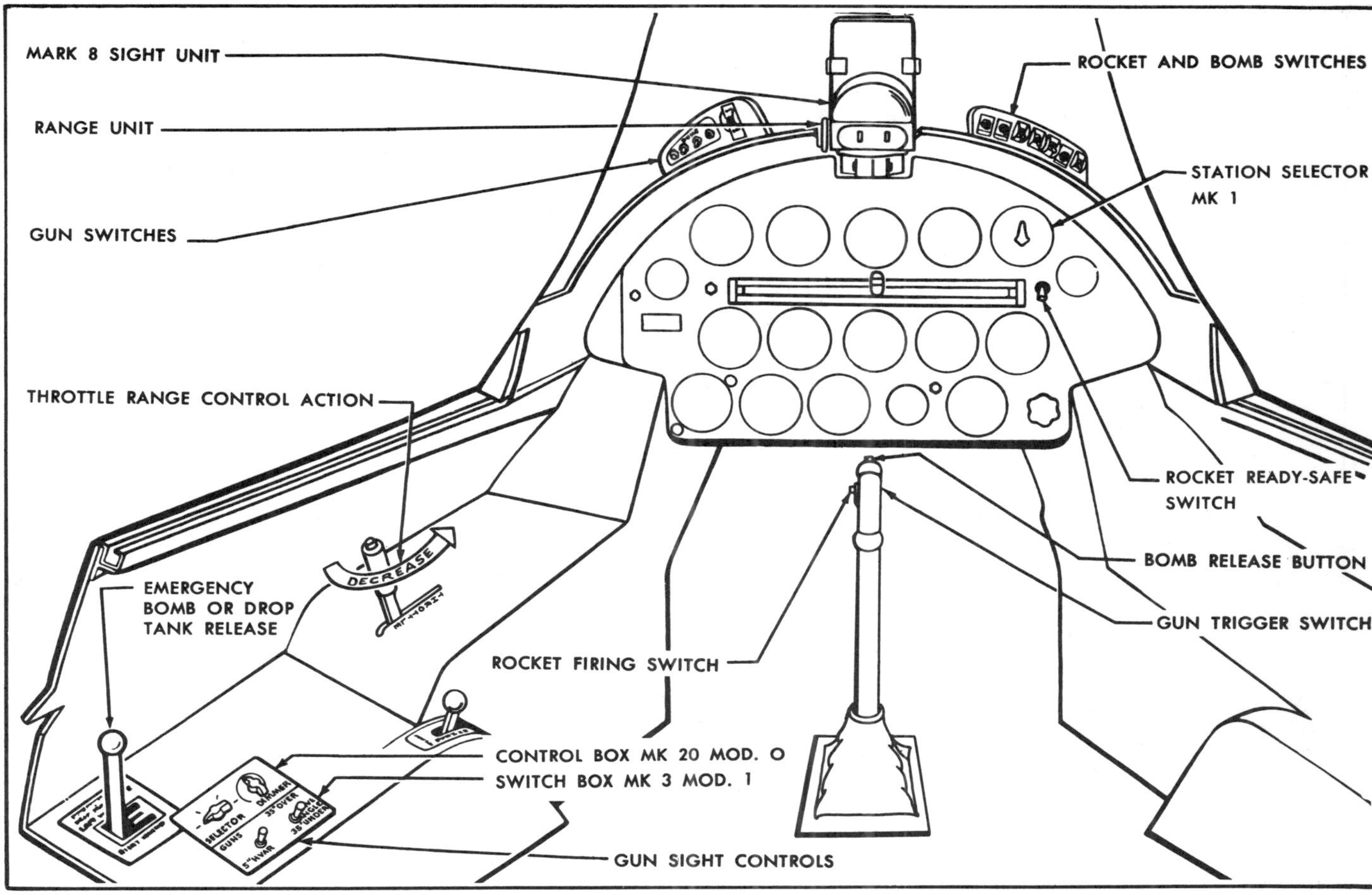

Figure 4—2. Armament and Gun Sight Controls

4–10. The ranging control installation consists of a ranging throttle grip, a gun sight controller (servo motor), and a flexible driveshaft. The Mk. 8 sight unit is supported on a mount bolted to the cockpit cowling. A rubber crash-pad is located on the sighting head for protection of the pilot. Directly below the crash-pad there is a sight lamp cover. The lamps are readily accessible so that should one fail in flight, it could be easily replaced with one of the two spare bulbs which are held in clips just below the sight.

4—11. GUN SIGHT CONTROL PANEL. When the master armament switch is turned to the "ON" position electrical current is transmitted to the sight by way of the gun sight switch panel installed on the left hand console. The four switches mounted on the panel are the gun sight selector, the gun sight rheostat, the gun sight armament switch and the dive angle switch.

4—12. GUN SIGHT SELECTOR SWITCH. The gun sight selector switch permits the pilot to select his sight image. When the switch is in the "OFF" position neither reticle image is illuminated. In the "FIXED" position only the fixed reticle appears. When the selector switch is in the "FIXED AND GYRO" position, both the fixed and gyro reticles are illuminated. In the "GYRO" position only the gyro image is visible.

4—13. The gun sight dimmer is a rheostat which controls the light intensity of the reticle images. The gun sight armament switch is a toggle switch with "GUNS" and "HVAR" positions. The dive angle switch is a two position toggle switch with "ABOVE 35°" and "BELOW 35°" positions.

4—14. GUN SIGHT RANGE CONTROL. Ranging is controlled by rotating the ranging throttle grip. The grip is capable of a 60° rotation to permit range adjustments from 600 to 2400 feet. Range is increased by clockwise rotation of the throttle and is decreased by counterclockwise rotation. The range unit MK 17 Mod. O is rotated in proportion to the throttle grip rotation by a flexible shaft connecting it to the Gun Sight Controller Aero 2B. A window in the Range Unit permits visual inspection of the range being fed into the gunsight.

4—15. TESTING THE FIRE CONTROL SYSTEM. Ground test the Mk. 6 fire control system as follows:

a. Power control and master armament switches on.

b. Gun sight armament switch—"GUNS."

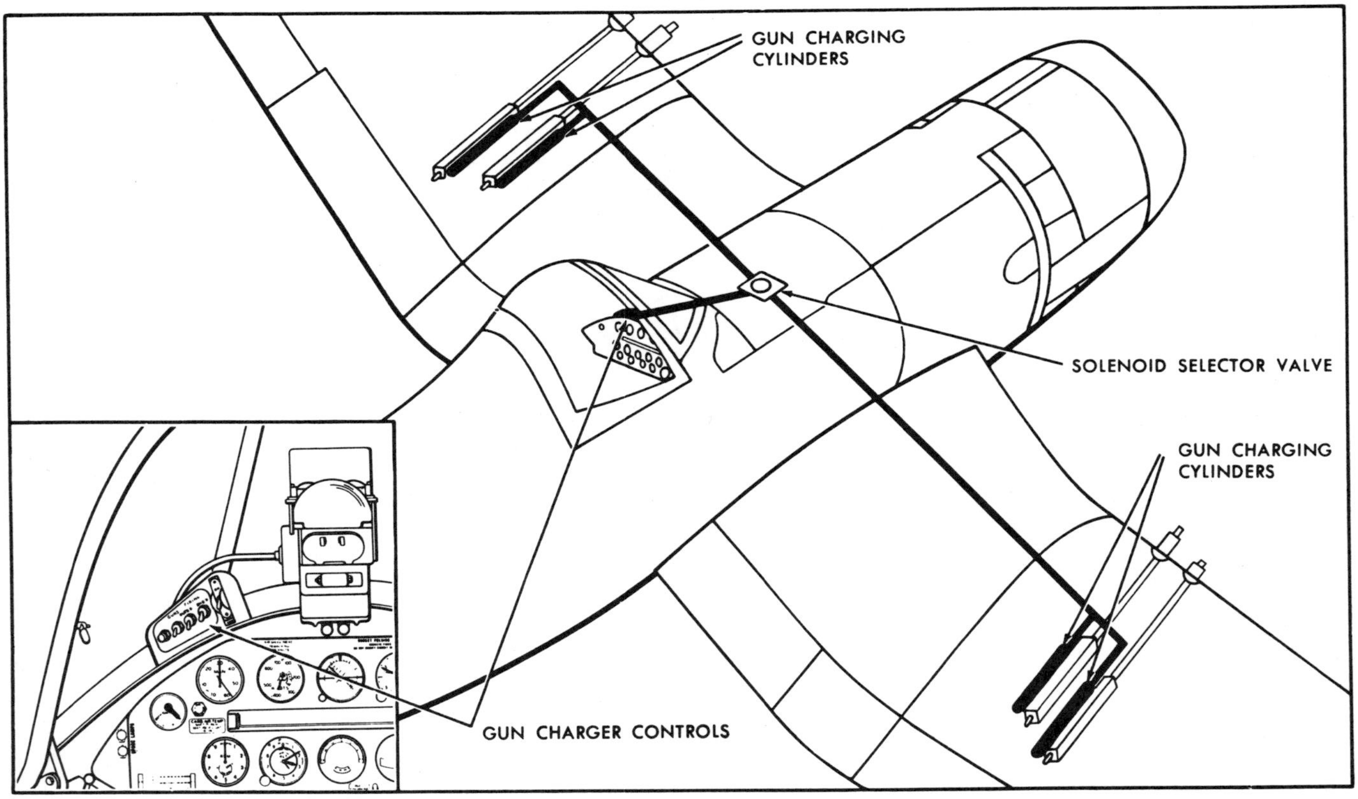

Figure 4-3. Gun Charging Control Hydraulic System Diagram

c. Gun sight selector switch–"FIXED." Only the fixed reticle image should be visible.

d. Move reticle masking lever up to check that it blacks out arcs below the fixed cross. Check lever for freedom of travel.

e. Gun sight selector switch–"FIXED AND GYRO." Both reticle images should be visible. Check gun sight dimmer.

f. Gun sight selector switch–"GYRO." Only the gyro image should be visible.

g. Check for image parallax. Examine one image at a time, moving the eye from side to side over the width of the lens opening. There should be no apparent shift of the reticle image with respect to the target as the eye is moved. If the image shifts more than 3 mils in any direction, the lens is out of focus and the sighting head should be replaced.

h. Operate the throttle ranging control grip. The gyro image diameter should decrease as the grip is rotated clockwise, and increase when the grip is rotated counterclockwise.

i. Place throttle ranging grip in extreme counterclockwise position and look through window on the Range Unit MK 17 Mod. 0. The range drum should be positioned so that the numeral "6" is adjacent to the index mark. Rotate grip to extreme clockwise position. The range drum should be positioned so the numeral "24" is aligned with the index mark. Check grip for freedom of movement.

j. Check movement of span-setting handle over the span dial. Movement should be free throughout range. With handle at extreme left (high) end of scale, turn the range drum to minimum range (600 feet). The handle should not move as the drum is turned. If the handle moves, there is not sufficient friction between the handle and the crash-pad plate. Pressing against the crash-pad to bend the plate slightly will usually remedy this condition.

k. Open gun sight lamp cover and examine lamps. If they show signs of blackening replace them. Make certain two new spare bulbs are installed in stowage clips.

l. Check operation of armament safety switch which is actuated by the arresting hook handle. With both gun sight images visible, operate the arresting hook handle. If images go out, it is indication that the armament safety switch is operating properly.

4–15A. GUN CAMERA. The camera mechanism is electrically operated whenever the gun, bomb or rocket trigger switches are depressed. No separate camera switch is provided.

4–16. BOMBS AND ROCKETS.

4–17. DESCRIPTION. Either bombs, 11.75" rockets, or Mk. 5 Mod. 4 external auxiliary fuel tanks can be carried on the electrically operated Mk. 51, Mod. 12 bomb racks within the two center section and the centerline pylons, while eight 3.5-inch or 5-inch rockets can be carried on the four Mk. 9, Mod. 3 launchers on each outer wing panel (see figure 4–1). The Mk. 55, Mod. 0 bomb rack is interchangeable with the Mk. 9, Mod. 3 rocket launchers in the outer panel so that eight bombs can be carried, if necessary. The right- and left-hand center section pylons can accommodate bombs up to 1600 pounds and the centerline pylon can carry bomb sizes up to 2000 pounds. The master armament switch located on the left-hand armament switch box and toggle switches on the right-hand armament switch box control selection and arming of the bombs and rockets. A bomb release button and a rocket firing button are located on the control stick grip (see figure 4–4). Bombs and drop tanks may be released manually should the electrical system fail (see paragraph 3–25).

4–18. The right-hand armament switch box (see figure 4–5) contains the following: three switches for selecting bombs on the left, center, or right-hand bomb racks, a bomb arming switch, a selector switch for launching outer panel rockets or bombs in pairs or singles, a switch for arming outer panel rockets or bombs, and a pylon release switch for releasing the two center section pylons. This switch is inoperative on this installation.

4–19. BOMB AND 11.75″ ROCKETS. Bombs or 11.75″ rockets are selected for dropping by three switches which are labeled "LEFT," "CENTER," and "RIGHT." Each switch has an "OFF" and "ON" position. The bomb arming switch has three positions, "TAIL ARM," "NOSE AND TAIL ARM," and a neutral or safe position. These switches are not effective unless the master armament switch is "ON." The pilot selects the type of arming depending upon the use of the bomb. When the arming switch is thrown to "NOSE AND TAIL ARM," both the nose and tail fuzes on all of the bombs will be armed when the bomb is released. With the switch in "TAIL ARM" only the tail fuze will be armed. If the bomb is not armed it will fall safe. It is not necessary to arm 11.75″ rockets as they arm themselves automatically after being released from the pylon.

4–20. BOMB RELEASE. Bombs, 11.75″ rockets and external auxiliary tanks can be released either manually or electrically. Note that the position of the arming switch has no effect on the drop tank. Arm and release bombs electrically as follows: (See paragraph 3–25 for manual emergency release.)

a. Master armament switch–"ON."

b. Bomb arming switch–"NOSE AND TAIL ARM," "TAIL ARM," or to the neutral position if the bomb is to be dropped safe.

c. Desired bomb selector switch–"ON."

d. Press the bomb release button on the control stick.

4–21. OUTER PANEL ROCKETS OR BOMBS. Four rockets (either 3.5- or 5-inch rockets) or bombs can be carried on each outer panel. In airplanes Bureau Serial No. 121793 through 124560, the rocket or bomb stations are numbered consecutively from inboard to outboard on each wing. In airplanes Bureau Serial No. 124666 and subsequent, the rocket or bomb stations are numbered consecutively from left outboard to right outboard. The following switches control rocket arming and firing:

a. A MASTER ARMAMENT switch, located on the left-hand armament switch box, is an "ON-OFF" switch breaker and is used to energize all armament circuits.

b. A SAFE-READY switch is located on the instrument panel in airplanes Bureau Serial No. 121793 through 124560 and on the right-hand armament switch box in airplanes Bureau Serial No. 124666 and subsequent. This switch prevents inadvertent firing of the rockets when the MASTER ARMAMENT switch is "ON." Rockets cannot be fired unless this switch is tripped from "SAFE" to "READY."

c. A rocket selector switch is located on the right-hand armament switch box in airplanes Bureau Serial No. 121793 through 124560 and is not used in airplanes Bureau Serial No. 124666 and subsequent. This switch has two positions, "PAIRS" and "FOUR SINGLES." To launch rockets in pairs, the switch must be tripped to "PAIRS" position. With the switch in "FOUR SINGLES" position, only four rockets will be launched and the switch must be tripped to "PAIRS" to launch the remaining four rockets.

d. An outer panel bomb or rocket arming switch is located on the right-hand armament switch box. It is a three-position "NOSE AND TAIL ARM," "TAIL ARM," and "SAFE" toggle switch and is used to arm the rocket or bomb fuzes. Bombs may be released in any of the three conditions. Rockets are never launched in a SAFE condition because the tail fuze is automatically armed when a rocket is launched; rockets may, therefore, be launched with either nose and tail armed or with tail armed but never safe.

e. A MK 1 STATION SELECTOR is used in airplanes Bureau Serial No. 121793 through 124560 and is mounted on the instrument panel. This is a four-position ("PAIRS," "2-2-4," "2-6" and "SALVO") switch. The station selector pointer moves or steps automatically to the next clockwise station each time the rocket firing

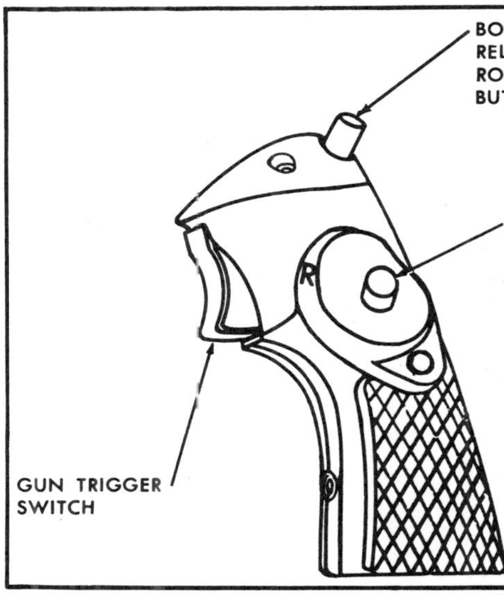

Figure 4-4. Trigger Switches

button is depressed and released. The pointer may be freely moved counterclockwise but the "SALVO RESET" button must be depressed to move the pointer clockwise. Launching of more than two rockets at a time is not permitted on this airplane; therefore, the station selector must always be started at "PAIRS."

f. A MK 2 STATION SELECTOR is used in airplanes Bureau Serial No. 124666 and subsequent and is located on the instrument panel. It is an eight-position switch marked clockwise with stations "1" through "8." Station "1" is marked "START SINGLES" and station "5" is marked "START PAIRS." After each launching, the pointer automatically moves to the next clockwise position. If the pointer is preset to "START SINGLES," the eight rockets are launched singly. If the pointer is preset to "START PAIRS," the rockets are launched in pairs. This switch does not permit firing more than two rockets at one time.

g. A ROCKET firing button is located on the control stick grip. This switch is depressed to launch rockets either singly or in pairs at pilot-controlled intervals.

WARNING

Do not place the "READY-SAFE" switch in the "READY" position until ready to fire the rockets or bombs. Upon completion of rocket or bomb firing, return the switch to the "SAFE" position.

4–22. THROUGH 4–26. DELETED.

4–27. OPERATION WITH MK 1 SELECTOR SWITCH. Present restrictions on the airplane permit the launching of rockets singly or in pairs in the following manner:

a. Throw master armament switch "ON."

b. If nose-arming is desired, place outer panel bomb or rocket arming switch in "NOSE AND TAIL ARM" position.

c. Set MK 1 station selector switch to "PAIRS."

WARNING

Always set MK 1 station selector switch to "PAIRS." Partial salvo may inflict severe damage on the wings, flaps, and ailerons.

d. To fire eight rockets singly after observing steps a, b, and c above:

(1) Throw rocket selector switch to "FOUR SINGLES."

(2) Place ready-safe switch in "READY" position.

(3) Depress and release rocket firing button four times. This will cause No. 1 left, No. 2 right, No. 3 left, and No. 4 right rockets to be fired and will cause the MK 1 station selector switch to step clockwise to "SALVO."

(4) Return MK 1 station selector switch to "PAIRS."

(5) Place rocket selector switch at "PAIRS."

(6) Depressing and releasing the rocket firing button will cause the remaining four rockets to be released in the following order: No. 1 right, No. 2 left, No. 3 right, No. 4 left.

e. To fire eight rockets in pairs after observing steps a, b, and c above:

(1) Throw rocket selector switch to "PAIRS."

Figure 4-5. Armament Switch Boxes

(2) Place ready-safe switch at "READY."

(3) Depress and release the rocket firing button four times. This will cause the rockets to be launched in pairs, commencing with the rockets on No. 1 right and left launchers.

4–28. OPERATION WITH MK 2 SELECTOR SWITCH. Rockets may be launched singly or in pairs in the following manner:

a. Throw master armament switch "ON."

b. If nose arming is desired, place outer panel bomb or rocket arming switch in "NOSE AND TAIL ARM" position.

c. To fire eight rockets singly, turn rocket selector switch indicator to "1" position, throw "READY-SAFE" switch to "READY," and depress rocket firing button eight times. The launcher sequence of fire is 1, 7, 3, 5, 8, 2, 6, 4. Launchers are numbered in sequence from left outboard to right outboard.

d. To fire eight rockets in pairs, turn rocket selector switch indicator to "5" position, throw "READY-SAFE" switch to "READY," and depress rocket firing button four times. The launcher sequence of fire is 1 and 8, 2 and 7, 3 and 6, 4 and 5.

Note

The rocket firing circuit is inoperative when the arresting hook control handle is in the "DOWN" position.

4–29. TABLE OF ELECTRONIC EQUIPMENT.

Type	*Designation*	*Use*	*Illustration of Controls*	*Remarks*
VHF	AN/ARC-1	Two-way voice communication	Fig. 4-6	Frequency range 100 to 156 megacycles
Range Receiver	AN/ARC-5	Low-frequency range reception	Fig. 4-6	Frequency range 190 to 550 kilocycles
Navigation Equipment	AN/ARR-2A	Navigation receiver	Fig. 4-6	Frequency range 234 to 258 megacycles
IFF	AN/APX-1 (F4U-5 and F4U-5P aircraft)	Identification	Fig. 4-6	
Radio Altimeter	AN/APN-1	Measure absolute altitude over terrain	Fig. 1-6 Fig. 1-7	High range cannot be used below 400 feet

4–30. OPERATION OF RADIO EQUIPMENT.

4–31. UPON ENTRANCE INTO COCKPIT. The radio console panel, containing all the controls for operating the communication, navigation, and identification radio equipment is on the right-hand control shelf (see figures 1–6 and 4–6). The headphone and microphone extension is plugged into the radio jack plug located on the bulkhead aft of the pilot's right shoulder (see figure 4–7). The power control switch must be "ON" and the engine must be running above generator cutout speed to avoid draining the battery. With the master radio switch "ON," power is provided to all radios except the IFF equipment. The radio gear requires a one-minute warm-up period.

4–32. VHF RECEPTION.

4–33. GENERAL. The VHF receiver is the RT-18 ARC-1 with a frequency range of 100 to 156 megacycles. A selector switch permits transmission and reception on either the "GUARD" or "MAIN T/R" channels separately, or reception on "BOTH" simultaneously with transmission on the main channel. VHF volume is controlled by the COMM VOLUME knob on the MASTER panel. VHF signals are received exclusively by turning down NAVIG and RECVR volume which are controlled by their respective SENS knobs. Navigation and range signals will be heard simultaneously with VHF signals when their respective volumes are turned up.

Note

For an actual operating test of this equipment it is necessary that signals be present on the channels to be operated. In the absence of signals, the squelch circuit reduces receiver output to zero so that it is impractical to gage receiver performance.

4–34. VHF GUARD CHANNEL RECEPTION. With the GUARD-BOTH-MAIN T–R selector switch on the VHF panel turned to "GUARD," "T/R" will appear in the left-hand window indicating the equipment is set for transmission and reception on the guard channel only. "OFF" will appear in the right-hand window indicating a disabled main channel. If a signal is present, regulate the volume with the COMM VOLUME knob on the MASTER panel. If no signal is present, increase COMM VOLUME to the full volume position.

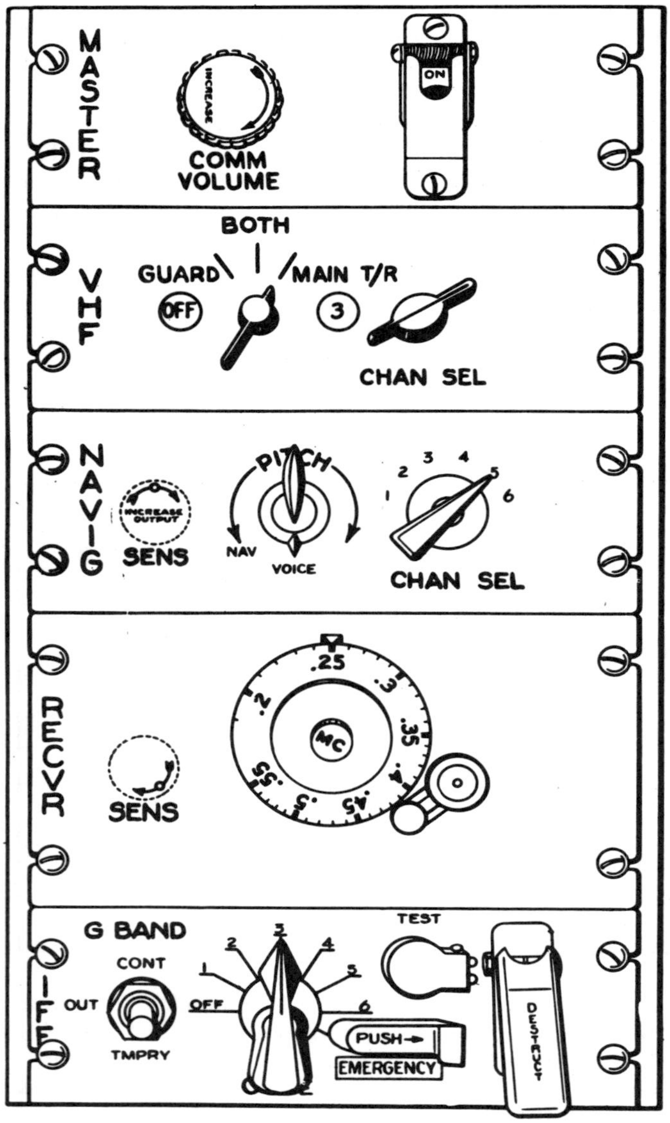

Figure 4—6. Radio Console Control Panel

4—35. MAIN T/R CHANNEL RECEPTION. To transmit and receive on any one of the main channels turn the GUARD-BOTH-MAIN T/R switch to "MAIN" and rotate the CHAN SEL switch until the assigned channel number appears in the right hand window. "OFF" will appear in the left hand window indicating a disabled guard channel. Volume is adjusted as described above.

4—36. NORMAL OPERATION When the GUARD-BOTH-MAIN T/R switch is turned to "BOTH," the equipment will monitor simultaneously on both the guard and the main channels. If signals are heard simultaneously, turn the switch to "GUARD" or "MAIN T/R" to select the desired channel without interference.

4—37. LF RECEPTION. The low frequency R-23A/ARC-5 range receiver, with a frequency range of 190 to 550 kilocycles is controlled from the RECVR panel. Stations are selected with the tuning knob. Volume is controlled by the SENS knob. To receive LF signals exclusively, turn down VHF and NAVIG volume, controlled by the COMM VOLUME and the NAVIG SENS knob respectively. VHF and NAVIG signals will be heard simultaneously with radio range signals when their respective volumes are turned up.

Note

Volume should be kept at a minimum when working with radio range signals, as high volume can produce incorrect course indications.

4—38. NAVIGATION RECEPTION. The navigation receiver is a R-4A/ARR-2 with a frequency range from 234 to 258 megacycles. To receive navigation signals exclusively, turn down the VHF and RECVR volume, controlled by the COMM VOLUME and RECVR SENS knobs respectively. To hear VHF and radio range signals simultaneously with navigation signals turn up their respective volumes. To operate the navigation equipment:

a. Set the CHAN SEL indicator on the NAVIG panel to the assigned channel number.

b. Turn the VOICE-NAV indicator to "NAV."

c. Increase volume by rotating the SENS knob, from its extreme counterclockwise position slowly clockwise, to obtain a usable weak signal or a fairly strong background hiss.

d. Adjust PITCH control for clear tone.

e. Readjust SENS knob to minimum volume to receive the strongest single signal.

Note

MINIMUM volume is essential for accurate interpretation of navigation signals. Loud signals can be inaccurate.

4—39. TRANSMISSION. A microphone button is provided on the throttle for use with a lip or mask microphone.

WARNING

These instructions are subject to local limitations regarding radio silence.

4—40. COMMUNICATION TRANSMISSION. The communication equipment includes an RT 18/ARC-1 transmitter with a frequency range of 100 to 156 megacycles for VHF transmission. To transmit:

a. Turn CHAN SEL switch to desired main channel.

b. Turn GUARD-BOTH-MAIN T/R switch as required.

Note

With the switch in either the "BOTH" or "MAIN T/R" position, transmission is possible on the main channel selected.

4–41. IFF EQUIPMENT (AN/APX-1). The IFF equipment in the F4U-5 and F4U-5P airplanes consists of an RT-22A/APX-1 transmitter-receiver. For information on the IFF equipment used in F4U-5N airplanes, refer to paragraph B-16.

Note

Before take-off, check with service crew to see that a complete destructor circuit test has been made.

All the IFF controls are on the IFF control panel. To operate:

a. Set CODE indicator to the desired position of any of the six available. Set to position No. 1 if no other has been previously specified.

b. Throw G BAND toggle switch to "CONT" or "TMPRY" only when required.

c. To destroy equipment, raise red switch guard labeled DESTRUCT and throw the switch "ON."

d. To secure equipment, be certain CODE indicator is "OFF."

Note

Additional information concerning operation of identification equipment should be obtained from the communications officer-in-charge.

4–41A. AN/APN-1 RADIO ALTIMETER. *(See figure 1–7.)* The primary function of the radio altimeter is to provide direct measurement of "absolute altitude" (terrain clearance) during flight. The altimeter equipment is designed to measure altitude accurately in two ranges, a low range of 0 to 400 feet and a high range of 400 to 4,000 feet. The 28-volt d-c power supply to the radio altimeter is controlled by the radio altimeter circuit breaker on the circuit breaker panel. The altitude indicator incorporates a power switch (knob marked "ON" with clockwise arrow) and a range switch (knob marked "RANGE"). The power switch controls the entire 28-volt d-c current input to the altimeter system. The range switch controls the input to a range relay in the altimeter transmitter-receiver and operates in conjunction with the altitude limit switch. When the range switch is in the low range (counterclockwise) position, the face of the indicator reads from 0 to 400 feet. In the high range (clockwise) position the indicator reads from 0 to 4,000 feet. The indicator scale numerals change from 0, 1, 2, 3, 4 for low range to 0, 10, 20, 30, 40 for high range.

Figure 4-7. Pilot's Jack Plug

Note

When on the ground, always set the range switch in low range (counterclockwise) before turning on the radio altimeter system.

4–41B. The altitude limit switch is located on the right console directly inboard of the wing folding and locking control in F4U-5 and F4U-5P airplanes (see figure 1–6), and on the instrument board in F4U-5N airplanes (see figure B–4). A red warning light located above and to the left of the radio altitude indicator in F4U-5 and F4U-5P airplanes and on the left side of the radar indicator in F4U-5N airplanes will go on when the aircraft descends below the altitude set on the altitude limit switch. The pilot may select the minimum altitude point for the light to go on by setting the altitude limit switch at the altitude step desired. In the low range, altitude from 50 to 300 feet is designated in 25-foot steps; in the high range, altitude from 500 to 3,000 feet is designated in 250-foot steps. To put the radio altimeter in operation proceed as follows:

a. Place power control switch and radio altimeter circuit breaker in "ON" position.

b. Set the range switch in low or high range depending on whether the airplane is above or below 400 feet.

WARNING

The high range is not calibrated for, and must not be used at, altitudes below 400 feet. Under conditions of poor visibility always use low range when flying at altitudes below 600 feet.

c. Set the altitude limit switch for the desired "preset altitude" (altitude below which the red light should go on).

d. Turn indicator power switch "ON." If the airplane is on the ground, the red light will go "on" after the equipment warms up as lowest setting is 50 feet.

Note

When airplane is on the ground, the indicator may not indicate zero altitude exactly.

4–42. PILOT'S CHECK-OFF LIST. Before take-off, the pilot shall make the following radio equipment check:

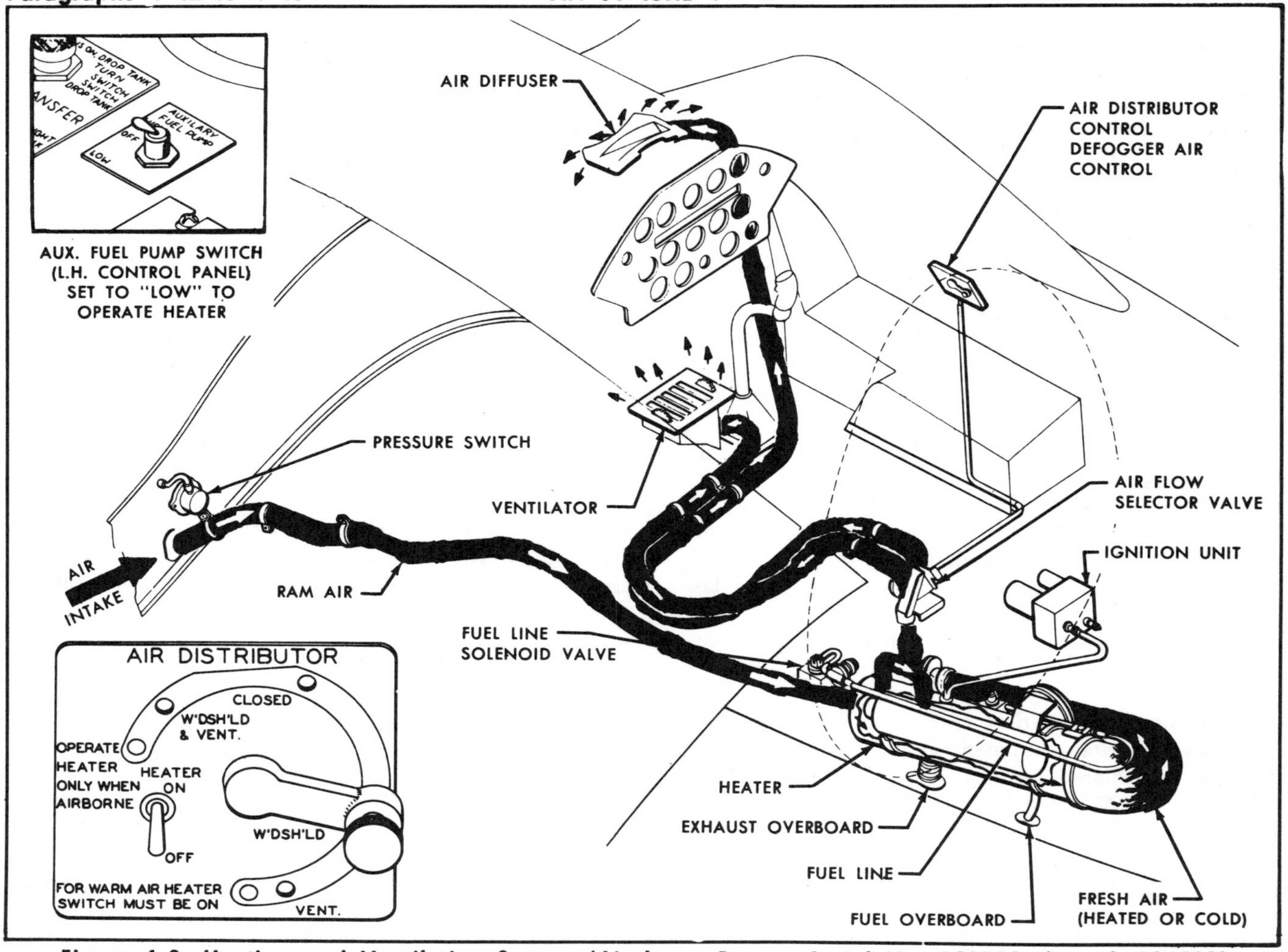

Figure 4-8. Heating and Ventilating System (Airplanes Bureau Serial No. 121793 through 124503)

a. Check with the ground service to make sure that a complete destructor circuit test has been made for IFF equipment.

b. Plug in headset and mask or lip microphone, if one is to be used.

c. Turn power control switch and master radio switch on.

d. Set up VHF receiver and adjust COMM VOLUME on MASTER panel.

e. Set up range receiver.

f. Set up navigation receiver.

g. Set controls for simultaneous reception of communication and navigation receivers.

h. If security instructions permit, select desired transmitter channel and make test transmission with base station on VHF.

i. Turn radio altimeter circuit breaker on and set altitude limit switch for any desired altitude.

j. Set the range switch for low range (turn counterclockwise).

k. Turn indicator power switch "ON." Warning light will go on after equipment warms up. Indicator should deflect.

l. Change to high range (turn clockwise). Indicator deflection should be different from that for low range.

4-42A. After landing and parking the airplane, make the following check:

a. Turn radio master switch "OFF."

b. Turn indicator power switch "OFF."

c. Turn power control switch to "OFF."

d. On IFF panel—turn CODE indicator "OFF."

4-43. HEATING AND VENTILATION.

4-44. DESCRIPTION. *(See figure 4-8)* There are two hot and fresh air outlets in the cockpit. One is a register on the floor for heating and ventilating the cockpit; the other is a diffuser on the windshield cowl for defrosting or defogging the windshield. The air distributor, containing the master heater switch and the air flow control, is mounted on the right side of the cockpit. The master heater switch has an "OFF" and "ON" position. The air flow control handle has four positions, "WINDSHIELD," "VENTILATOR," "CLOSED," and "WINDSHIELD AND VENTILATOR."

4-45. The amount of air and the angle at which it enters the cockpit is regulated by two control treadles on the register. These treadles are notched for easy control by the pilot with his feet. The amount of air

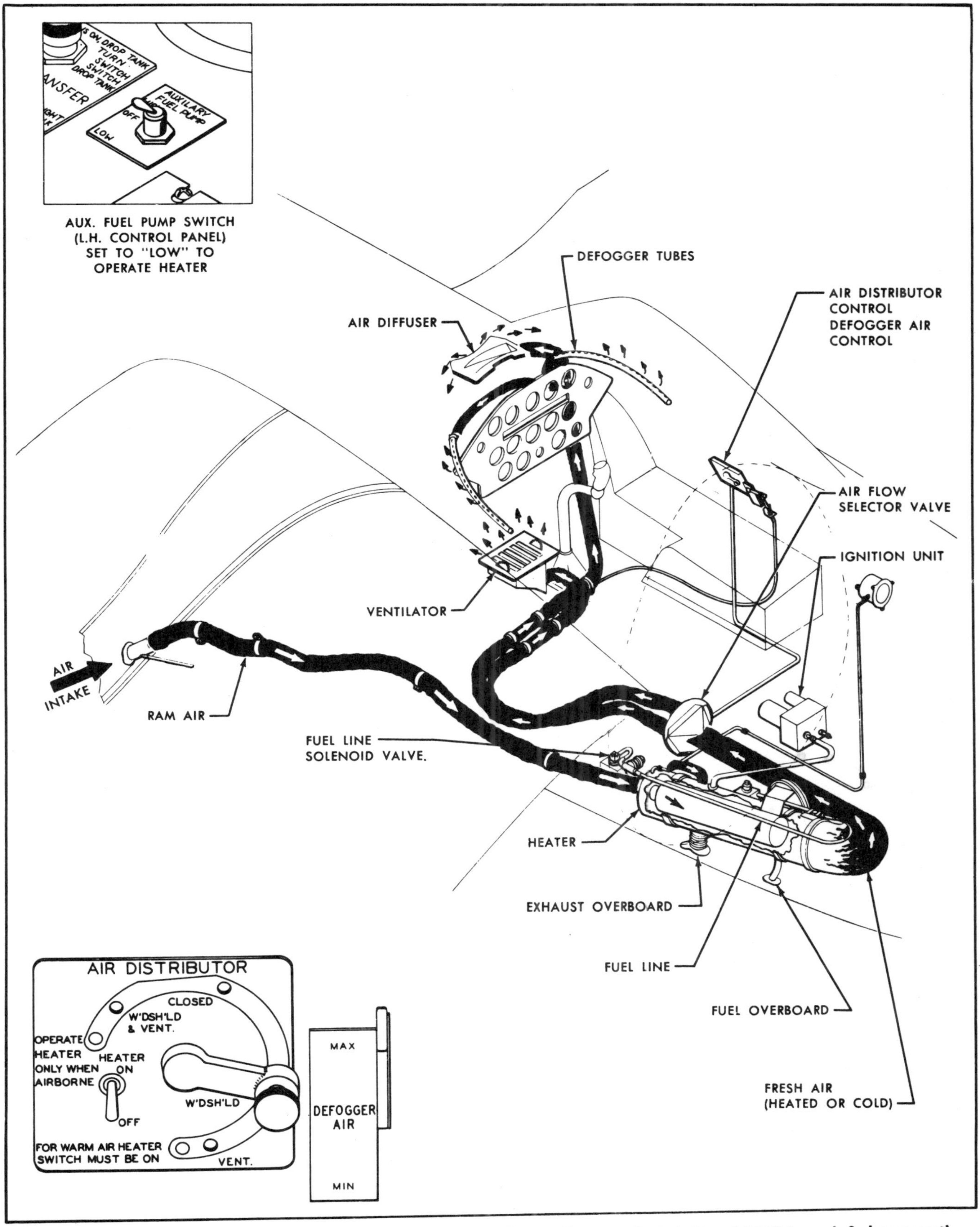

Figure 4-8A. Heating and Ventilating System (Airplanes Bureau Serial No. 124504 and Subsequent)

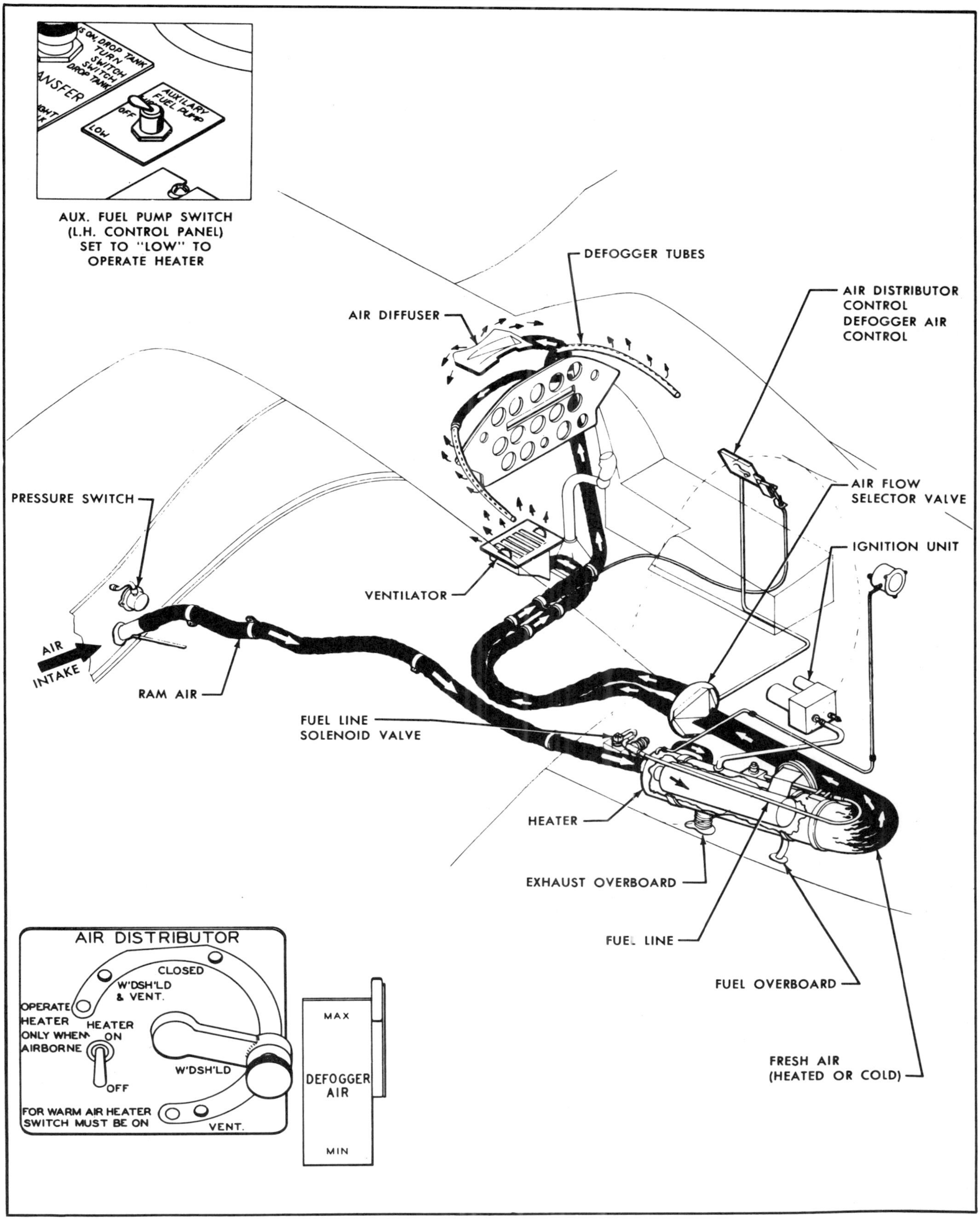

Figure 4-8A. Heating and Ventilating System (Airplanes Bureau Serial No. 124504 and Subsequent)

Figure 4-9. Anti-Blackout Suit Connection

(heated or cold) passing through the register is controlled with the right-hand treadle. Rotating it forward opens the register; rotating it aft, closes it. The angle at which the air enters the cockpit is controlled by rotating the deflector control treadle on the left side of the register either forward or aft.

4–46. Other units in the system are: the heater itself which is located underneath the radio equipment in the compartment behind the cockpit, an ignition unit located on the underside of the radio compartment shelf to supply high voltage to the spark plug in the heater, a pressure switch which permits the heater to function only at airspeeds above 120 knots, and two solenoid shut-off valves (both in fuel line, one mounted on the heater and the other mounted just ahead of the heater) which stop fuel flow to the heater when its output exceeds certain temperature limits. The heater burns gasoline tapped from the main fuel system at the fuel selector valve. Fresh air is taken through an inlet in the left wing and is passed through the heater and thence to the cockpit outlets. When heated air is desired, the heater is turned on warming the air as it passes over a heated jacket in the heater.

4–47. The heater is turned on by first setting the auxiliary (booster) fuel pump to "LOW" operation and then turning on the master heater switch on the air distributor. This switch has an "OFF" and "ON" position. When this switch is on, the spark plug within the heater is energized, the fuel shutoff solenoid in the fuel line is energized permitting fuel to flow to the heater provided that the pressure switch is closed (airplane traveling at least 120 knots), and the fuel cycling solenoid on the heater is energized allowing fuel to flow to the heater combustion chamber.

CAUTION

Operate the heater only when airborne.

4–48. Should the master heater switch be left on while the flow of ram air is prevented from flowing through the system (by turning the control handle on the air distributor to "CLOSED") the heater is kept from overheating by two thermal switches. One shuts off the fuel cycling solenoid on the heater when the temperature exceeds 250°F. Should the heater continue to function because of some defect in the circuit, the other thermal switch shuts off the fuel line solenoid valve at 350°F preventing fuel flow to the heater.

4–49. OPERATION OF ANTI-BLACKOUT SUIT EQUIPMENT.

4–50. GENERAL. The airplane is equipped with facilities (see figure 4–9) which permit use of an anti-blackout suit to increase the pilot's tolerance for high sustained gravity accelerations. Pressure, taken from the discharge side of the engine-driven vacuum pump, is exerted against the legs, thighs, and abdomen of the pilot.

WARNING

A pilot using an anti-blackout suit must realize that the suit has increased his resistance to the effects of high acceleration. If he has depended previously on "greying out" to gage the severity of his air maneuvers, he must develop a new sense when using these suits if structural failure of the airplane is to be prevented. Pilots should, therefore, practice combat maneuvers, such as rolling pullouts, flipper turns and severe evasive maneuvers and determine with the aid of the accelerometer the number of g's attained on each maneuver, staying within the acceleration restrictions of the airplane (see paragraphs 2–84 to 2–86).

4–51. QUICK-DISCONNECT. A quick-disconnect fitting is located on the aft end of the left-hand control shelf. An accelerometer is installed on the main instrument panel to enable the pilot to make a visual check of the number of g's attained during maneuvers.

Note

The fitting is plugged with a quick-disconnect plug at all times when the hose is not connected with the anti-blackout g system. This prevents air from being blown into the cockpit when the g-operated valve is actuated by the maneuvering of the airplane.

The function of the suit is completely automatic once the hose is connected.

CAUTION

On airplanes Bureau Serial No. 124404 and subsequent, the switch-breaker on the left-hand console must be on before the anti-blackout system will operate.

4–52. DELETED.

4–53. OXYGEN.

4–54. DESCRIPTION. The airplane is equipped with a diluter-demand oxygen system (see figure 4–11).

There are two 514-cubic-inch oxygen cylinders in the system; one located on the right-hand side of the cockpit compartment beneath the right-hand control shelf and the other located aft of the cockpit (between fuselage stations 227 and 248 in F4U-5 and -5N airplanes and between fuselage stations 253 and 274 in F4U-5P airplanes). The forward oxygen cylinder is mounted in a near vertical position so that the oxygen valve on the top of the cylinder is accessible to the pilot through a small door on the aft end of the right-hand control shelf. The door is labeled "OXYGEN BOTTLE INSIDE, LIFT PANEL FOR CONTROL." The rear oxygen bottle is accessible through the radio compartment access door. The oxygen supply can be replenished either by replacing the depleted cylinders with new ones or by refilling the installed cylinders. The manifold interconnecting the two cylinders enables them to be filled at the same time. A filler neck and check valve unit is located underneath the floor and is accessible through the lower cockpit access panel.

4-55. DILUTER-DEMAND REGULATOR. The diluter-demand regulator is located on the left-hand control shelf. The regulator air-valve lever has two positions, "NORMAL OXYGEN" and "100 PERCENT OXYGEN." At low altitude, with the air-valve in the normal oxygen position, the regulator dilutes the pure oxygen in the system with a relatively large volume of air, producing the proper breathing mixture. As altitude increases, the ratio of air in the breathing mixture is progressively decreased until at 30,000 feet undiluted oxygen is delivered to the mask. When the air-valve is in the "100 PERCENT OXYGEN" position, undiluted oxygen is delivered at any altitude. With the air valve set to "NORMAL OXYGEN" or "100 PERCENT OXYGEN" an air-oxygen mixture of undiluted oxygen flows only on inhalation. In aircraft Bu. No. 123144 and subsequent, an automatic positive pressure regulator is provided. This regulator incorporates an additional aneroid which expands as the atmospheric pressure decreases. At 30,000 feet this action depresses a diaphragm which causes the internal regulator pressure to rise, providing a continuous supply of pure oxygen at high altitudes.

4-56. DELETED.

4-57. OXYGEN FLOW INDICATORS. Two blinker-type oxygen flow indicators blink in unison with the breathing of the pilot when the regulator is functioning properly in supplying normal oxygen or 100 percent oxygen. One indicator is incorporated in the composite regulator under the left-hand console and the other is located so as to be visible on the left-hand console forward of the master water injection switch.

4-58. OXYGEN SYSTEM PRESSURE GAGES. Oxygen system pressure is indicated on pressure gages. One gage is incorporated in the composite regulator under the left-hand console and the other is located forward of the master water injection switch on the left-hand console.

4-59. BREATHING TUBE. A standard breathing tube with a quick-disconnect female coupling is stowed in a pan beneath the pilot's seat. The end of the breathing tube protrudes through a horn in the forward end of the pan and is within easy reach. The tube can be pulled from the pan, and the tube end of the mask quickly and easily coupled to it. When disconnected from the mask, the breathing tube can be pushed back into the pan.

4-60. PREFLIGHT CHECK PROCEDURE. The following check should be made prior to each flight in which oxygen is to be or likely to be used:

WARNING

The valve on the forward oxygen cylinder, located in the right-hand control shelf, should always be kept open to permit the consumption of oxygen from both cylinders. If the valve is closed, oxygen will be supplied from, and the pressure gage will indicate the pressure of, the rear cylinder only.

a. Oxygen system pressure should read 1,800 (±50) psi if cylinders are fully charged, at 70°F or equivalent. If the cylinder pressure has decreased by more than 25 psi in 24 hours, after the temperature correction noted below has been applied, the system should be subjected to a "Ground Crew Test" prior to use.

Note

The allowance for temperature change is 3.5-psi increase for each degree (Fahrenheit) that temperature rises; 3.5-psi decrease for each degree (Fahrenheit) that temperature drops.

b. Test breathing tube couplings, regulator diaphragm, and diluter check valve for leakage by inserting a spare mask tube quick-disconnect fitting (AN6043) into open end of disconnect until flow indicator face opens. Seal end of disconnect with tongue. If flow indicator does not close within 5 seconds, the leakage is within acceptable limits. If leakage exists, check couplings, outlet elbow, and breather tube hose clamps for tightness.

c. Put on mask. Check fit by placing thumb over disconnect at end of mask tube and inhaling lightly. If mask is leakproof, it will adhere tightly to the face and inhalation will be resisted. If mask leaks, tighten mask suspension straps. DO NOT USE MASK THAT LEAKS.

d. Fully engage mating portion of the disconnect coupling to connect mask to the oxygen system breathing tube.

e. Attach breathing tube clothing clamp to parachute harness or clothing, allowing free head movement. *Do not clamp to shoulder harness.*

f. Breathe several times with regulator air valve in the "NORMAL" and "100 PERCENT OXYGEN" positions in turn, to check regulator operation, and observe oxygen flow indicator for "blink," verifying positive flow of oxygen.

OXYGEN CONSUMPTION TABLE APPROXIMATE HOURS OF OXYGEN—ONE MAN—AIR VALVE AT "NORMAL OXYGEN" (This table is to be used only for airplanes with type 2863-A1 regulators; data for type 2862-B1 regulators which have an automatic positive pressure system will be supplied when available.)								
CYLINDER PRESSURE	ALTITUDE IN FEET							
	5,000	10,000	15,000	20,000	25,000	30,000	35,000	40,000
1800	16.0	18.0	17.0	13.8	8.1	6.2	8.4	13.8
1500	12.8	14.4	13.6	11.0	6.6	5.0	6.8	11.0
1200	9.6	10.8	10.2	8.2	4.8	3.8	5.0	8.2
900	6.4	7.2	6.8	5.6	3.2	2.4	3.4	5.6
600	3.2	3.6	3.4	2.8	1.6	1.2	1.2	2.8
300	Descend Below 10,000 Feet							
	Two 514-Cubic-Inch Cylinders—One Diluter-Demand Regulator							

Figure 4–10. Oxygen System Consumption Table

Note

Since oxygen flow at sea level is negligible when the regulator is in the "NORMAL" or diluted oxygen position, the indicator may not operate on the ground when the regulator handle is in that position. In this case, turn the air-valve to the "100 PERCENT OXYGEN" position, and test again. The air-valve should be turned to "NORMAL OXYGEN" again after the check.

4–61. NORMAL OPERATION AND USE.

a. Oxygen shall be used constantly, during day flights when above 10,000 feet and during night flights when above 5,000 feet, when on combat missions and training missions simulating combat.

b. Pressure gage should read approximately 1,800 psi for fully charged cylinders.

c. Set air valve to "NORMAL OXYGEN" for normal flight conditions. Only when the presence of carbon monoxide or other noxious gases is suspected should the air valve be set to "100 PERCENT OXYGEN."

d. Put on A-13A Oxygen Mask, fully engage disconnect coupling and attach clip to parachute harness or clothing sufficiently high enough on the chest to permit unimpeded movement of the head. *Do not clamp to shoulder harness.*

e. Check mask fit periodically.

f. Breathe normally and check the following at frequent intervals:

(1) Cylinder pressure gage for amount of oxygen remaining.

(2) Oxygen flow indicator to verify flow of oxygen through the regulator.

Note

The oxygen flow indicator blinks upon the intermittent application of from 5 to 7 inches of water pressure created by the flow of oxygen. The automatic pressure breathing oxygen regulator delivers a pressure of 5 to 7 inches of water to the mask at approximately 41,000 feet, and this pressure is likewise transmitted to the flow indicator which will remain open as long as this pressure is applied. Accordingly the flow indicator will not "blink" above this altitude; however, the positive pressure in the mask is an unmistakable indication that oxygen is being delivered to the mask and no apprehension should be felt as long as the flow indicator remains open.

(3) Mask fit by squeezing tube and inhaling.

(4) Disconnect coupling to insure that it is fully engaged.

CAUTION

Do not exhaust cylinder supply below 300 psi except in emergency.

4–62. EMERGENCY OPERATION. Refer to paragraph 3–34.

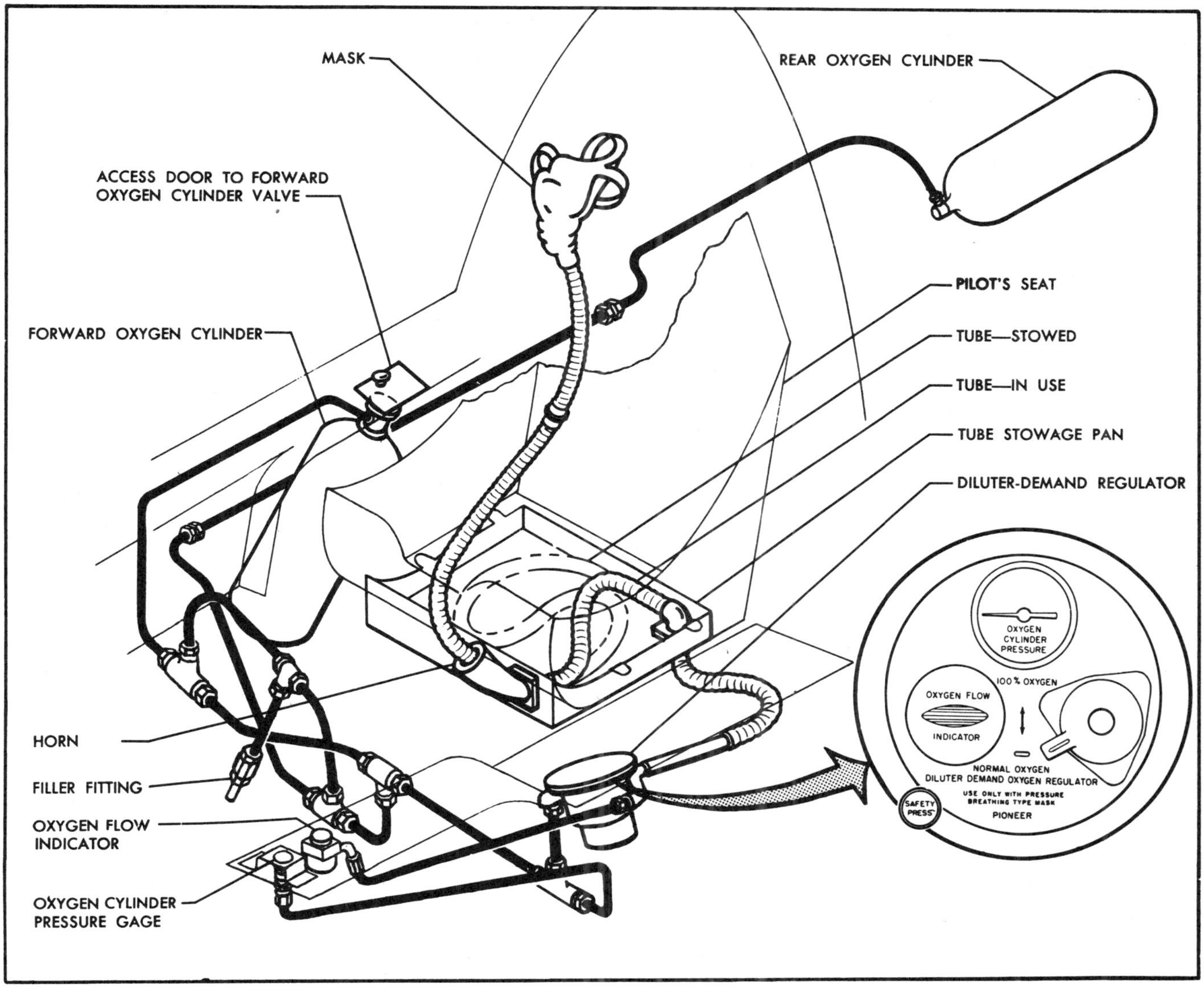

Figure 4–11. Oxygen System

Appendix I

OPERATING CHARTS

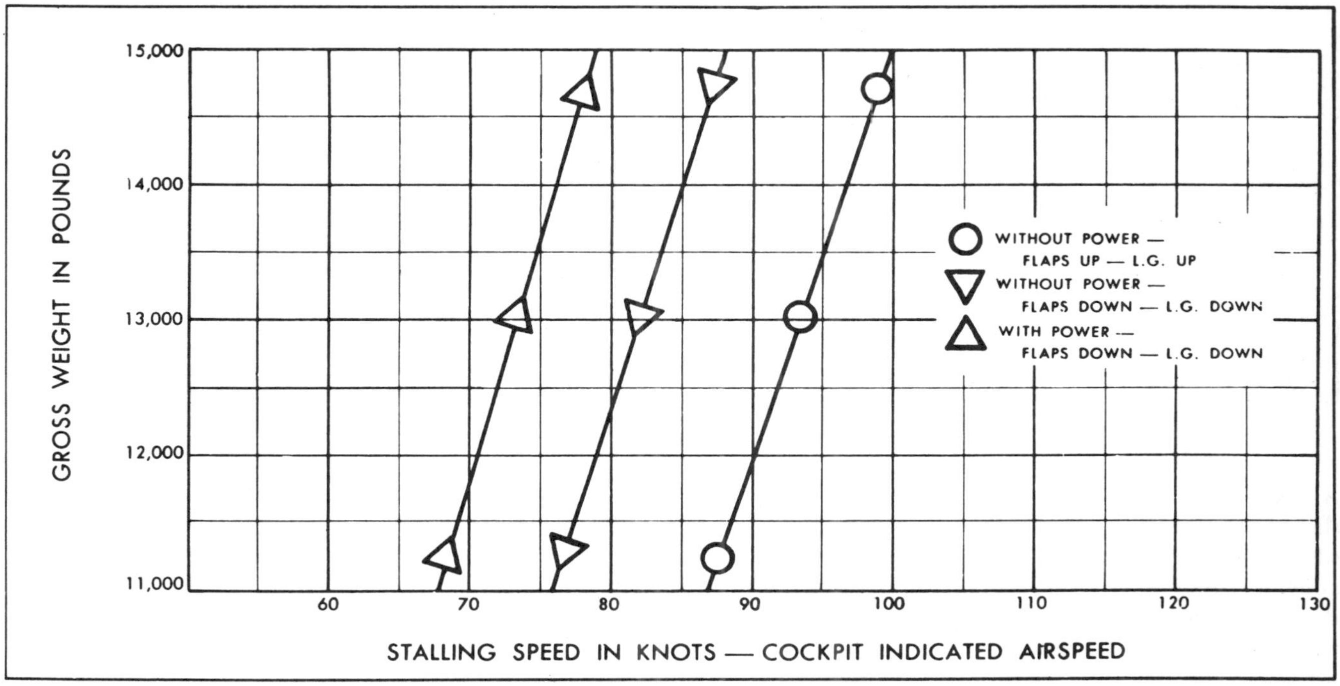

Figure A-1. Stalling Speed vs. Gross Weight Relationship Curve

CLEAN CONDITION **FLAPS RETRACTED**		LANDING CONDITION **FLAPS EXTENDED**	
I.A.S.	CORRECTION	I.A.S.	CORRECTION
70 KNOTS	ADD 0 KNOTS	70 KNOTS	ADD 0 KNOTS
80 KNOTS	ADD 0 KNOTS	80 KNOTS	SUBTRACT 2 KNOTS
90 KNOTS	ADD 0 KNOTS	90 KNOTS	SUBTRACT 3 KNOTS
100 KNOTS	ADD 0 KNOTS	100 KNOTS	SUBTRACT 4 KNOTS
200 KNOTS	ADD 0 KNOTS	110 KNOTS	SUBTRACT 5 KNOTS
300 KNOTS	ADD 0 KNOTS	120 KNOTS	SUBTRACT 5 KNOTS
400 KNOTS	ADD 0 KNOTS	130 KNOTS	SUBTRACT 3 KNOTS

Figure A-2. Airspeed Installation Correction Table

A-1. ENGINE CALIBRATION CURVE.

A-2. The Engine Calibration Curve has been deleted. It is not possible to make up a usable Engine Calibration Curve for this engine from which horsepower can be obtained at various combinations of rpm, manifold pressure, and altitude. In its place, charts showing data for two representative cruising manifold pressures for various rpm's are included. The performance characteristics of this engine are such that for a given power output, fuel consumption remains essentially constant for all altitudes up to the critical altitude (altitude at which full throttle is reached). The choice of the rpm-manifold pressure combination in chart A is such as to give an average BMEP of 155 psi, which is very close to the BMEP recommended for continuous cruising by the engine manufacturer. Chart B is based on a lower BMEP value.

Manifold Pressure: 35 in. Hg. (Sea level to critical altitude)	
RPM	**Fuel Consumption** *(gal. per hr.)*
1200	63
1400	71
1600	82
1800	96
2000	114

CHART A

Manifold Pressure: 30 in. Hg. (Sea level to critical altitude)	
RPM	**Fuel Consumption** *(gal. per hr.)*
1200	55
1400	61
1600	69
1800	78
2000	87
2200	97

CHART B

Figure A-3. Fuel Consumption Data

A-2A. For more precise flight planning, reference should be made to the Flight Operation Instruction Charts since miles per gallon of fuel consumed (under no-wind conditions) is a function of the aerodynamic characteristics of the airplane, the propeller efficiency as well as engine power output.

A-2B. It may not be possible to operate the engine at as low an rpm and manifold pressure for cruising as desired when flying at intermediate and high altitudes due to engine surge. The necessity of increasing rpm and manifold pressure to eliminate this condition will, of course, result in higher fuel consumption. This is a limitation that cannot be avoided and is characteristic of all highly supercharged engines. It is not possible to include fuel consumption data to cover this contingency because of the widely varying surge characteristics exhibited by different airplanes. Reliable fuel consumption data can be obtained only through experience with a particular airplane.

POWER PLANT CHART

AIRCRAFT MODEL(S)	PROPELLER(S)	ENGINE MODEL(S)
F4U-5, -5N, -5P	BLADE: 6837A-0 HUB: 24E60-159	R-2800-32W CARBURETOR: STROMBERG PR64-B2

GAGE READING	FUEL PRESS.	OIL PRESS.	OIL TEMP.	COOLANT TEMP.	OIL CONS.
DESIRED	25	125	75		
MAXIMUM	26	150	85		
MINIMUM	24	90	20		
IDLING	14	40			

MAXIMUM PERMISSIBLE DIVING RPM: 3120 (30 Sec.)
MINIMUM RECOMMENDED CRUISE RPM: 1200

OIL GRADE: (s) 1120 (w) 1100
FUEL GRADE: 115/145; REFER TO NOTE 1.

COMBAT POWER (War Emergency)			MILITARY POWER (Non-Combat Emergency)			OPERATING CONDITIONS			NORMAL RATED (Maximum Continuous)			MAXIMUM CRUISE (Normal Operation)		
MINUTES 232°C			30 MINUTES 248°C			TIME LIMIT MAX. CYL. HD. TEMP.			UNLIMITED 232°C OR 248°C FOR ½ HOUR			UNLIMITED 232°C		
RICH OR NORMAL 2800			NORMAL 2800 (Note 2)			MIXTURE RPM			NORMAL 2600 (Note 2)			NORMAL 2200 (Note 2)		
MANIF. PRESS.	SUPER-CHARGER	FUEL Gal/Min.	MANIF. PRESS.	SUPER-CHARGER	FUEL Gal/Min.	STD. TEMP. °C	PRESSURE ALTITUDE (Feet)	STD. TEMP. °F	MANIF. PRESS.	SUPER-CHARGER	FUEL Gal/Hr.	MANIF. PRESS.	SUPER-CHARGER	FUEL Gal/Hr. (Note 4)
	REFER TO NOTE 3		F.T.	REFER TO NOTE 3	3.3	— 55.0	40,000	— 67.0	F.T.	REFER TO NOTE 3	190	F.T.	REFER TO NOTE 3	112
			F.T.		3.8	— 55.0	38,000	— 67.0	F.T.		210	F.T.		127
			F.T.		4.4	— 55.0	36,000	— 67.0	F.T.		235	F.T.		135
			F.T.		4.9	— 52.4	34,000	— 62.3	F.T.		260	F.T.		138
			F.T.		5.4	— 48.4	32,000	— 55.1	53.0		280	35.0		138
F.T.		3.0	64.0		5.7	— 44.4	30,000	— 48.0	53.0		280	35.0		136
F.T.		3.1	64.0		5.9	— 40.5	28,000	— 40.9	53.0		280	35.0		134
F.T.		4.1	64.0		5.8	— 36.5	26,000	— 33.7	53.0		280	35.0		133
F.T.		4.2	64.0		5.7	— 32.5	24,000	— 26.5	53.0		280	35.0		131
F.T.		4.4	64.0		5.7	— 28.6	22,000	— 19.4	53.0		280	35.0		129
F.T.		4.6	64.0		5.8	— 24.6	20,000	— 12.3	53.0		280	35.0		127
F.T.		4.7	64.0		5.8	— 20.7	18,000	— 5.2	53.0		280	35.0		125
F.T.		4.8	64.0		5.8	— 16.7	16,000	2.0	53.0		280	35.0		123
F.T.		4.8	64.0		5.8	— 12.7	14,000	9.1	53.0		280	35.0		121
F.T.		4.9	64.0		5.8	— 8.8	12,000	16.2	53.0		280	35.0		119
F.T.		5.0	64.0		5.7	— 4.8	10,000	23.4	53.0		280	35.0		116
70		5.0	64.0		5.7	— 0.8	8,000	30.5	53.0		280	35.0		113
70		5.0	64.0		5.7	3.1	6,000	37.6	53.0		280	35.0		110
70		5.0	64.0		5.8	7.1	4,000	44.7	53.0		280	35.0		108
70		5.0	64.0		5.8	11.0	2,000	51.8	53.0		280	35.0		105
70		5.0	64.0		5.9	15.0	SEA LEVEL	59.0	53.0		280	35.0		101

TAKE-OFF CONDITIONS: 64.0 IN. HG., MANIFOLD PRESSURE
2800 RPM, RICH MIXTURE
248°C CYLINDER HEAD TEMP.

CONDITIONS TO AVOID: ENGINE SURGE. If surge occurs, increase rpm and then advance throttle until surge ceases.

GENERAL NOTES

F.T. = full throttle operation.
For combat power data, values are for level flight with ram.
For complete cruising data, see figure A-6.

SPECIAL NOTES

1. When operating on grade 100/130 fuel do not exceed 56 in. Hg manifold pressure at take-off or at military power, or 50 in. Hg manifold pressure at normal rated power, or 35 in. Hg at maximum cruise power. When necessary it is permissible to mix 100/130 fuel with 115/145 fuel but manifold pressures established for 100/130 fuel must be used.
2. If cylinder temperature cannot be maintained, move mixture to rich position.
3. Supercharger speed controlled automatically.
4. Maximum cruise is defined as the maximum power that can be used continuously and still have the carburetor meter at the most economical fuel-air ratio. Higher powers up through normal rated may be used for continuous cruising but the fuel-air ratio becomes progressively higher, resulting in greatly increased fuel consumption with a consequent reduction in range.

Figure A–4. Power Plant Chart

AIRCRAFT MODEL
F4U-5

TAKE-OFF, CLIMB & LANDING CH

TAKE-OFF DISTANCE IN FEET

GROSS WEIGHT LB.	HEAD WIND		HARD SURFACE RUNWAY						SOD TURF RUNWAY			
			AT SEA LEVEL		AT 3000 FEET		AT 6000 FEET		AT SEA LEVEL		AT 3000 FEET	
	MPH	KTS	GROUND RUN	TO CLEAR 50' OBJ.	GROUND RUN	TO CLEAR 50' OBJ.	GROUND RUN	TO CLEAR 50' OBJ.	GROUND RUN	TO CLEAR 50' OBJ.	GROUND RUN	TO CLE. 50' OB
12,800	0	0	730	1370	840	1610	1000	1930	760	1400	880	1650
	17	15	500	1010	580	1180	700	1450	520	1020	600	1210
	35	30	300	670	360	810	450	1020	310	680	370	820
	52	45	140	390	190	490	250	640	160	400	200	500
14,000	0	0	900	1740	1050	2080	1260	2530	940	1780	1120	2150
	17	15	630	1230	740	1560	900	1920	660	1320	770	1600
	35	30	390	880	470	1090	590	1370	400	900	490	1120
	52	45	210	540	260	670	350	880	220	550	280	690
15,000	0	0	1080	2150	1280	2630	1530	3250	1140	2210	1360	2710
	17	15	760	1610	910	1990	1100	2480	800	1660	960	2040
	35	30	480	1120	600	1410	730	1780	500	1140	630	1440
	52	45	270	700	340	900	450	1160	280	710	360	920
18,300	0	0	1760	4210	2120	5740	2550	7740	1890	4330	2280	5900
	17	15	1280	3270	1570	4520	1900	6170	1370	3360	1690	4640
	35	30	850	2380	1060	3330	1320	4670	910	2435	1140	3410
	52	45	520	1590	670	2270	860	329C	550	1620	720	2320

NOTE: INCREASE CHART DISTANCES AS FOLLOWS: 75°F + 10%; 100°F + 20%; 125°F + 30%; 150°F + 40% OPTIM

DATA AS OF: 1 JUNE 1951

CLIMB DATA (NORMAL RATED POWER)

GROSS WEIGHT LB.	AT SEA LEVEL				AT 5000 FEET					AT 10000 FEET					AT 15000 FEET					A	
	BEST I.A.S.		RATE OF CLIMB F.P.M.	GAL. OF FUEL USED	BEST I.A.S.		RATE OF CLIMB F.P.M.	FROM SEA LEVEL		BEST I.A.S.		RATE OF CLIMB F.P.M.	FROM SEA LEVEL		BEST I.A.S.		RATE OF CLIMB F.P.M.	FROM SEA LEVEL		BEST I.A.S.	
	MPH	KTS			MPH	KTS		TIME MIN.	FUEL USED	MPH	KTS		TIME MIN.	FUEL USED	MPH	KTS		TIME MIN.	FUEL USED	MPH	K
12800	175	150	3100	48	170	145	3000	2	55	165	145	3000	3	63	165	140	2900	5	71	160	14
14000	170	150	2700	48	165	145	2600	2	56	165	145	2600	4	65	160	140	2500	6	75	160	14
15000	170	145	2200	48	165	145	2100	2	58	165	140	2100	5	69	160	140	2000	7	82	160	13
18300	165	140	1300	48	160	140	1300	4	65	160	140	1300	8	88	155	135	1200	12	103	155	13

POWER PLANT SETTINGS: (DETAILS ON POWER PLANT CHART)

NOTE: INCREASE ELAPSED CLIMBING TIME 6% FOR EACH 10°C. (20°F.) ABOVE 15°C. (59°F.) FREE AIR TEMPERATURE

DATA AS OF: 1 JUNE 1951

LANDING DISTANCE IN FEET

GROSS WEIGHT LB.	BEST I.A.S. APPROACH POWER OFF		HARD DRY SURFACE						FIRM DRY SOD			
			AT SEA LEVEL		AT 3000 FEET		AT 6000 FEET		AT SEA LEVEL		AT 3000 FEET	
	MPH	KTS	GROUND ROLL	TO CLEAR 50' OBJ.	GROUND ROLL	TO CLEAR 50' OBJ.	GROUND ROLL	TO CLEAR 50' OBJ.	GROUND ROLL	TO CLEAR 50' OBJ.	GROUND ROLL	TO CLEAR 50' OBJ.
11,000	105	90	960	1830	1050	1990	1150	2160	1060	1940	1160	2110
12,000	110	95	1050	2000	1150	2170	1250	2340	1150	2100	1270	2280
15,000	125	110	1310	2500	1430	2680	1560	2860	1440	2630	1570	2820

NOTE: FOR GROUND TEMPERATURES ABOVE 35°C. (95°F.) INCREASE APPROACH I.A.S. 10% AND ALLOW 20% INCREASE IN GROUND ROLL

DATA AS OF: 1 JUNE 1951

REMARKS:

TAKE-OFF AND CLIMB DATA INCLUDE THE EFFECT OF THE DRAG INCREMENT OF EITHER ONE 150 U.S. GAL. DROP TANK OR ONE 1000 POUND BOMB IN THE 14000 POUND CONDITION. FOR THE 15000 POUND CONDITION, THE EFFECT OF THE DRAG INCREMENT FOR ANY COMBINATION OF TWO UNITS (TANKS, BOMBS, 11.75" ROCKETS) IS INCLUDED.

NOTE: TO DETERMINE FUEL CONSUMPTION IN BRITISH IMPERIAL GALLONS MULTIPLY BY 10, THEN DIVIDE BY 12

Figure A-5. Tak

ENGINE MODEL
R-2800-32W

EET	SOFT SURFACE RUNWAY					
	AT SEA LEVEL		AT 3000 FEET		AT 6000 FEET	
TO CLEAR 50′ OBJ.	GROUND RUN	TO CLEAR 50′ OBJ.	GROUND RUN	TO CLEAR 50′ OBJ.	GROUND RUN	TO CLEAR 50′ OBJ.
1980	840	1480	990	1760	1200	2130
1490	570	1080	680	1290	840	1590
1040	340	720	420	870	540	1100
650	180	420	230	530	300	690
2600	1070	1500	1270	2300	1540	2810
1970	740	1410	890	1710	1100	2130
1400	450	950	560	1180	720	1500
900	240	570	320	740	420	960
3350	1300	2370	1560	2910	1900	3620
2550	910	1770	1110	2190	1380	2770
1820	570	1220	720	1540	910	1960
1180	330	750	430	980	560	1270
7950	2300	4750	2840	6460	3540	8730
6330	1670	3660	2100	5050	2540	6810
4780	1110	2640	1420	3690	1830	5180
3360	680	1750	900	2500	1190	3620

WITH 2800 R.P.M., 64 IN. HG. & 50 DEG. FLAP IS 100% OF CHART VALUES
TE: DO NOT EXCEED 56 IN. HG. FOR TAKE-OFF USING 100/130 GRADE FUEL

T		AT 25000 FEET					AT 30000 FEET				
FROM EA LEVEL		BEST I.A.S.		RATE OF CLIMB F.P.M.	FROM SEA LEVEL		BEST I.A.S.		RATE OF CLIMB F.P.M.	FROM SEA LEVEL	
ME IN.	FUEL USED	MPH	KTS		TIME MIN.	FUEL USED	MPH	KTS		TIME MIN.	FUEL USED
7	80	160	140	2500	9	89	155	135	2200	11	99
8	85	155	135	2100	10	96	155	135	1800	13	107
0	94	155	135	1600	13	109	155	135	1300	16	124
6	124	150	130	1000	21	147	150	130	700	27	173

FUEL USED (U.S. GAL.) INCLUDES WARM-UP AND TAKE-OFF ALLOWANCE

'FEET	WET OR SLIPPERY					
	AT SEA LEVEL		AT 3000 FEET		AT 6000 FEET	
O CLEAR 50′ OBJ.	GROUND ROLL	TO CLEAR 50′ OBJ.	GROUND ROLL	TO CLEAR 50′ OBJ.	GROUND ROLL	TO CLEAR 50′ OBJ.
2300	2180	3060	2390	3340	2630	3640
2460	2410	3360	2640	3650	2870	3960
3020	2960	4150	3230	4480	3530	4830

OPTIMUM LANDING IS 100% OF CHART VALUES

LEGEND

I.A.S.	INDICATED AIR SPEED
M.P.H.	MILES PER HOUR
KTS.	KNOTS
F.P.M.	FEET PER MINUTE

FIGURES ARE PRELIMINARY DATA, SUBJECT TO REVISION AFTER FLIGHT CHECK

nb, and Landing Chart

AIRCRAFT MODEL
F4U-5
ENGINE: R-2800-32W

LIMITS	R.P.M.	M.P. IN. HG.	MIXTURE POSITION	TIME LIMIT	CYL. TEMP.	G
COMBAT POWER	2800	70	RICH OR NORMAL		232°C	
MILITARY POWER	2800	64 56 (100/130 GRADE FUEL)	NORMAL	30 MIN.	248°C	5 3

COLUMN I		FUEL U.S. GAL.	COLUM
RANGE IN AIRMILES			RANGE IN
STATUTE AT S.L.	NAUTICAL AT S.L.		STATUTE
		234	
270	235	210	440
245	210	190	400
220	190	170	355
190	165	150	315
165	145	130	275
140	120	110	230
115	100	90	190
90	80	70	145
65	55	50	105
40	35	30	65

MAXIMUM CONTINUOUS						PRESS. ALT. FEET	(2.1 STAT. (1.8 NAU		
R.P.M.	M.P. IN-CHES	MIX-TURE	APPROX. TOT. G.P.H.	T.A.S. M.P.H.	T.A.S. KTS.		R.P.M.	M.P. IN-CHES	MIX-TURE
2600	53	NORM.	280	445	386	30000	2550	47	NORM.
2600	53	NORM.	280	431	374	25000	2500	43	NORM.
2600	53	NORM.	280	411	357	20000	2400	43	NORM.
2600	53	NORM.	280	390	339	15000	2400	42	NORM.
2600	53	NORM.	280	369	320	10000	2300	40	NORM.
2600	53	NORM.	280	347	301	5000	2350	37	NORM.
2600	53	NORM.	280	328	284	S. L.	2200	40	NORM.

(1) MAKE A
CLIMB (
CHART)
COMBAT

(2) THESE D
NOT NE
AIRPLAN
IS AS C
EN ON
ER CON
CHECKE

DATA AS OF: 1 JUNE 1951
Data Basis: NATC Report FT 31-187

Figure A-6. (Sheet 1 of 4 Sheets) F

OPERATION INSTRUCTION CHART

SHEET 1 OF 4 SHEETS

RT WEIGHT LIMITS: 12800 TO 11400 LB.

EXTERNAL LOAD ITEMS

NONE

POWER PLANT CHART, APPENDIX I.

INSTRUCTIONS FOR USING CHART: SELECT FIGURE IN FUEL COLUMN EQUAL TO OR LESS THAN AMOUNT OF FUEL TO BE USED FOR CRUISING. MOVE HORIZONTALLY TO RIGHT OR LEFT AND SELECT RANGE VALUE EQUAL TO OR GREATER THAN THE STATUTE OR NAUTICAL AIRMILES TO BE FLOWN. VERTICALLY BELOW AND OPPOSITE VALUE NEAREST DESIRED CRUISING ALTITUDE (ALT.) READ R.P.M., MANIFOLD PRESSURE (M.P.), AND MIXTURE SETTING REQUIRED.

NOTES: COLUMN I IS FOR EMERGENCY HIGH SPEED CRUISING ONLY. COLUMNS II, III, IV, AND V GIVE PROGRESSIVE INCREASE IN RANGE AT A SACRIFICE IN SPEED. AIRMILES PER GALLON (MI./GAL.) (NO WIND), GALLONS PER HR. (G.P.H.) AND TRUE AIR SPEED (T.A.S.) ARE APPROXIMATE VALUES FOR REFERENCE. RANGE VALUES ARE FOR AN AVERAGE AIRPLANE FLYING ALONE (NO WIND). TO OBTAIN BRITISH IMPERIAL GAL. (OR G.P.H.): MULTIPLY U.S. GAL. (OR G.P.H.) BY 10, THEN DIVIDE BY 12.

COLUMN III		COLUMN IV		FUEL U.S. GAL.	COLUMN V	
RANGE IN AIRMILES		RANGE IN AIRMILES			RANGE IN AIRMILES	
STATUTE	NAUTICAL	STATUTE	NAUTICAL		STATUTE AT S.L.	NAUTICAL AT S.L.
BTRACT FUEL ALLOWANCES NOT AVAILABLE FOR CRUISING (1)				234		
570	495	705	610	210	705	610
515	450	640	555	190	640	555
460	400	570	495	170	570	495
410	355	505	435	150	505	435
355	305	435	380	130	435	380
300	260	370	320	110	370	320
245	215	305	265	90	305	265
190	165	235	205	70	235	205
135	120	170	145	50	170	145
80	70	100	90	30	100	90

	(2.7 STAT. (2.4 NAUT.) MI/GAL.)						(3.4 STAT. (2.9 NAUT.) MI./GAL.)						PRESS. ALT. FEET	MAXIMUM AIR RANGE					
	R.P.M.	M.P. IN-CHES	MIX-TURE	APPROX. TOT. G.P.H.	T.A.S. M.P.H.	T.A.S. KTS.	R.P.M.	M.P. IN-CHES	MIX-TURE	APPROX. TOT. G.P.H.	T.A.S. M.P.H.	T.A.S. KTS.		R.P.M.	M.P. IN-CHES	MIX-TURE	APPROX. TOT. G.P.H.	T.A.S. M.P.H.	T.A.S. KTS.
KTS.																			
347	2200	36	NORM.	129	357	308	1900	35	NORM.	100	334	290	30000	1850	32	NORM.	82	295	256
340	2200	36	NORM.	126	348	302	1800	35	NORM.	95	316	274	25000	1700	31	NORM.	77	274	238
319	2100	36	NORM.	119	330	286	1800	35	NORM.	90	298	259	20000	1600	32	NORM.	75	263	228
302	2100	37	NORM.	114	314	272	1750	35	NORM.	85	282	245	15000	1500	31	NORM.	70	244	212
280	2200	36	NORM.	108	300	260	1700	35	NORM.	81	270	234	10000	1500	31	NORM.	67	233	202
272	2200	35	NORM.	106	293	254	1650	35	NORM.	76	254	220	5000	1500	30	NORM	66	225	195
261	2100	35	NORM.	101	279	242	1500	34	NORM.	71	235	204	S. L.	1500	29	NORM.	62	208	180

AL NOTES

OR WARM-UP, TAKE-OFF, AND
E-OFF, CLIMB AND LANDING
ANCE FOR WIND, RESERVE AND
D.
ONE AIRPLANE ONLY AND ARE
DRRECT FOR ANY MODEL F4U-5
E THAT THE FUEL CONSUMPTION
SIBLE TO THE TEST RESULTS GIV-
, THE ENGINE AUTOMATIC POW-
LATION SHOULD BE CAREFULLY
; TO EXISTING INSTRUCTIONS.

EXAMPLE

AT 12000 LB. GROSS WEIGHT WITH 171 GAL. OF FUEL (AFTER DEDUCTING TOTAL ALLOWANCES OF 63 GAL.) TO FLY 500 STAT. AIRMILES AT 10000 FT. ALTITUDE, MAINTAIN 1700 R.P.M. AND 35 IN. MANIFOLD PRESSURE WITH MIXTURE SET: NORMAL.

LEGEND

ALT: PRESSURE ALTITUDE
M.P.: MANIFOLD PRESSURE
G.P.H.: U.S. GAL. PER HOUR
G.P.M.: U.S. GAL. PER MINUTE
KTS.: KNOTS
S.L.: SEA LEVEL
T.A.S.: TRUE AIR SPEED

RED FIGURES ARE PRELIMINARY DATA, SUBJECT TO REVISION AFTER FLIGHT CHECK.

AIRCRAFT MODEL
F4U-5
ENGINE: R-2800-32W

FLIGHT OPERATION INSTRUCTION

SHEET 2 OF 4 SHEETS

CHART WEIGHT LIMITS: 14000 TO 1170

LIMITS	R.P.M.	M.P. IN. HG.	MIXTURE POSITION	TIME LIMIT	CYL. TEMP.	TOTAL G.P.M.
COMBAT POWER	2800	70	RICH OR NORMAL		232°C	5.0 S.L.
MILITARY POWER	2800	64 56 (100/130 GRADE FUEL)	NORMAL	30 MIN.	248°C	5.9-S.L. 5.7-30000'

FOR DETAILS SEE POWER PLANT CHART, APPENDIX I.

INSTRUCTIONS FOR USING CHART: SELECT F
UMN EQUAL TO OR LESS THAN AMOUNT
FOR CRUISING. MOVE HORIZONTALLY TO
SELECT RANGE VALUE EQUAL TO OR GREATE
OR NAUTICAL AIRMILES TO BE FLOWN. VER
OPPOSITE VALUE NEAREST DESIRED CRUIS
READ R.P.M., MANIFOLD PRESSURE (M.P.), A
REQUIRED.

COLUMN I RANGE IN AIRMILES STATUTE AT S.L.	COLUMN I RANGE IN AIRMILES NAUTICAL AT S.L.	FUEL U.S. GAL.	COLUMN II RANGE IN AIRMILES STATUTE	COLUMN II RANGE IN AIRMILES NAUTICAL	COLUMN III RANGE IN AIRMILES STATUTE	COLUMN III RANGE IN AIRMILES NAUTICAL
		384	SUBTRACT FUEL ALLOWANCES NOT AVAILABLE FO			
425	370	350	660	570	845	735
380	330	315	590	515	760	660
340	295	280	525	455	675	585
295	255	245	460	400	595	515
255	220	210	395	340	510	440
210	185	175	330	285	425	370
170	145	140	265	230	340	295
125	110	105	200	170	255	220
85	75	70	130	115	170	145
40	35	35	65	55	85	75

MAXIMUM CONTINUOUS						PRESS. ALT. FEET	(1.9 STAT. (1.6 NAUT.) MI/GAL.)						(2.4 STAT. (2.1 NAUT.) MI./GAL.)					
R.P.M.	M.P. IN-CHES	MIX-TURE	APPROX. TOT. G.P.H.	APPROX. T.A.S. M.P.H.	APPROX. T.A.S. KTS.		R.P.M.	M.P. IN-CHES	MIX-TURE	APPROX. TOT. G.P.H.	APPROX. T.A.S. M.P.H.	APPROX. T.A.S. KTS.	R.P.M.	M.P. IN-CHES	MIX-TURE	APPROX. TOT. G.P.H.	APPROX. T.A.S. M.P.H.	APPROX. T.A.S. KTS.
2600	53	NORM.	280	419	363	30000	2500	46	NORM.	197	375	326	2250	37	NORM.	143	346	300
2600	53	NORM.	280	408	354	25000	2450	43	NORM.	193	366	318	2300	36	NORM.	137	332	288
2600	53	NORM.	280	392	340	20000	2400	44	NORM.	184	350	304	2250	37	NORM.	132	318	276
2600	53	NORM.	280	370	321	15000	2350	42	NORM.	172	327	284	2200	37	NORM.	126	304	264
2600	53	NORM.	280	348	302	10000	2350	43	NORM.	163	310	269	2200	37	NORM.	122	295	256
2600	53	NORM.	280	330	286	5000	2350	38	NORM.	158	301	261	2300	35	NORM.	118	286	248
2600	53	NORM.	280	306	266	S. L.	2200	40	NORM.	155	294	255	2300	34	NORM.	114	277	240

SPECIAL NOTES

(1) MAKE ALLOWANCE FOR WARM-UP, TAKE-OFF, AND CLIMB (SEE THE TAKE-OFF, CLIMB AND LANDING CHART) PLUS ALLOWANCE FOR WIND, RESERVE AND COMBAT AS REQUIRED.

(2) THESE DATA ARE FOR ONE AIRPLANE ONLY AND ARE NOT NECESSARILY CORRECT FOR ANY MODEL F4U-5 AIRPLANE. TO INSURE THAT THE FUEL CONSUMPTION IS AS CLOSE AS POSSIBLE TO THE TEST RESULTS GIVEN ON THESE CHARTS, THE ENGINE AUTOMATIC POWER CONTROL INSTALLATION SHOULD BE CAREFULLY CHECKED ACCORDING TO EXISTING INSTRUCTIONS.

AT 13500 LB.
GAL. OF FU
TOTAL ALLO
FLY 900 STAT
ALTITUDE, MA
35 IN. MANIF
TURE SET: NO

DATA AS OF: 1 JUNE 1951
Data Basis: NATC Report FT 31-187

Figure A-6. (Sheet 2 o

EXTERNAL LOAD ITEMS
ONE 150 GAL. DROP TANK OR ONE 1000 LB. BOMB OR ONE 11.75" ROCKET

L COL-
E USED
T AND
TATUTE
W AND
(ALT.)
ETTING

NOTES: COLUMN I IS FOR EMERGENCY HIGH SPEED CRUISING ONLY. COLUMNS II, III, IV, AND V GIVE PROGRESSIVE INCREASE IN RANGE AT A SACRIFICE IN SPEED. AIRMILES PER GALLON (MI./GAL.) (NO WIND), GALLONS PER HR. (G.P.H.) AND TRUE AIR SPEED (T.A.S.) ARE APPROXIMATE VALUES FOR REFERENCE. RANGE VALUES ARE FOR AN AVERAGE AIRPLANE FLYING ALONE (NO WIND). TO OBTAIN BRITISH IMPERIAL GAL. (OR G.P.H.): MULTIPLY U.S. GAL. (OR G.P.H.) BY 10, THEN DIVIDE BY 12.

IV RMILES NAUTICAL	FUEL U.S. GAL.	COLUMN V RANGE IN AIRMILES STATUTE AT S.L.	NAUTICAL AT S.L.
(1)	384		
900	350	1100	955
810	315	990	860
720	280	880	765
630	245	770	670
540	210	660	575
450	175	555	480
360	140	440	380
270	105	330	285
180	70	220	190
90	35	110	96

(2.6 NAUT.) MI./GAL.)				PRESS. ALT. FEET	MAXIMUM AIR RANGE					
MIX-TURE	APPROX. TOT. G.P.H.	T.A.S. M.P.H.	KTS.		R.P.M.	M.P. IN-CHES	MIX-TURE	APPROX. TOT. G.P.H.	T.A.S. M.P.H.	KTS.
NORM.	101	303	263	30000	1850	33	NORM.	88	277	240
NORM.	98	293	254	25000	1700	32	NORM.	82	260	225
NORM.	94	280	243	20000	1600	33	NORM.	79	248	215
NORM.	89	265	230	15000	1500	32	NORM.	73	230	200
NORM.	86	256	222	10000	1500	32	NORM.	71	225	195
NORM.	82	244	212	5000	1500	32	NORM.	69	219	190
NORM.	78	234	203	S. L.	1500	30	NORM.	64	202	175

T WITH 319
EDUCTING
5 GAL.) TO
T 10000 FT.
R.P.M. AND
WITH MIX-

LEGEND

ALT: PRESSURE ALTITUDE
M.P.: MANIFOLD PRESSURE
G.P.H.: U.S. GAL. PER HOUR
G.P.M.: U.S. GAL. PER MINUTE
KTS.: KNOTS
S.L.: SEA LEVEL
T.A.S.: TRUE AIR SPEED

RED FIGURES ARE PRELIMINARY DATA, SUBJECT TO REVISION AFTER FLIGHT CHECK.

ts) Flight Operation Instruction Chart

AIRCRAFT MODEL
F4U-5
ENGINE: R-2800-32W

LIMITS	R.P.M.	M.P. IN. HG.	MIXTURE POSITION	TIME LIMIT	CYL. TEMP.	G. TO
COMBAT POWER	2800	70	RICH OR NORMAL		232°C	5 5
MILITARY POWER	2800	64 56 (100/130 GRADE FUEL)	NORMAL	30 MIN.	248°C	5.9 5 30

COLUMN I		FUEL U.S. GAL.	COLUMN
RANGE IN AIRMILES			RANGE IN AI
STATUTE AT S.L.	NAUTICAL AT S.L.		STATUTE
		384	
400	345	350	595
360	310	315	535
319	280	280	475
280	240	245	415
240	210	210	355
200	175	175	300
160	140	140	240
120	105	105	180
80	70	70	120
40	35	35	60

MAXIMUM CONTINUOUS						PRESS. ALT. FEET	(1.7 STAT. (1.5 NAUT			
R.P.M.	M.P. IN-CHES	MIX-TURE	APPROX. TOT. G.P.H.	T.A.S. M.P.H.	T.A.S. KTS.		R.P.M.	M.P. IN-CHES	MIX-TURE	TO G.
2600	53	NORM.	280	386	335	30000	2500	46	NORM.	2
2600	53	NORM.	280	382	331	25000	2500	44	NORM.	1
2600	53	NORM.	280	369	320	20000	2450	44	NORM.	1
2600	53	NORM.	280	347	301	15000	2400	44	NORM.	1
2600	53	NORM.	280	326	283	10000	2400	44	NORM.	1
2600	53	NORM.	280	304	264	5000	2400	39	NORM.	1
2600	53	NORM.	280	284	246	S. L.	2100	42	NORM.	1

(1) MAKE AL
CLIMB (SE
CHART) P
COMBAT
(2) THESE DA
NOT NEC
AIRPLANE
IS AS CL
EN ON TH
ER CONT
CHECKED

DATA AS OF 1 JUNE 1951
Data Basis: NATC Report FT 31-187

Figure A-6. (Sheet 3 of 4 Sheets) Fli

OPERATION INSTRUCTION CHART

SHEET 3 OF 4 SHEETS

T WEIGHT LIMITS: 15000 TO 12700 LB.

EXTERNAL LOAD ITEMS

ANY COMBINATION OF TWO UNITS (BOMBS, TANKS, 11.75" ROCKETS)

POWER PLANT CHART, APPENDIX I.

INSTRUCTIONS FOR USING CHART: SELECT FIGURE IN FUEL COLUMN EQUAL TO OR LESS THAN AMOUNT OF FUEL TO BE USED FOR CRUISING. MOVE HORIZONTALLY TO RIGHT OR LEFT AND SELECT RANGE VALUE EQUAL TO OR GREATER THAN THE STATUTE OR NAUTICAL AIRMILES TO BE FLOWN. VERTICALLY BELOW AND OPPOSITE VALUE NEAREST DESIRED CRUISING ALTITUDE (ALT.) READ R.P.M., MANIFOLD PRESSURE (M.P.), AND MIXTURE SETTING REQUIRED.

NOTES: COLUMN I IS FOR EMERGENCY HIGH SPEED CRUISING ONLY. COLUMNS II, III, IV, AND V GIVE PROGRESSIVE INCREASE IN RANGE AT A SACRIFICE IN SPEED. AIRMILES PER GALLON (MI./GAL.) (NO WIND), GALLONS PER HR. (G.P.H.) AND TRUE AIR SPEED (T.A.S.) ARE APPROXIMATE VALUES FOR REFERENCE. RANGE VALUES ARE FOR AN AVERAGE AIRPLANE FLYING ALONE (NO WIND). TO OBTAIN BRITISH IMPERIAL GAL. (OR G.P.H.): MULTIPLY U.S. GAL. (OR G.P.H.) BY 10, THEN DIVIDE BY 12.

COLUMN III		COLUMN IV		FUEL U.S. GAL.	COLUMN V	
RANGE IN AIRMILES		RANGE IN AIRMILES			RANGE IN AIRMILES	
STATUTE	NAUTICAL	STATUTE	NAUTICAL		STATUTE AT S.L.	NAUTICAL AT S.L.
TRACT FUEL ALLOWANCES NOT AVAILABLE FOR CRUISING (1)				384		
745	645	900	780	350	990	860
670	580	810	705	315	895	775
595	515	720	625	280	795	690
520	450	630	545	245	700	605
450	390	540	470	210	595	515
375	325	450	390	175	495	430
300	260	360	310	140	400	345
225	195	270	235	105	300	260
150	130	180	155	70	195	170
75	65	90	80	35	99	86

	(2.1 STAT. (1.8 NAUT.) MI./GAL.)						2.6 STAT. (2.2 NAUT.) MI./GAL.)						PRESS. ALT. FEET	MAXIMUM AIR RANGE					
	R.P.M.	M.P. IN-CHES	MIX-TURE	APPROX.			R.P.M.	M.P. IN-CHES	MIX-TURE	APPROX.				R.P.M.	M.P. IN-CHES	MIX-TURE	APPROX.		
				TOT.	T.A.S.					TOT.	T.A.S.						TOT.	T.A.S.	
KTS.				G.P.H.	M.P.H.	KTS.				G.P.H.	M.P.H.	KTS.					G.P.H.	M.P.H.	KTS.
303	2400	40	NORM.	137	291	252	2000	35	NORM.	109	277	240	30000	1900	35	NORM.	100	260	225
293	2400	39	NORM.	148	310	269	1900	36	NORM.	108	274	238	25000	1800	34	NORM.	90	242	210
283	2300	39	NORM.	140	294	255	2000	36	NORM.	107	270	234	20000	1700	34	NORM.	84	230	200
269	2250	39	NORM.	137	287	249	2000	37	NORM.	103	261	226	15000	1600	35	NORM.	81	225	195
259	2100	40	NORM.	126	268	232	2000	36	NORM.	100	254	220	10000	1550	34	NORM.	76	213	185
247	2050	35	NORM.	120	255	221	2000	35	NORM.	97	246	213	5000	1550	34	NORM.	73	208	180
237	1850	39	NORM.	116	247	214	2000	34	NORM.	94	238	207	S. L.	1500	33	NORM.	71	202	175

L NOTES

R WARM-UP, TAKE-OFF, AND
OFF, CLIMB AND LANDING
ICE FOR WIND, RESERVE AND

ONE AIRPLANE ONLY AND ARE
RECT FOR ANY MODEL F4U-5
THAT THE FUEL CONSUMPTION
BLE TO THE TEST RESULTS GIV-
THE ENGINE AUTOMATIC POW-
TION SHOULD BE CAREFULLY
TO EXISTING INSTRUCTIONS.

EXAMPLE

AT 14500 LB. GROSS WEIGHT WITH 302 GAL. OF FUEL (AFTER DEDUCTING TOTAL ALLOWANCE OF 82 GAL.) TO FLY 600 STAT. AIRMILES AT 15000 FT. ALTITUDE, MAINTAIN 2250 R.P.M. AND 39 IN. MANIFOLD PRESSURE WITH MIXTURE SET: NORMAL.

LEGEND

ALT: PRESSURE ALTITUDE
M.P.: MANIFOLD PRESSURE
G.P.H.: U.S. GAL. PER HOUR
G.P.M.: U.S. GAL. PER MINUTE
KTS.: KNOTS
S.L.: SEA LEVEL
T.A.S.: TRUE AIR SPEED

AIRCRAFT MODEL
F4U-5
ENGINE: R-2800-32W

FLIGHT OPERATION INSTRUCTION

SHEET 4 OF 4 SHEETS
CHART WEIGHT LIMITS: 18300 TO 170

LIMITS	R.P.M.	M.P. IN. HG.	MIXTURE POSITION	TIME LIMIT	CYL. TEMP.	TOTAL G.P.M.	FOR DETAILS SEE POWER PLANT CHART APPENDIX I.
COMBAT POWER	2800	70	RICH OR NORMAL		232°C	5.0 S.L.	
MILITARY POWER	2800	64 56 (100/130 GRADE FUEL)	NORMAL	30 MIN.	248°C	5.9-S.L. 5.7-30000′	

INSTRUCTIONS FOR USING CHART: SELECT
UMN EQUAL TO OR LESS THAN AMOUNT
FOR CRUISING. MOVE HORIZONTALLY TO
SELECT RANGE VALUE EQUAL TO OR GREA
OR NAUTICAL AIRMILES TO BE FLOWN. V
OPPOSITE VALUE NEAREST DESIRED CRU
READ R.P.M., MANIFOLD PRESSURE (M.P.),
REQUIRED.

COLUMN I RANGE IN AIRMILES STATUTE AT S.L.	COLUMN I RANGE IN AIRMILES NAUTICAL AT S.L.	FUEL U.S. GAL.	COLUMN II RANGE IN AIRMILES STATUTE	COLUMN II RANGE IN AIRMILES NAUTICAL	COLUMN III RANGE IN AIRMILES STATUTE	COLUMN III RANGE IN AIRMILES NAUTICAL	S
		234		SUBTRACT FUEL ALLOWANCES NOT AVAILABLE			
205	175	210	250	220	315	275	
185	160	190	230	200	285	250	
165	145	170	205	175	255	220	
145	125	150	180	155	225	195	
125	110	130	155	135	195	170	
105	90	110	130	115	165	145	
85	75	90	110	95	135	115	
70	60	70	85	75	105	90	
50	40	50	60	50	75	65	
30	25	30	35	30	45	40	

MAXIMUM CONTINUOUS R.P.M.	M.P. INCHES	MIXTURE	APPROX. TOT. G.P.H.	T.A.S. M.P.H.	T.A.S. KTS.	PRESS. ALT. FEET	(1.2 STAT. (1.0 NAUT.) MI./GAL.) R.P.M.	M.P. INCHES	MIXTURE	APPROX. TOT. G.P.H.	T.A.S. M.P.H.	T.A.S. KTS.	(1.5 STAT. (1.3 NAUT.) MI./GAL.) R.P.M.	M.P. INCHES	MIXTURE	APPROX. TOT. G.P.H.	T.A.S. M.P.H.	T.A.S. KTS.
2600	53	NORM.	280	265	230	30000												
2600	53	NORM.	230	283	246	25000	2600	47	NORM.	230	276	240						
2600	53	NORM.	280	289	251	20000	2550	46	NORM.	227	272	236	2500	40	NORM.	159	239	208
2600	53	NORM.	280	281	244	15000	2550	46	NORM.	223	268	233	2450	40	NORM.	161	241	209
2600	53	NORM.	280	272	237	10000	2550	47	NORM.	218	261	227	2450	41	NORM.	161	241	209
2600	53	NORM.	280	268	233	5000	2550	41	NORM.	212	255	222	2500	36	NORM.	157	235	204
2600	53	NORM.	280	262	228	S. L.	2500	45	NORM.	208	249	216	2350	39	NORM.	154	231	201

SPECIAL NOTES

(1) MAKE ALLOWANCE FOR WARM-UP, TAKE-OFF, AND CLIMB (SEE THE TAKE-OFF, CLIMB AND LANDING CHART) PLUS ALLOWANCE FOR WIND, RESERVE AND COMBAT AS REQUIRED.

(2) THESE DATA ARE FOR ONE AIRPLANE ONLY AND ARE NOT NECESSARILY CORRECT FOR ANY MODEL F4U-5 AIRPLANE. TO INSURE THAT THE FUEL CONSUMPTION IS AS CLOSE AS POSSIBLE TO THE TEST RESULTS GIVEN ON THESE CHARTS, THE ENGINE AUTOMATIC POWER CONTROL INSTALLATION SHOULD BE CAREFULLY CHECKED ACCORDING TO EXISTING INSTRUCTIONS.

AT 18000 LE
GAL. OF F
TOTAL ALL
FLY 235 ST.
ALTITUDE, A
31 IN. MAN
TURE SET: N

DATA AS OF: 1 JUNE 1951
Data Basis: NATC Report FT 31-187

Figure A-6. (Sheet 4 of 4 Sheets) Flight Operation Instruction Chart

EXTERNAL LOAD ITEMS
TWO 1000-LB. BOMBS
ONE 2000-LB. BOMB
EIGHT 5-INCH ROCKETS

EL COL-
BE USED
FT AND
STATUTE
OW AND
E (ALT.)
SETTING

NOTES: COLUMN I IS FOR EMERGENCY HIGH SPEED CRUISING ONLY. COLUMNS II, III, IV, AND V GIVE PROGRESSIVE INCREASE IN RANGE AT A SACRIFICE IN SPEED. AIRMILES PER GALLON (MI./GAL.) (NO WIND), GALLONS PER HR. (G.P.H.) AND TRUE AIR SPEED (T.A.S.) ARE APPROXIMATE VALUES FOR REFERENCE. RANGE VALUES ARE FOR AN AVERAGE AIRPLANE FLYING ALONE (NO WIND). TO OBTAIN BRITISH IMPERIAL GAL. (OR G.P.H.): MULTIPLY U.S. GAL. (OR G.P.H.) BY 10, THEN DIVIDE BY 12.

N IV AIRMILES NAUTICAL	FUEL U.S. GAL.	COLUMN V RANGE IN AIRMILES STATUTE AT S.L.	NAUTICAL AT S.L.
G (1)	234		
330	210	445	390
300	190	405	350
265	170	360	315
235	150	320	275
205	130	275	240
170	110	235	200
140	90	190	165
110	70	150	130
80	50	105	90
45	30	65	55

T. (1.6 NAUT.) MI./GAL.				PRESS. ALT. FEET	MAXIMUM AIR RANGE					
MIX-TURE	APPROX. TOT. G.P.H.	T.A.S. M.P.H.	KTS.		R.P.M.	M.P. IN-CHES	MIX-TURE	APPROX. TOT. G.P.H.	T.A.S. M.P.H.	KTS.
				30000	2600	47	NORM.	221	250	219
				25000	2500	41	NORM.	170	230	200
				20000	2450	37	NORM.	139	220	191
				15000	2300	36	NORM.	119	210	182
NORM.	119	214	186	10000	2200	29	NORM.	101	190	165
NORM.	118	212	184	5000	2050	31	NORM.	96	190	165
NORM.	117	210	182	S. L.	1750	36	NORM.	80	170	148

HT WITH 146
DEDUCTING
38 GAL.) TO
AT 10000 FT.
) R.P.M. AND
E WITH MIX-

LEGEND

ALT: PRESSURE ALTITUDE
M.P.: MANIFOLD PRESSURE
G.P.H.: U.S. GAL. PER HOUR
G.P.M.: U.S. GAL. PER MINUTE
KTS.: KNOTS
S.L.: SEA LEVEL
T.A.S.: TRUE AIR SPEED

RED FIGURES ARE PRELIMINARY DATA, SUBJECT TO REVISION AFTER FLIGHT CHECK.

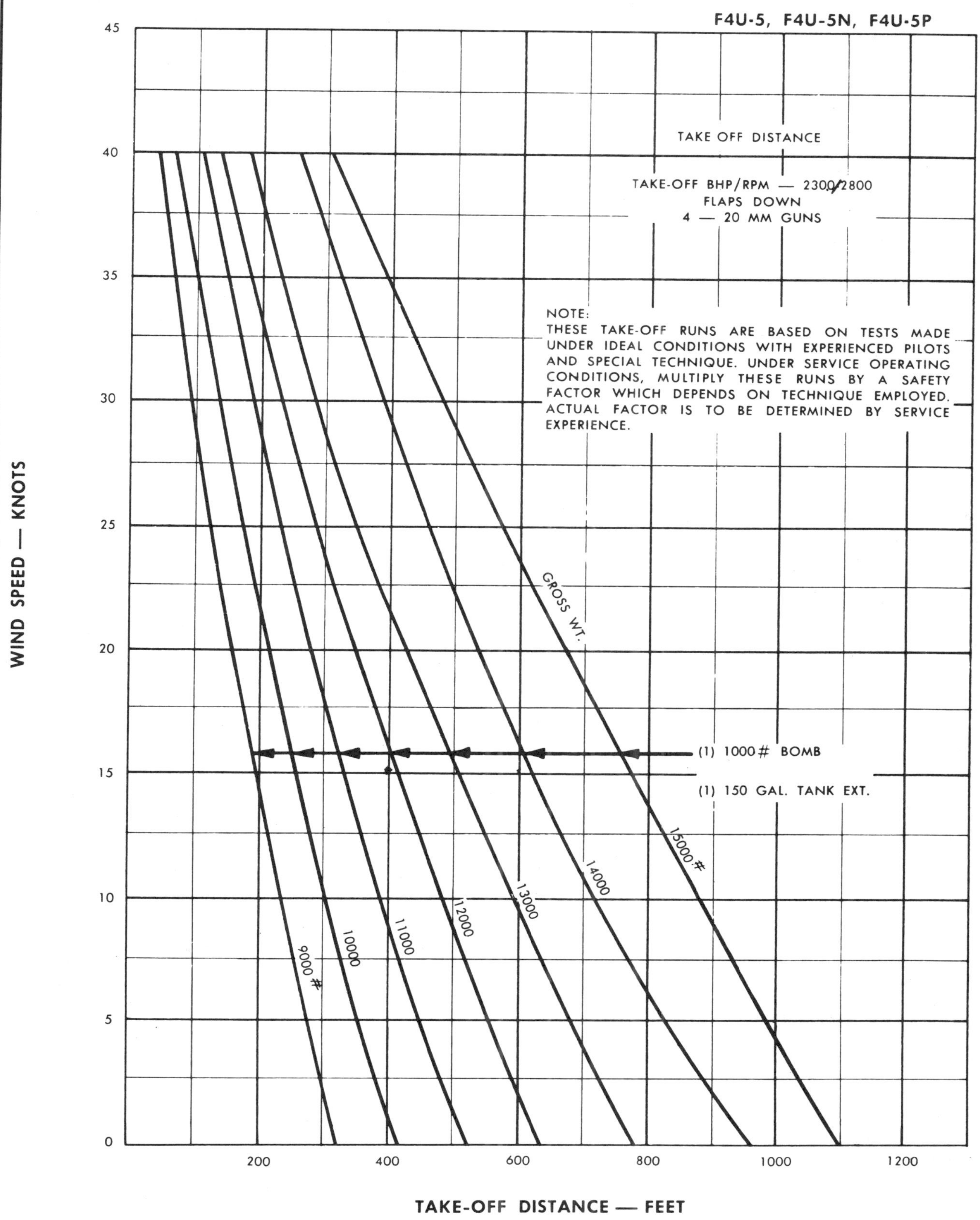

Figure A-7. Take-Off Distance Curves (Sheet 1 of 2 Sheets)

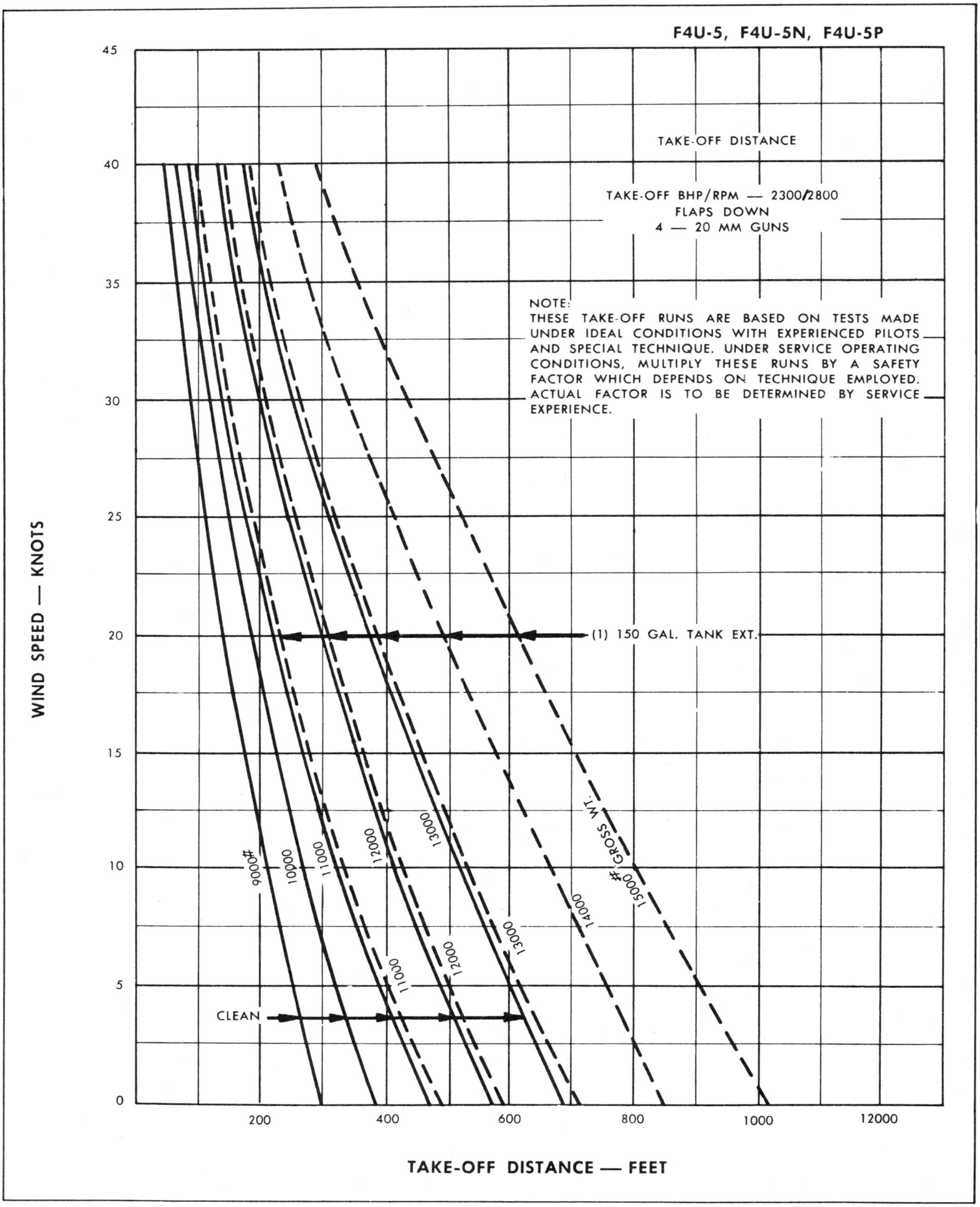

Figure A-7. Take-Off Distance Curves (Sheet 2 of 2 Sheets)

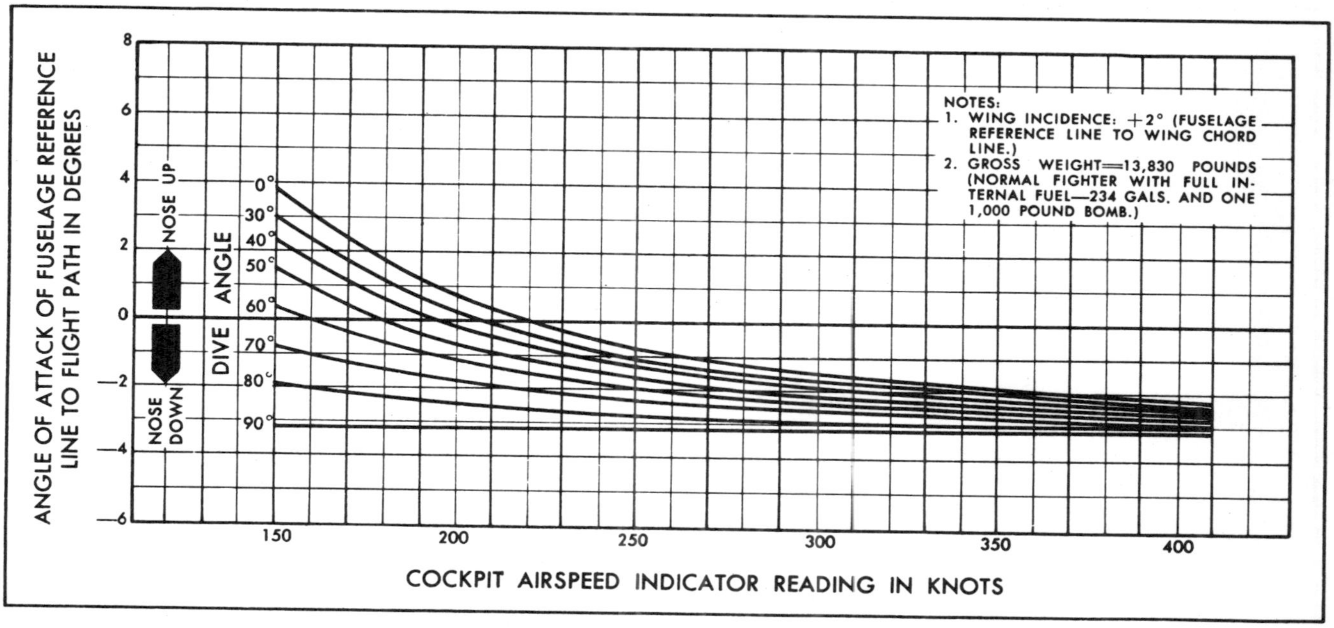

Figure A-8. Angle of Attack in Dives vs. Indicated Airspeed Curves

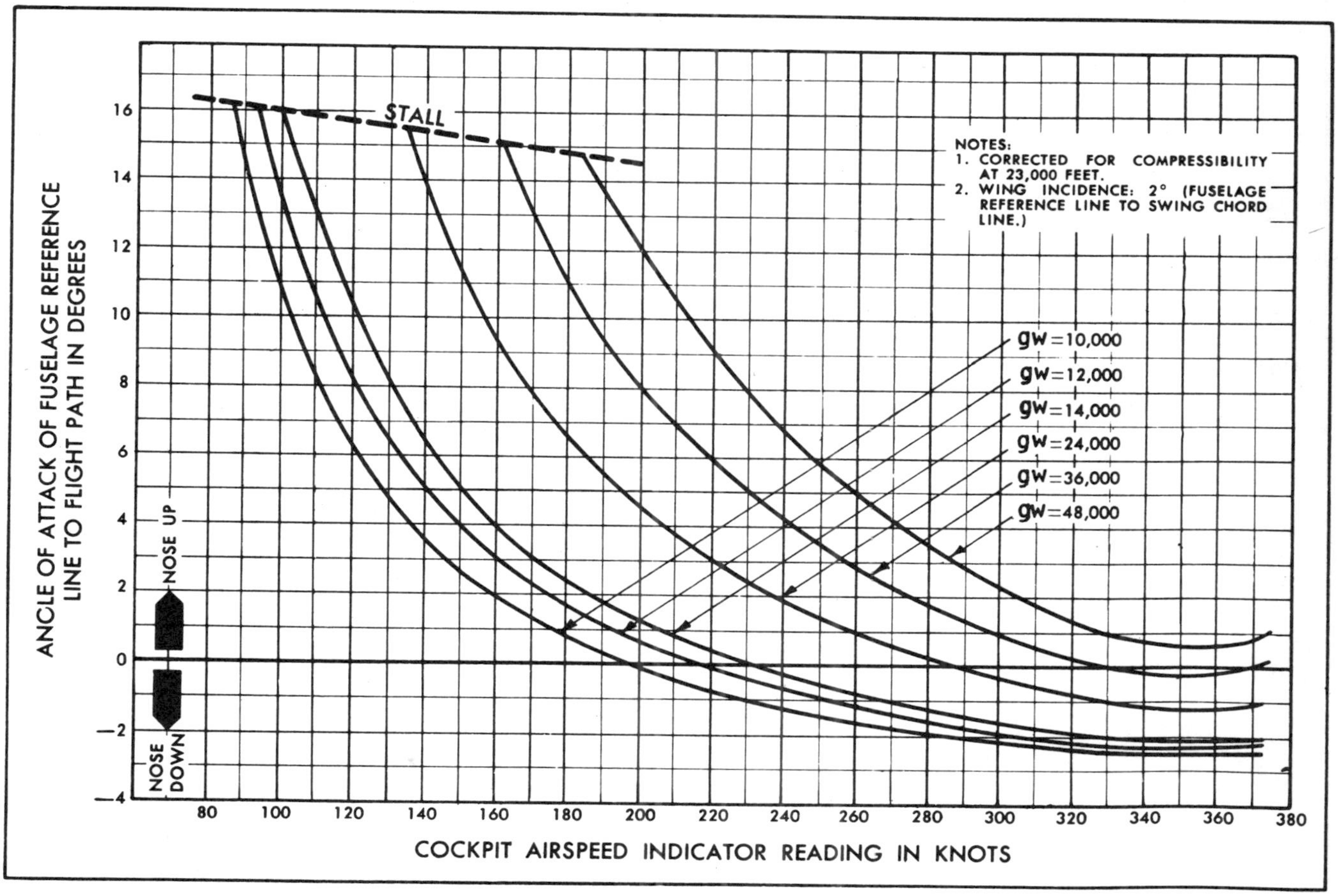

Figure A-9. Angle of Attack vs. Indicated Airspeed for Various Accelerations

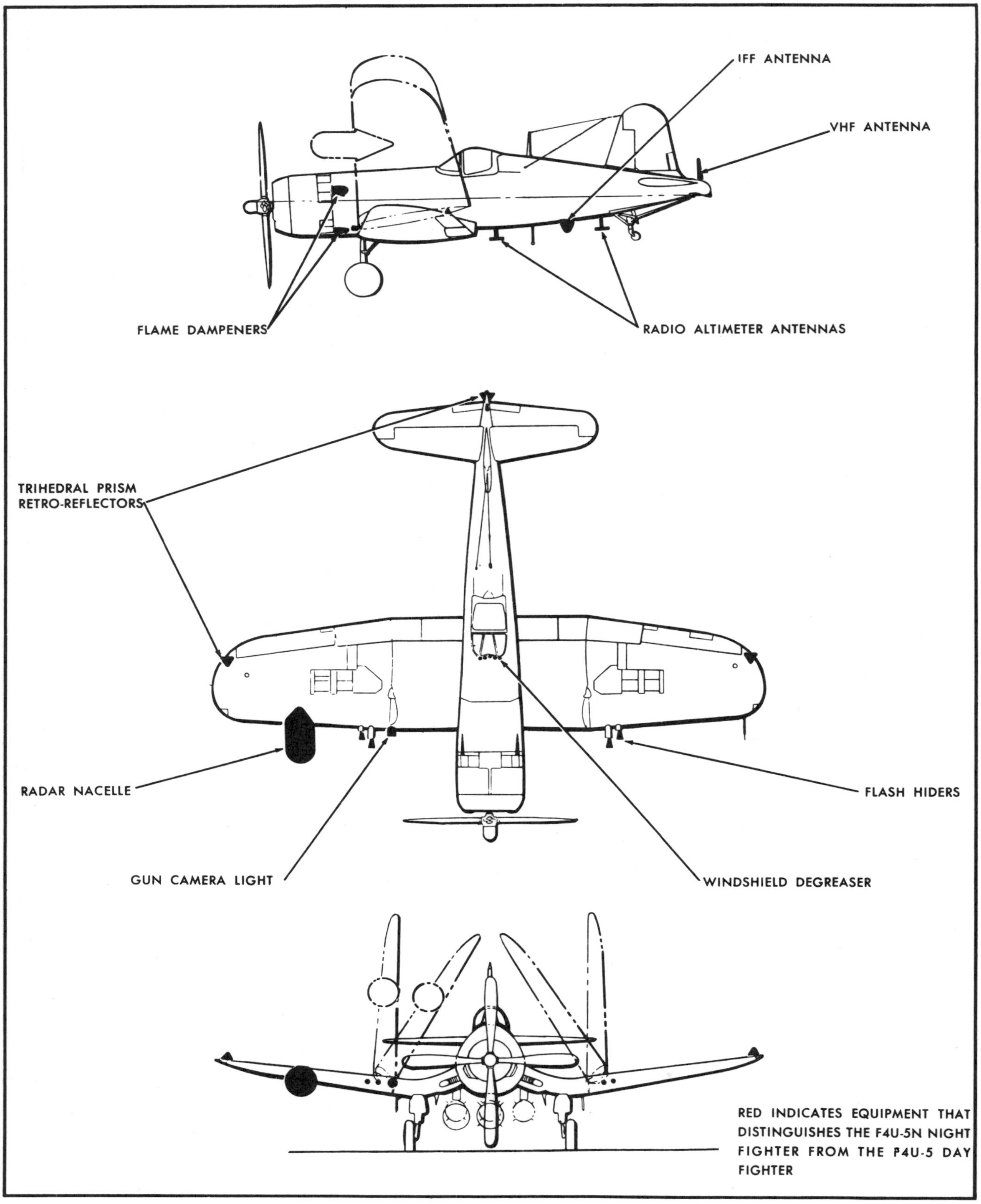

Figure B-1. General Arrangement of F4U-5N Airplane

Appendix II

NIGHT FIGHTER EQUIPMENT

B-1. F4U-5N NIGHT FIGHTER.

B–2. DESCRIPTION. The F4U-5N airplane is a completely equipped single seat night fighter which can easily be distinguished from the F4U-5 day fighter by the radar nacelle on the right wing. This airplane incorporates the following systems and miscellaneous units which are not installed in the F4U-5 day fighter: (1) P-1 Auto Pilot, (2) AN/APS-19A Radar Set, (3) AN/ARC-28 Communication (VHF) Equipment, (4) AN/APX-6 IFF Equipment, (5) Windshield Degreaser, (6) MK 20 Gunsight, (7) T-20 Flash Hiders mounted on the gun muzzles, and (8) Exhaust Collector Flame Dampeners. The flash hiders and flame dampeners minimize at night the visible gun flash and exhaust flame. The throttle ranging grip used on the F4U-5 airplane is replaced by a conventional throttle grip and microphone switch.

B–3. FLIGHT CHARACTERISTICS. The F4U-5N airplane has essentially the same flight characteristics as the day fighter except for the items discussed below.

B–3A. STALLS. The stalling characteristics of the F4U-5N airplane are significantly different from those previously presented for the day fighter. Positive stall warning, consisting of a longitudinal stick shaking and airplane buffeting, occurs at a reasonable margin above the actual stall. For this airplane, the stall begins on the right wing, resulting in a strong tendency for a roll-off to the right accompanied by a positive swerve of the airplane to the right. This characteristic is evident in both clean and landing configurations but is more pronounced with flaps deflected. Because of the increasing right wing heaviness as the stall is approached, and because the lateral trim change due to reducing power is in a direction to increase the right wing dropping tendency, caution should be exercised when the engine is cut at speeds close to the stall on making a carrier landing.

CAUTION

Flight at speeds close to the stall, as evidenced by the "feeling" of fore and aft stick shaking and airframe buffeting, should be avoided or entered upon with extreme caution during low-altitude operations.

In turning or accelerated flight, the roll-off to the right at the stall is so violent as to be initially uncontrollable by the pilot. IT IS RECOMMENDED THAT THE PILOT SECURELY RESTRAIN HIMSELF BY MEANS OF HIS SHOULDER HARNESS WHENEVER A POSSIBILITY OF ENCOUNTERING THIS FLIGHT CONDITION EXISTS.

Characteristics in a spin and the recovery techniques to be applied in this condition are similar in general to those discussed for the F4U-5 in paragraphs 2-74 and 2-76.

B–3B. MAXIMUM PERMISSIBLE INDICATED AIRSPEEDS AND ACCELERATIONS. The operating flight strength limitations are those shown in figure 2-6.

B–3C. A-C POWER SUPPLY. A-C power is supplied by an inverter which generates three-phase 400-cycle 115-volt alternating current. On airplanes Bureau Serial No. 124519, 124551 and subsequent, a stand-by inverter and a "MAIN"—"STAND-BY" inverter control switch is installed. In case of failure of the main inverter, a warning light indicates that the pilot should switch to the stand-by inverter. This inverter supplies a-c power to the a-c instruments and lights only. All other a-c circuits will be inoperative.

B–3D. On airplanes Bureau Serial No. 124666 and subsequent the cockpit is rearranged as indicated in figure B–2A. The gun firing circuit breakers are now located in the main junction box and are the automatic reset type. A modified exterior lights control panel, cockpit flood light and individually controlled flight and engine instrument lights are installed. The rocket selector system is completely controlled by the MK-2 station selector, thus eliminating the "Pairs-Single" toggle switch. A G-2 master compass indicator and its components are installed on these airplanes. The master direction indicator dial consists of the following:

a. A calibrated dial to indicate the stabilized heading of the aircraft at all times.

b. A correspondence indicator to indicate the unstabilized heading of the aircraft.

c. A resetting knob for rapid initial setting of the gyro.

B–3E. To operate the G-2 master direction indicator, proceed as follows:

a. Start the gyro by setting the G-2 compass switch to "COMPASS CONTROL."

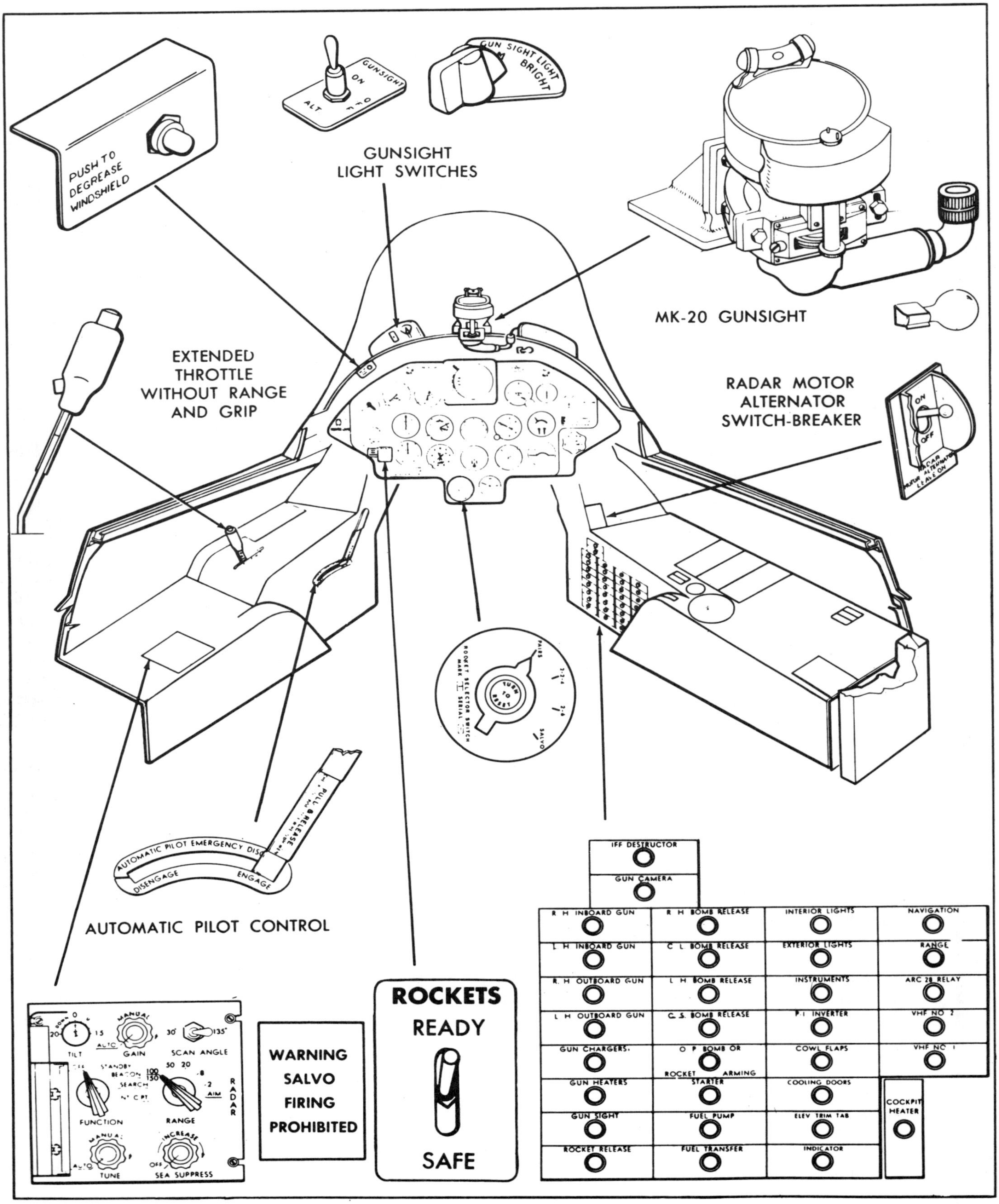

Figure B-2. Cockpit—Looking Forward (Airplanes Bureau Serial No. 121816 through 124560)

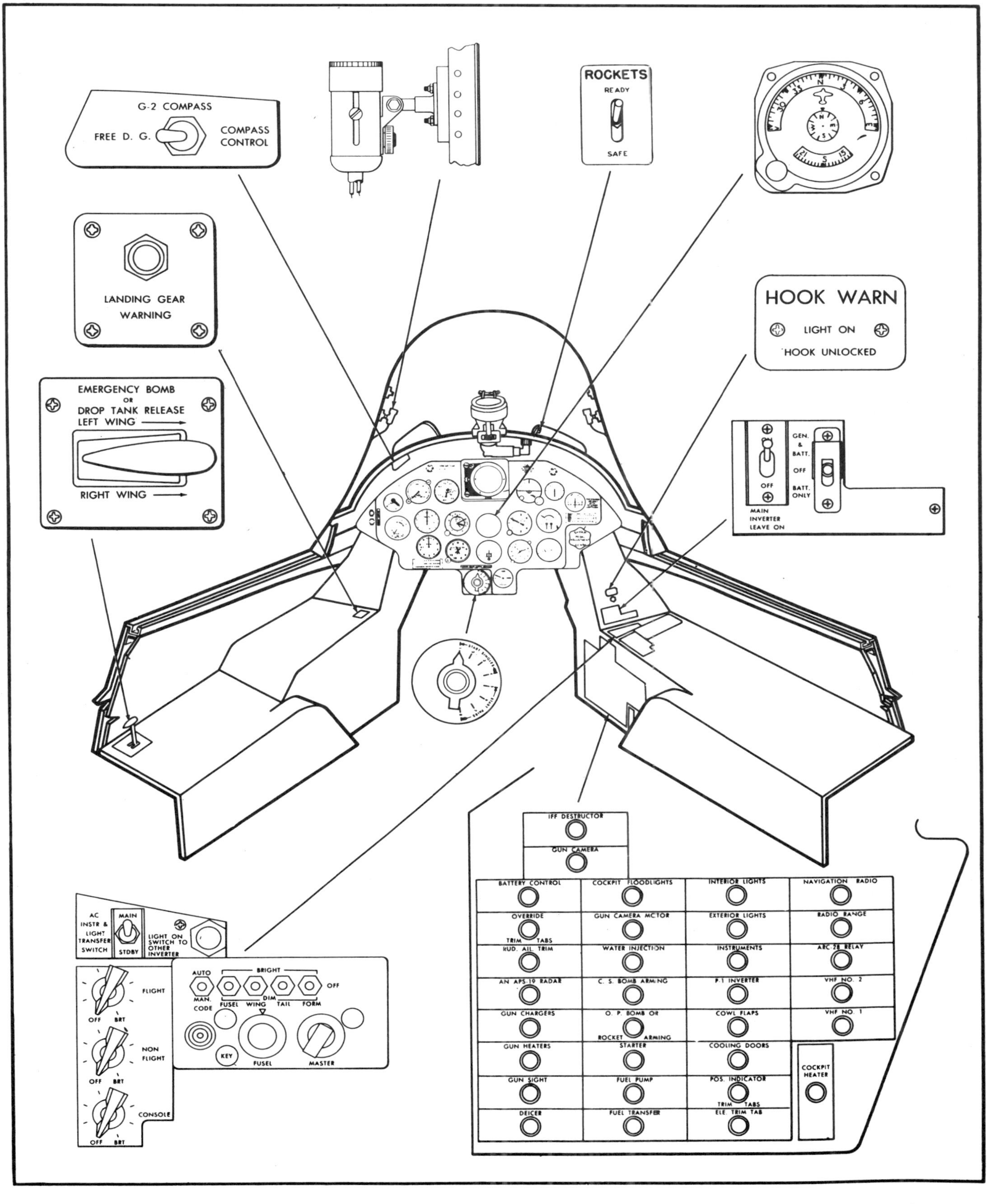

Figure B-2A. Cockpit—Looking Forward (Airplanes Bureau Serial No. 124666 and Subsequent)

b. After 3 minutes, set the master direction indicator heading to agree with the correspondence-indicator heading.

c. Maintain course of airplane on desired dial heading.

d. If auto pilot is to be used, it may be turned on after 3 minutes.

B-4. P-1 AUTOMATIC PILOT.

B-5. DESCRIPTION. The P-1 automatic pilot is a system of automatic controls which hold the aircraft on any selected heading, bring it back without overswing when momentary displacements occur, and simultaneously keep the airplane stabilized in pitch and bank. While under automatic control, the aircraft can also be made to climb, dive, and execute perfectly banked turns. The automatic pilot is engaged and disengaged from the surface controls electrically, by means of a clutch switch. It can also be disconnected by a cable system in an emergency. When the auto pilot is engaged with the surface controls, it maintains the airplane in the same heading and flight attitude it was in prior to engagement. Changes in heading, and flight attitude can be made with the auto pilot by operating the controller unit. The auto pilot is controlled by a number of autosyn transmitters located in the compass, turn and bank, and gyro horizon indicators. As the indicators register changes in direction, pitch, bank, and turn, they simultaneously actuate the autosyns which send out signals to the system. These signals cause the auto pilot servo motors to move the control surfaces in a manner which will enable the airplane to regain its original heading, flight attitude, and flight track.

Note

The G-2 compass switch has two positions, "COMPASS CONTROL" and "FREE DG." The compass control position provides control of the gyros in the system. The "FREE DG" position frees the gyros and should be used when flying over a magnetic field such as the north or south pole.

B-6. AUTO PILOT CONTROLS.

B-7. DESCRIPTION. *(See figure B-2.)* The auto pilot control switches with the exception of the caging knob are located on the right-hand control panel. They are as follows:

a. INVERTER CIRCUIT BREAKER. This switch is located on the circuit breaker panel and is normally closed. It completes the 28-volt d-c power circuit to the a-c inverter.

b. AUTO PILOT CIRCUIT BREAKER. This circuit breaker is located on the circuit breaker panel and is normally closed. It completes the 28-volt d-c power circuit to certain units in the auto pilot and gyro compass system. When "out" this switch breaks the holding circuit to the clutch switch, preventing the clutch switch from being pushed "ON."

c. MAIN — STAND-BY INVERTER SWITCH. When the inverter warning light is on, switch to "STAND-BY." This switch should be in "MAIN" position for normal operation.

d. CAGING KNOB. The caging knob located on the gyro horizon indicator is used to cage this instrument before flight and prevents the automatic pilot clutch from being pushed "ON" when the gyros are caged. The cage knob also automatically cages the P-3 compass transmitter if it is not the self-erecting type.

e. AUTO PILOT POWER SWITCH. This is an ON-OFF switch which controls the 115-volt a-c current from the inverter to the auto pilot. It also controls the clutch switch holding circuit so that when it is "OFF" the clutch switch cannot be pushed "ON." Note that the power switch must be on 30 seconds prior to engaging the clutch switch to permit the auto pilot amplifiers to warm up. If the clutch switch is engaged immediately after power switch is placed in the "ON" position, controls will creep and control stick movement may be violent.

f. CLUTCH SWITCH. This is a push-button switch which, when depressed, closes its own holding circuit to keep it in the "ON" position. The clutch switch will "pop" out if the gyros are caged or if the power switch or auto pilot circuit breaker is "OFF." The clutch switch engages the auto pilot system to the controls.

Normally, the controls are neutralized prior to engaging the clutch switch.

g. CONTROLLER. The controller is employed to maneuver the airplane, change the heading (direction of flight), or fly in a set course other than a straight heading (circle) with the auto pilot. The controller consists essentially of a turn control, bank-trim control, and pitch-trim control. The turn control (knob on top of controller) operates all control surfaces to make a coordinated turn of the airplane with the auto pilot. The pitch-trim and bank-trim controls can be operated to adjust individually the position of the elevators and ailerons for climbing, diving, or banking. The controller is provided with three adjustments which must be made whenever a new controller is installed (see figure B-5). All three adjustment screws are trimmed so that the turn control will make a correctly coordinated turn. After a ground adjustment, further adjustments must be made while the airplane is in flight.

h. EMERGENCY DISCONNECT HANDLE. This handle is located on the vertical face of the engine control unit. It actuates a cable system which manually disengages the auto pilot from the control surfaces, should the auto pilot fail to do so normally.

Note

After the emergency disconnect handle has been pulled, the auto pilot cannot be re-engaged while in flight

B–8. OPERATION IN FLIGHT. To engage the auto pilot while in flight proceed as follows:

a. Check to see that inverter circuit breaker and auto pilot circuit breaker are "ON."

b. Turn auto pilot power switch "ON" and wait from 30 seconds to 1 minute for auto pilot system to warm up.

c. Set controller so that turn control, pitch-trim, and bank-trim controls are in neutral.

d. Set rudder and control stick for straight and level flight and on the heading desired.

e. Depress clutch button. Auto pilot is now engaged with surface controls. Any change now in heading flight track or altitude will be corrected by auto pilot.

CAUTION

Do not engage the auto pilot while in a turn, or in climbs, dives, or banks of more than 10 degrees because to do so may result in insufficient trim adjustment being available, at the controller, to return the airplane to level flight.

f. If desired to maneuver the airplane or to make coordinated turns with the auto pilot, operate the knobs on the controller.

WARNING

Do not attempt to adjust the trim tabs while the auto pilot is engaged. The auto pilot will merely correct for trim tab movement. If the trim tabs are adjusted while the auto pilot is engaged, the airplane flight attitude may change violently when the auto pilot is disengaged.

g. To disengage the auto pilot yet permit it to remain in operation, pull the clutch switch "OFF." To disengage the auto pilot and discontinue operation, throw the power switch "OFF" making certain that the clutch switch goes "OFF" automatically.

h. To disengage the auto pilot in an emergency, pull the emergency disconnect handle to the "DISENGAGE" position. Note that the auto pilot cannot now be re-engaged while in flight.

CAUTION

After any sudden change in load, disengage the auto pilot (using clutch switch), retrim the airplane while in manual flight, then re-engage the auto pilot. Generally, when flying on auto pilot it is well to retrim the airplane in manual flight every hour.

B–9. PREFLIGHT OPERATIONAL TEST. The auto pilot should be checked prior to flight as follows:

a. Connect an auxiliary power supply to the aircraft or have engines running at high enough rpm to insure 28-volt d-c generator output.

b. Make certain that P-1 inverter circuit breaker and auto pilot circuit breaker are "ON."

c. Turn caging knob on gyro horizon indicator to cage gyros. Leave in caged position until indicator dial rocks back and forth and moves within 30 degrees of airplane's heading.

d. Uncage gyros and jar instrument panel to make certain indicator gyro is uncaged. Allow compass dial to settle on correct heading. This will take as long as 15 minutes on an east or west heading, and approximately 5 minutes on a north or south heading if airplane is in a 3-point position.

e. Check freedom of all control surfaces.

f. Turn auto pilot power switch "ON." Wait for 30 seconds to 1 minute for servo amplifier to warm up.

g. Set controller so that turn control, pitch-trim, and bank-trim controls are in neutral.

h. Neutralize all control surfaces with control stick. Surface controls and auto pilot are now aligned for engagement.

AUTO PILOT CONTROLLER OPERATING POSITIONS

CONTROL BEING OPERATED	TURNING DIRECTION OF CONTROL	CORRECT MOVEMENT OF SURFACE CONTROLS
TURN CONTROL (knob on top of controller)	To Right	Right Aileron — "UP" Rudder — "RIGHT" Elevators — "UP"
	To Left	Left Aileron — "UP" Rudder — "LEFT" Elevators — "UP"
PITCH-TRIM CONTROL (small wheel, right-hand side of controller)	To Left Toward "UP"	Elevators — "UP"
BANK-TRIM CONTROL (large wheel under knob)	To Left	Left Aileron — "UP"

i. Depress clutch button. Auto pilot should now be engaged with controls. To check, overpower auto pilot by manually operating control stick and rudder pedals. Auto pilot should cause definite drag, particularly strong on rudder pedals. If any control drags, then lets go, then drags, etc., it is an indication that a servo disconnect is not properly engaged.

j. Pull clutch switch "OFF." All controls should go free. Make certain all controls are free by moving control stick and rudder pedals around.

k. Return controls to neutral, and depress clutch switch again. Make certain again that auto pilot is engaged by checking for drag. Check for disengagement of auto pilot from controls when caging knob is turned to "CAGE," when power switch is turned "OFF" and when auto pilot circuit breaker is pulled "OFF." Repeat the same procedure used for the clutch switch. Clutch switch should also "pop" out when any of the three switches above are positioned as directed.

l. With the auto pilot re-engaged to the neutralized controls after the check above, operate controller as shown in table above.

Note

After checking each control on the controller, return it to neutral before checking the next control. The control surfaces should move proportionately with the movement of the controls on the controller.

m. If desired, the emergency operation may be checked by overpowering auto pilot for drag and at the same time pulling the emergency disconnect handle to "DISENGAGE." All controls should go free. Note that auto pilot servos must be manually reset after this operation.

B–10. TABLE OF ELECTRONIC EQUIPMENT.

TYPE	*DESIGNATION*	*USE*	*RANGE*	*ILLUSTRATION OF CONTROLS*	*REMARKS*
1. Radar	AN/APS-19 or AN/APS-19A			Fig. B-2. Fig. B-4.	Allow three minutes for set to become operative.
a. Beacon		Navigation.	150 miles.		
b. Search		Detection and location of targets.	100 miles.		
c. Intercept		Detection of air-borne targets.	20 miles		
d. Aim		Aim fixed guns.	1500 yds. (.85 miles)		
2. IFF	AN/APX-6	Identification; distress.	Line of sight.	Fig. B-3.	Check for proper mode setting.
3. VHF	AN/ARC-28	Relay for two-way radio communication; local two-way operation.	Line of sight.	Fig. B-3.	Allow 30 seconds for set to become operative.
4. Navigation Equipment	AN/ARR-2A	Navigation receiver.		Fig. 4-6.	Frequency range 234 to 258 megacycles
5. Range Receiver	AN/ARC-5	Low-frequency range reception.		Fig. 4-6.	Frequency range 190 to 550 kilocycles.
6. Radio Altimeter	AN/APN-1	Measure absolute altitude over terrain.	Low: 0-400 ft. High: 400-4000 ft.	Fig. 1-6 Fig. 1-7.	High range cannot be used below 400 feet.

B–11. AN/APS-19 RADAR SET.

B–12. DESCRIPTION. *(See figure B-2.)* F4U-5N aircraft Bureau Serial No. 121816 through 122206 are equipped with AN/APS-19 radar equipment; F4U-5N aircraft Bureau Serial No. 123144 and subsequent are equipped with AN/APS-19A radar equipment. The AN/APS-19A radar indicator is equipped with adjustments which were not included on the AN/APS-19 set. These adjustments allow the pilot to alter the focus and brilliance of the radar scope and the brilliance of the radio altimeter limit light on the radar scope bezel by turning the three knobs located on the radar scope bezel. The radar equipment is employed for search, intercept, aim, and beacon purposes. Search operation is used when the pilot wishes to detect targets on the earth's surface. The targets may be water-borne or located on the ground, and may be as far away as 100 miles. Intercept operation is used to look for airborne targets. The equipment should enable the pilot to detect other aircraft at distance up to 20 nautical miles. Aim operation is used when the pilot wishes to shoot down a target. Fifteen hundred yards is the maximum range of effectiveness for aim operation. Beacon operation is for homing navigation and can be used on ranges up to 150 nautical miles. Power for the radar system is supplied by a motor generator. (Refer to paragraph B–3A for complete a-c power information.) A pilot's control unit is located on the left control panel. Before operation of the control unit is effective, the motor generator power switch and the radar circuit breaker must be "ON." The motor generator switch is located on the inclined section of the right-hand control panel. The radar circuit breaker is located on the horizontal face of the right control panel. The control unit is provided with a hinged cover which may be placed over the TILT, FUNCTION and TUNE controls during aim operation. A detachable hood for the radar scope is stowed around the control stick when not in use. The switches on the pilot's control unit are as follows:

a. FUNCTION. This switch turns the radar equipment on and off and selects for "BEACON," "SEARCH," or "INT'C'PT" operation. If the pilot desires temporarily to discontinue operation, turn to "STANDBY" until another tactical operation is wanted.

b. TUNE. When this control is in the extreme clockwise "AUTO" position the AFC (automatic frequency control) is in operation and will maintain maximum echoes automatically. If the AFC becomes inoperative, turn this control to "MANUAL" and tune the receiver until maximum echoes are seen.

c. GAIN. This control regulates the strength of the signals coming from the receiver and the amount of "snow" that is applied to the indicator screen. Manipulation of the GAIN control is seldom necessary if it is left in the "AUTO" position. At short ranges from surface and beacon targets, use of the "MANUAL" position will allow finer azimuth bearing readings. In manual operation gain is low if signals disappear, high if "snow" tends to blot out signals.

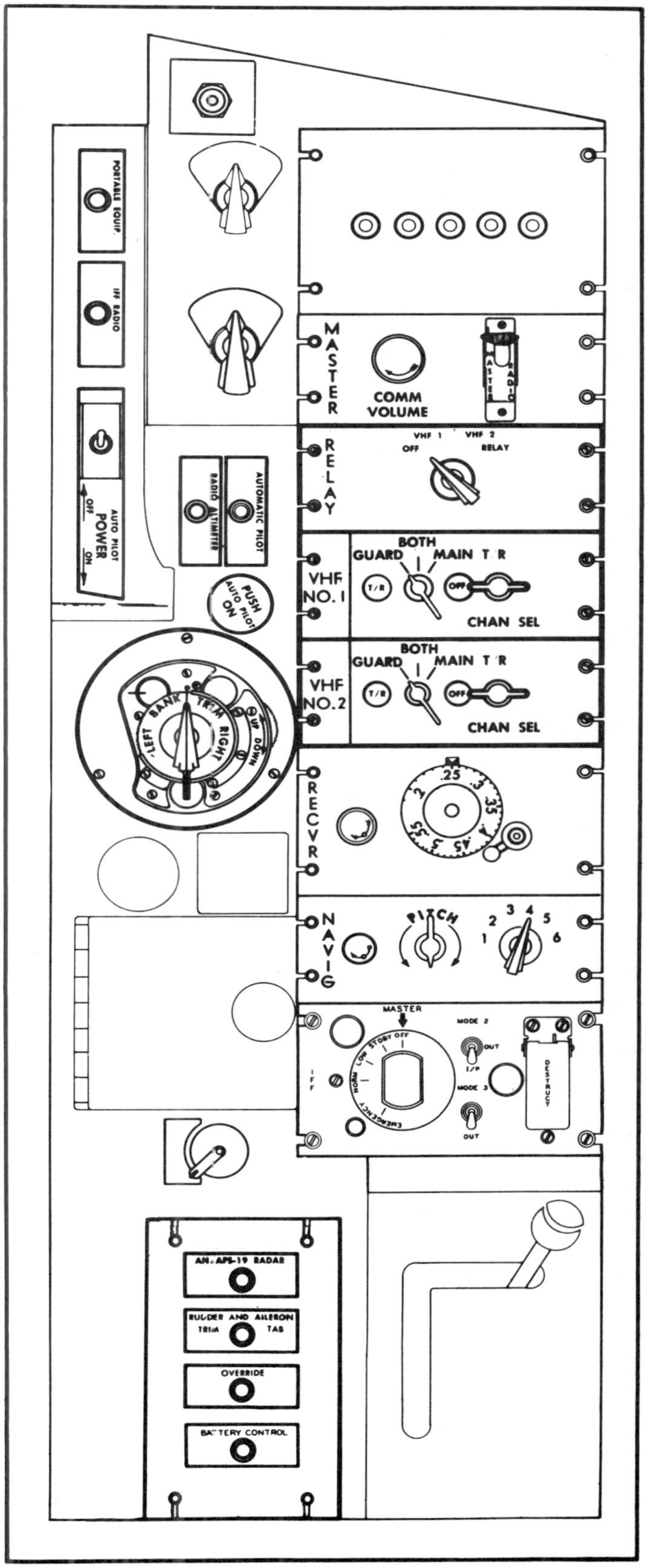

Figure B-3. Right-Hand Console

d. TILT. There is a screwdriver adjustment for changing the antenna tilt vertically. This adjustment must be made by qualified personnel only.

e. SCAN ANGLE. This controls the selection of the wide or narrow scan angle and has two positions: "30°" and "130°" for AN/APS-19 equipment and "30°" and "135°" for AN/APS-19A equipment.

f. RANGE. This switch sets the range within which the operation takes place. The ranges "100," "50," "20," "8," and "2" can be used on "SEARCH" and "INT'C'PT" FUNCTION control. Range "150" can be used on "BEACON" only, and "AIM" (1500 yds.) can be used on "INT'C'PT" only. A mechanical interlock prevents positioning of the RANGE switch on "AIM" whenever the FUNCTION control is not on "INT'C'PT."

g. SEA SUPPRESS. This control enables the operator to suppress signals received, particularly heavy sea return. Turning the control clockwise suppresses the returning signals. It is only usable on intercept, that is, when the scanner is in spiral operation.

B–13. SEARCH AND BEACON OPERATION. To operate the radar system, the radar motor generator switch (paragraph B–3A) and the radar circuit breaker must be "ON." Prior to operating the radar system the control switches must be in the following position: FUNCTION-"OFF," TUNE-"AUTO," GAIN-"AUTO," SCAN ANGLE-"130°" for AN/APS-19 equipment and "135°" for AN/APS-19A equipment, RANGE-"100," SEA SUPPRESS-"OFF." As "SEARCH" and "BEACON" operations are similar, they are both given in one procedure as follows:

a. Turn the function selector to "SEARCH" (or "BEACON"). Wait for three minutes for equipment to warm up.

b. SCAN ANGLE switch should be at "130°" for AN/APS-19 equipment and "135°" for AN/APS-19A equipment. When target is within the 30-degree sector, turn switch to "30°."

c. When a target echo appears on the screen, switch the RANGE control to the lowest one that will accommodate the signal. The sequence of operating ranges permits switching to lower ranges, as the airplane approaches closer to the target. On "SEARCH" the operating range sequence is "100," "50," "20," "8," and "2," for "BEACON" operation, RANGE switch can be positioned on "150."

d. Bring the target echo into zero azimuth as soon as possible.

e. Switch the SCAN ANGLE to "30°" if narrow beam is desired.

f. If the echo indication seems erratic, the TUNE will have to be a "MANUAL" adjustment. Observe echoes in "AUTO" position. Then tune for maximum echoes using the TUNE control manually. The signals in both cases should be of equal intensity.

g. If the "snow" indication is not satisfactory, or if target is lost in sea return, "MANUAL" operation of the GAIN control is necessary. Slowly turn the GAIN knob until "snow" begins to appear on the screen. Switch to "AUTO." Approximately the same intensity pattern should be obtained.

Note

Strong beacon signals may require manual reduction of the GAIN to prevent saturation with a resultant distortion of the echo on the scope.

h. When "SEARCH" operation is completed, turn all controls back to their original position unless further operations are to be made. In that case, switch the FUNCTION control to the next operation desired or to "STANDBY."

B–14. INTERCEPT AND AIM OPERATION. To operate the radar controls for intercept and aim see first part of paragraph above and then proceed as follows:

a. Turn the function selector to "INT'C'PT." After three minutes the equipment is ready for operation.

Note

If FUNCTION control was previously on "STAND-BY," equipment is ready for operation immediately after switching FUNCTION control to "INT'C'PT."

b. Turn the range selector to "20."

c. SCAN ANGLE switch should be at "130°" for AN/APS-19 equipment and "135°" for AN/APS-19A equipment when target is about two-thirds of a mile distant.

d. When an aircraft target echo appears on the screen, switch the RANGE control to the lowest one that will accommodate the signal. The reference of operating ranges permits switching to lower ranges as the airplane approaches closer to the target. On "INT'C'PT" the operating range sequence is "20," "8," and "2."

e. Bring the target echo into "dead ahead" position as soon as possible. The midpoint of the two images should center on zero azimuth, and the two dots should be aligned horizontally.

f. Continue "INT'C'PT" operation to within two-thirds of a mile from the target, which is about one-third the distance up from the scope's lower edge on the two-mile RANGE.

g. Switch the RANGE selector to "AIM" when the target is about two-thirds of a mile distant.

h. Continue approaching target on a collision course until the horizontal trace is halfway from the scope screen. If the horizontal trace does not cover the width of the screen the target is not dead ahead.

i. When the mission has been completed, turn all controls back to their original positions unless further operations are to be made. In that case, switch the FUNCTION selector to the next operation desired or to "STANDBY."

Note

If the sea return becomes troublesome, rotate the SEA SUPPRESS control slowly clockwise until sea return does not interfere with the intelligibility of the target echoes. The SEA SUPPRESS can be used only when functioning on "INT'C'PT." For GAIN control or TUNE adjustments, refer to paragraph B-12.

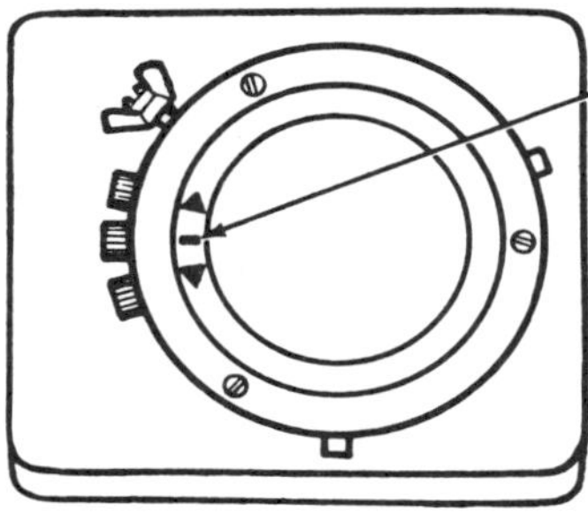

ID-158/APS-19 RADAR INDICATOR
(used on airplanes Bureau
Serial No. 121816 through 122206)

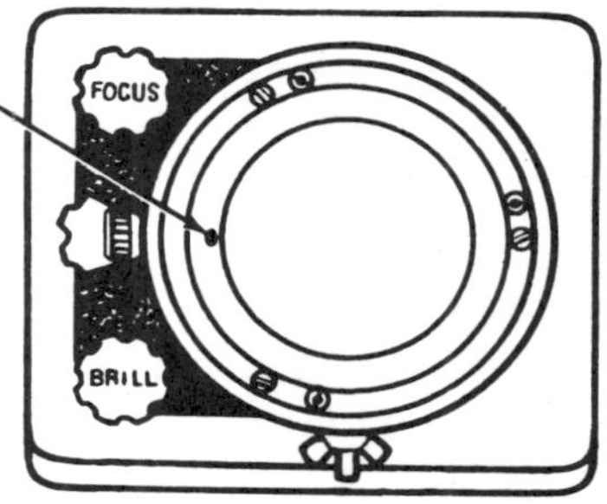

ID-158A/APS-19 RADAR INDICATOR
(used on airplanes Bureau
Serial No. 122207 and Subsequent)

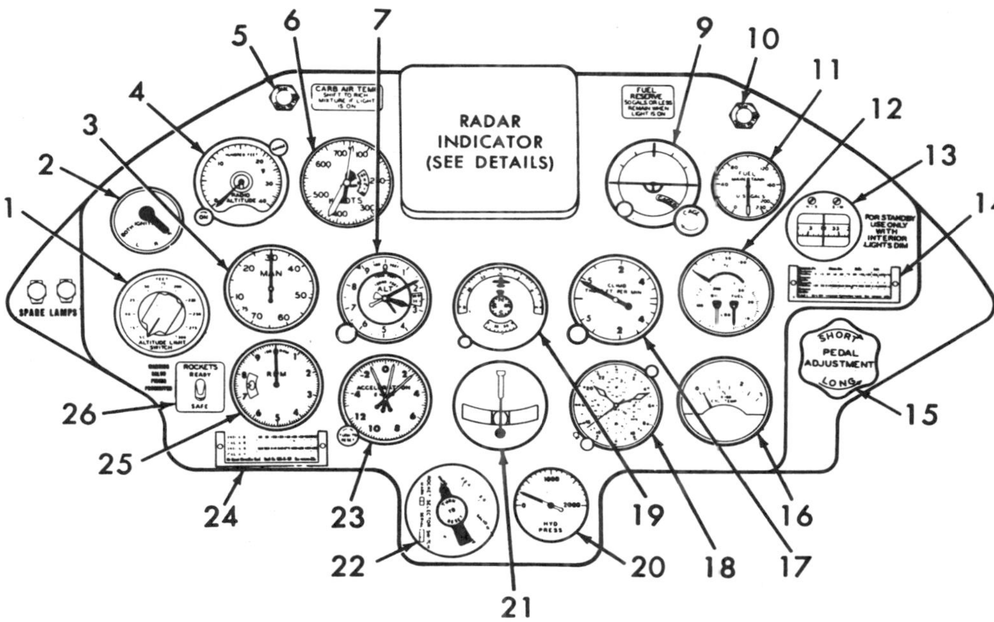

1. Radio Altitude Limit Switch
2. Ignition Switch
3. Manifold Pressure Gage
4. Radio Altitude Indicator
5. Carburetor Air Temperature Warning Light
6. Airspeed Indicator
7. Altimeter
8. Altitude Low Limit Indicator Light
9. Gyro Horizon Indicator (Vertical Gyro Control)
10. Fuel Reserve Warning Light
11. Fuel Quantity Indicator
12. Engine Gage Unit (Fuel Pressure, Oil Pressure, and Oil Temperature)
13. Stand-by Compass
14. Stand-by Compass Card Holder
15. Rudder Pedal Adjustment Knob
16. Engine Cylinder Temperature Indicator
17. Vertical Speed Indicator
18. Elapsed Time Clock
19. Master Direction Indicator
20. Hydraulic Pressure Gage
21. Turn and Bank Indicator
22. Rocket Selector Switch
23. Accelerometer
24. Airspeed Indicator Card Holder
25. Tachometer
26. Rocket Ready-Safe Switch

Figure B-4. Instrument Panel—F4U-5N Airplane

B–15. PREFLIGHT CHECK. The preflight check must be made with the engine running above generator cutout speed. Prior to checking the radar set the control switches must be in the following positions: FUNCTION—"OFF," TUNE—"AUTO," GAIN—"AUTO," SCAN ANGLE — "130°" for AN/APS-19 equipment and "135°" for AN/APS-19A equipment, RANGE — "2," SEA SUPPRESS—"OFF." Turn a-c power switch (paragraph B–3A) on and proceed as follows:

a. Turn the FUNCTION selector to "SEARCH." Wait 3 minutes before proceeding since a delay of 3 minutes is required by a time delay relay.

b. Note the appearance of the base and sweep lines. Clear lines indicate proper focus.

c. Check the alignment and the centering of the representation on the indicator.

d. A little "snow" indicates proper brilliance.

e. If the echo images disappear or appear erratic, AFC is not functioning properly and "MANUAL" operation of TUNE is necessary. This control is very sensitive and adjustments must be made carefully.

f. Turn the RANGE knob counterclockwise to increase the range. New images should appear and the old ones should lower on the screen. At sea it is possible that as the range is increased no new images will appear.

g. Vary the angle of tilt and note fading and reappearance of echoes.

h. Check other FUNCTION settings. Do not turn to "OFF" since the radar set will be inoperative for three minutes.

i. Change the SCAN ANGLE to "30°." The sweep should be more rapid.

B–16. AN/APX-6 IFF EQUIPMENT.

B–17. PURPOSE. The Radar Identification Set AN/APX-6 is an airborne transpondor and is one of several equipments which may be operated together to provide a system of electronic identification and recognition. The purposes of the AN/APX-6 are:

a. To identify the airplane in which it is installed as friendly when correctly challenged by an interrogator-responsor associated with friendly shore, shipboard, and airborne radars.

b. To permit surface tracking and control of aircraft in which it is installed.

Functionally, the AN/APX-6 receives challenges which are initiated by an interrogator-responsor, and transmits replies back to the interrogator-responsor where the replies are displayed, along with the associated radar targets, on the radar indicators. When a radar target is accompanied by a proper IFF reply, as transmitted by the AN/APX-6, that target is considered friendly.

B–18. Before operation of the C-544/APX-6 control unit is effective the a-c power (paragraph B-3A) must be on.

B–19. OPERATION. All controls required for operation of the AN/APX-6 equipment are located on Radar Set Control C-544/APX-6. This unit is located at the aft end of the right-hand control shelf (figure B-3). Operation is as follows:

a. To turn equipment on, rotate MASTER selector to "NORM."

b. To indicate emergency or distress, press red dial stop (figure B-3) and rotate MASTER selector to "EMERGENCY."

c. To maintain the equipment ready for instant use but inoperative, rotate the MASTER selector to "STDBY."

d. The detent position labeled "LOW" on the MASTER selector should not be used except upon proper authorization.

e. The switches labeled "MODE 2" and "MODE 3" should be set to their "OUT" positions unless otherwise directed by proper authority.

f. To explode destructors within the equipment, raise the switch guard labeled "DESTRUCT" and raise the switch handle to the "ON" position.

WARNING

Do not fire destructors unless the AN/APX-6 is in danger of falling into enemy hands. When in doubt about the security of the area you are *forced* to land in, fire the destructors.

WARNING

Destructors will be fired if the DESTRUCT switch is turned on or if the impact switch is tripped regardless of the setting of the MASTER selector.

g. To secure the equipment, rotate the MASTER selector to "OFF."

h. If destructors were fired during the flight, notify your Commanding Officer.

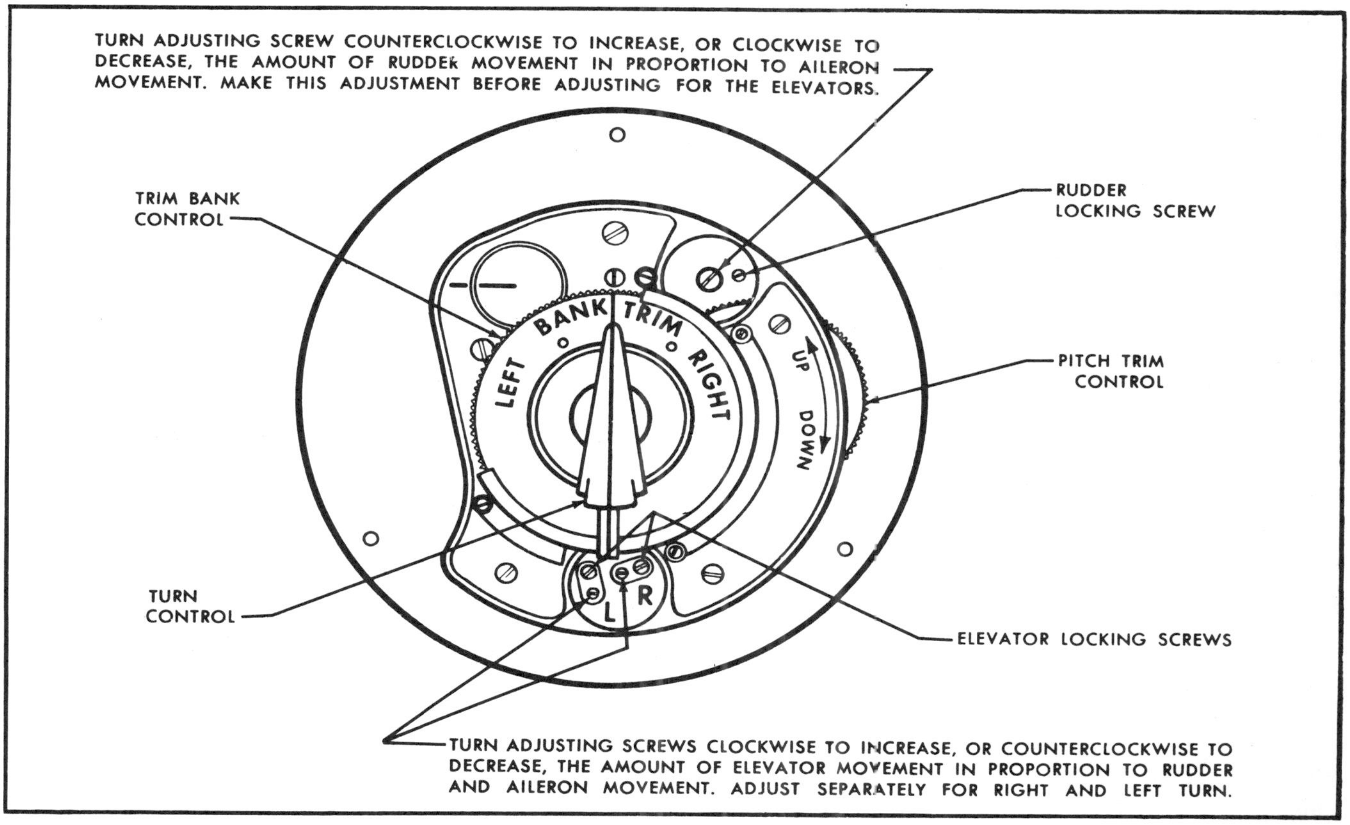

Figure B-5. Auto Pilot Controller Unit

B–20. AN/APN-1 RADIO ALTIMETER.

B–21. DESCRIPTION. The AN/APN-1 radio altimeter installation in the F4U-5N differs from that in the F4U-5 day fighter (refer to paragraph 4–41A) only in the location of the indicator, limit switch, and limit indicator light, as shown in figure B–4.

B–22. DELETED.

B–23. AN/ARC-28 COMMUNICATION (VHF).

B–24. DESCRIPTION. *(See figure B-3.)* The AN/ARC-28 communication equipment enables the airplane to serve as a relay point for extending the range of two-way VHF radio communication with modulated signals, as, for example, between a ground station or ship and a second aircraft in flight. By this method the equipment is capable of extending consistent VHF communication beyond the ordinary horizon limitation. The AN/ARC-28 equipment is made up of two Radio Transmitter-Receivers (RT-18/ARC-1) interconnected by a relay unit and three pilot control units located on the right-hand control panel and designated as: (1) RELAY, (2) VHF NO. 1, (3) VHF NO. 2. There are no individual transmitting-receiving facilities while the system is in "RELAY" operation. When not in "RELAY" operation, the pilot may select either the VHF NO. 1 or VHF NO. 2 transmitter-receiver for operation. Three protective circuit-breakers for the communication system are located on the circuit breaker panel. They are designated as "ARC-28 RELAY," "VHF NO. 1," and "VHF NO. 2." Power for the communication equipment is supplied when the three circuit breakers, the battery switch and the MASTER panel master radio switch are "ON." Reception volume is controlled by the "COM VOLUME" control also located on the MASTER panel. The engine must be running above generator cut-out speed to avoid draining the battery. The headphone and microphone extension is plugged into the radio jack plug. On airplanes Bureau Serial No. 121793 through 124480, the radio jack plug is located on the bulkhead aft of the pilot's right shoulder. On airplanes Bureau Serial No. 124481 and subsequent, the junction box and radio jack plug are located on the aft portion of the right-hand side panel. A microphone button is provided on the throttle for use with the microphone when transmitting.

B–25. AUTOMATIC RELAY OPERATION. For automatic relay operation, see figure B–3 and proceed as follows:

CAUTION

Each time the equipment is turned on, allow at least 30 seconds for the vacuum tubes to reach operating temperature before using the equipment for relay operation or before operating throttle switch if local control is desired.

a. Power control switch and master radio switch must be on. The ARC-28 RELAY, VHF NO. 1, and VHF NO. 2 circuit breakers must also be "ON." The engine must be running above generator cut-out speed or an external power source must be used when on the ground.

b. Rotate the RELAY control unit knob from "OFF" to "RELAY" position.

c. Rotate the channel selector switches on the VHF NO. 1 and VHF NO. 2 control units to the two frequency channels designated for relay operation, giving the desired frequency combination. The equipment will be ready for automatic relay operation as soon as the vacuum tubes reach operating temperature.

d. To change the frequency combination of the system, rotate the channel selector switches on the VHF NO. 1 and VHF NO. 2 control units.

e. Monitoring will give an indication to the operator that the equipment is operating properly.

B–26. LOCAL TRANSMITTER-RECEIVER OPERATION. To operate either the VHF NO. 1 or VHF NO. 2 transmitter-receiver individually, see figure B–3 and proceed as follows:

a. Power control switch and master radio switch must be on. The ARC-28 RELAY, VHF NO. 1 and VHF NO. 2 circuit breakers must also be "ON." The engine must be running above generator cut-out speed or an external power source must be used when on the ground.

b. Rotate the RELAY control unit knob to the "VHF 1" or "VHF 2" position, depending upon which transmitter-receiver is to be used.

CAUTION

Whenever switching from "OFF" to "VHF 1" or "VHF 2," or from "VHF 1" to "VHF 2" ("VHF 2" to "VHF 1") or "VHF 1" or "VHF 2" to "RELAY," allow 30 seconds for warm-up of transmitter-receiver before operation.

c. For further operational procedures using either the VHF NO. 1 or VHF NO. 2 transmitter-receiver see paragraphs 4–30 to 4–40.

B–27. PREFLIGHT CHECK. Engine must be running above generator cut-out speed. Turn the ARC-28 RELAY, VHF NO. 1, and VHF NO. 2 circuit breakers, the battery switch and the master radio switch "ON." Proceed as follows:

a. Rotate the RELAY control unit knob to "VHF 1" and check transmitting and receiving with ship or ground station or another airplane.

CAUTION

Each time the equipment is turned "on" allow at least 30 seconds for warm-up of vacuum tubes before using the equipment. When change of RELAY control is made allow 30 seconds before operation.

b. Switch to "VHF 2" and check transmitting and receiving.

c. Rotate RELAY control unit knob to "RELAY" and rotate channel selector switches on VHF NO. 1 and VHF NO. 2 control units to the two frequency channels designated for relay operation, giving the desired frequency combination.

d. Monitoring will indicate proper operation of equipment.

B–28. EMERGENCY OPERATING PROCEDURE.

B–28A. AUTOMATIC PILOT EMERGENCY DISCONNECT.

B–28B. To disconnect the automatic pilot mechanically, move the emergency disconnect handle to the aft position. The automatic pilot cannot be re-engaged while in flight.

B–28C. A-C POWER FAILURE.

B–28D. If the main inverter warning light indicates a-c power failure, move the "MAIN–STAND-BY" inverter switch to "STAND-BY" position. The automatic pilot, the IFF radar, and the AN/APS-19(A) radar are inoperative on stand-by inverter.

B–29. MANUAL RADAR CONTROLS.

B–30. Should the echo indication appear erratic, AFC is malfunctioning and careful "MANUAL" adjustment of the TUNE control is necessary for maximum echoes. Unsatisfactory "snow" indication necessitates "MANUAL" operation of the GAIN control. Slowly turn the GAIN knob until a little "snow" appears, then switch to "AUTO." If the sea return is troublesome, rotate the SEA SUPPRESS slowly clockwise until the sea return does not interfere with the intelligibility of the target echoes. SEA SUPPRESS can only be used on "INT'C'-PT."

B–31. IFF DESTRUCTOR.

B–32. In the event that the airplane may fall into enemy hands the IFF equipment must be destroyed. The destruction of the RT-24/APX-6 receiver-transmitter is accomplished by raising the guard latch on the IFF control panel and tripping the toggle switch "on."

B–33. IFF EMERGENCY SIGNAL.

B–34. Wide distress responses can be transmitted by pressing the dial stop on the IFF control panel and rotating the master control panel switch to the "EMERGENCY" position.

PLACE
STAMP
HERE

SCHIFFER PUBLISHING LTD
77 LOWER VALLEY RD
ATGLEN PA 19310-9717

Note

Should any piece of electronic equipment fail to operate (other than the difficulties discussed in paragraph B–30), turn that piece of equipment "off."

B–35. MK 20 GUNSIGHT AND CONTROLS.

B–36. DESCRIPTION. *(See figure B–2.)* The MK 20 gunsight is supported on a mount which is centrally located on the instrument cowl. The gunsight consists essentially of a rotatable reticle disc incorporating three reticle patterns, a reticle selector knob, a series of lenses and a quick-disconnect reticle lamp housing. A spare lamp is stowed on a clip to the right of the gunsight. The quick-disconnect lamp housing facilitates replacement of the double filament gunsight lamp while in flight. To replace the lamp it is only necessary to rotate the housing aft, out of the support clip, and then depress the snap fasteners which lock the housing to the gunsight. The lamp which is mounted in the housing can now be easily removed and replaced with the spare. The reticle selector knob on the gunsight permits the pilot to select one of the three reticle images, each of a different pattern.

B–37. OPERATION. *(See figure B-2.)* The gunsight is controlled primarily by the "ON-OFF" master armament switch in the gunnery switch box. The gunsight switches are also located in the gunnery switch box. They are the "ON"-"OFF"-"ALT" switch and the gunsight "DIMMER" rheostat. A gunsight circuit breaker is located on the circuit breaker panel. When the "ON"-"OFF"-"ALT" switch is "ON" it completes the circuit to one of the two filaments in the gunsight lamp. If this filament burns out the switch may be turned to "ALT" to complete the circuit to the alternate filament. The "DIMMER" is a rheostat which may be adjusted to vary the light intensity of the reticle image.

B–38. GUN CAMERA LIGHTS AND REFLECTORS.

B–39. DESCRIPTION. *(See figure B-1.)* The gun camera lights and reflector installation consists of three trihedral prism retro-reflectors and gun lights mounted around the gun camera opening. The purpose of the equipment is to indicate on the gun camera film the pilot's aim after he has made a firing run (training) on the tail of another airplane at night. The lights around the gun camera of the attacking airplane cause the reflectors on the airplane being attached to reflect back this same light onto the gun camera film in the attacking airplane. The firing run is recorded photographically by the simultaneous operation of the lights and the gun camera when the trigger switch is depressed. Note that there is no special switch for the lights, as they operate whenever the gun camera operates. The pilot should endeavor to simulate operation of the camera and lights with that of normal gunfire time. Between each intercept camera they should be operated momentarily to separate the film records of each firing run.

Note

F4U-5N aircraft Bureau Nos. 124471 and subsequent are not equipped with gun camera lights and trihedral prism retro-reflectors.

B–40. WINDSHIELD DEGREASING.

B–41. DESCRIPTION. *(See figure B-1.)* The windshield degreaser system is employed to clean the outside surfaces of the bullet-resistant center windshield and left-hand side windshield at night. The degreaser system is electrically operated by a push-button switch on the left-hand side of the instrument cowl. Note that the portable equipment circuit breaker must be closed for the degreaser switch to operate. Use fluid sparingly since the reservoir contains but 0.9 gallons of fluid.

B–42. FLAME DAMPENERS AND T-20 FLASH HIDERS.

B–43. DESCRIPTION. *(See figure B-1.)* The F4U-5N airplane is equipped with six flame dampeners clamped on the engine exhaust collectors. Their purpose is to minimize the visible exhaust flames at night. Each assembly consists of a flame dampener which dissipates the flame before it reaches the outer air, and a shield which hides the flame dampener. The shield is necessary since the dampener becomes cherry red due to heat induction. Four T-20 flash hiders are attached to the muzzle end of the guns to minimize the visible gun-flash when the guns are fired at night.

CAUTION

Flash hiders and flame dampeners must be installed for all night missions.

PHOTOGRAPHIC EQUIPMENT

Figure C-1. General View of F4U-5P Airplane

C-1. PHOTOGRAPHIC EQUIPMENT—GENERAL.

C-2. DESCRIPTION. The F4U-5P airplane is a photographic reconnaissance version of the F4U-5. It is basically the same airplane, the main difference being the incorporation of provisions for remote camera control, the installation of accommodations for either the "K" series cameras or the S-7S continuous strip camera, and the relocation of the remote indicating compass transmitter in the fin. Access to the camera compartment is obtained through the radio access door. The camera compartment and related equipment are designed to accommodate either the "K" series aerial cameras or the S-7S continuous strip camera. Conversion from one type camera to the other is provided for by the inclusion of a camera conversion kit in the camera compartment. All F4U-5P airplanes are equipped with one vertical and two oblique sliding camera doors, an oil deflector for each of the doors, a camera door actuating system, and a master camera switch.

The installation of the "K" series cameras is provided for by an adapter for mounting the camera, an electrical actuating motor for rotating the camera adapter, a solenoid actuated sway brace, four adjustable sway brace assemblies to secure the lens cones to the camera in position, a vacuum system to hold the film flat in the magazine, and the installation of an intervalometer in the cockpit. The S-7S continuous strip camera installation is provided for by installing a scanner unit in the lower fuselage at station 150, the installation of the strip camera remote control unit in the cockpit, an amplifier mounted at station 223 and a photo recorder mounted at station 253.

For detailed information on the photographic equipment, refer to paragraphs C-3 through C-17 for the "K" series installation, and to paragraphs C-18 through C-30 for the S-7S continuous strip camera installation.

Note

The effect of this modification on speed and other performance items is negligible.

C-3. INSTRUMENT PANEL. *(See figure C-4.)* The instrument panel in the F4U-5P airplane is the same as in the F4U-5 airplane except as follows: The climb indicator is above the elapsed time clock and the Mark 1 rocket selector switch is relocated below the stand-by compass. The P-3 compass correction card is located on the left side below the airspeed correction card. A B-3B intervalometer or remote control panel is installed above the climb indicator at the top of the instrument panel.

C-4. "K" SERIES CAMERA INSTALLATION.

C-5. "K" SERIES INTERVALOMETER. A B-3B type intervalometer is located on the instrument board above the climb indicator. The intervalometer is a 24 volt direct current electrical timing unit which automatically trips the camera shutter at pre-determined intervals. The controls for the intervalometer (see figure C-3) consist of the power supply toggle switch, setting knob, recycle knob and an "extra-picture" switch. A dial on the intervalometer is graduated in seconds for direct indication of the interval between film exposures. The setting hand can be rotated to any position between 2 and 120 seconds on the dial by depressing and turning the setting knob marked "INTERVAL," thereby indicating the selected time interval on the dial scale. The setting hand remains where set by the knob. The interval hand, indicating the remaining time portion of the set interval, returns to zero in one-second increments. Upon reaching the zero position it automatically snaps back to its original set position and starts again to return to zero. The camera is tripped the moment this interval hand reaches zero on the dial. The required time interval may be determined

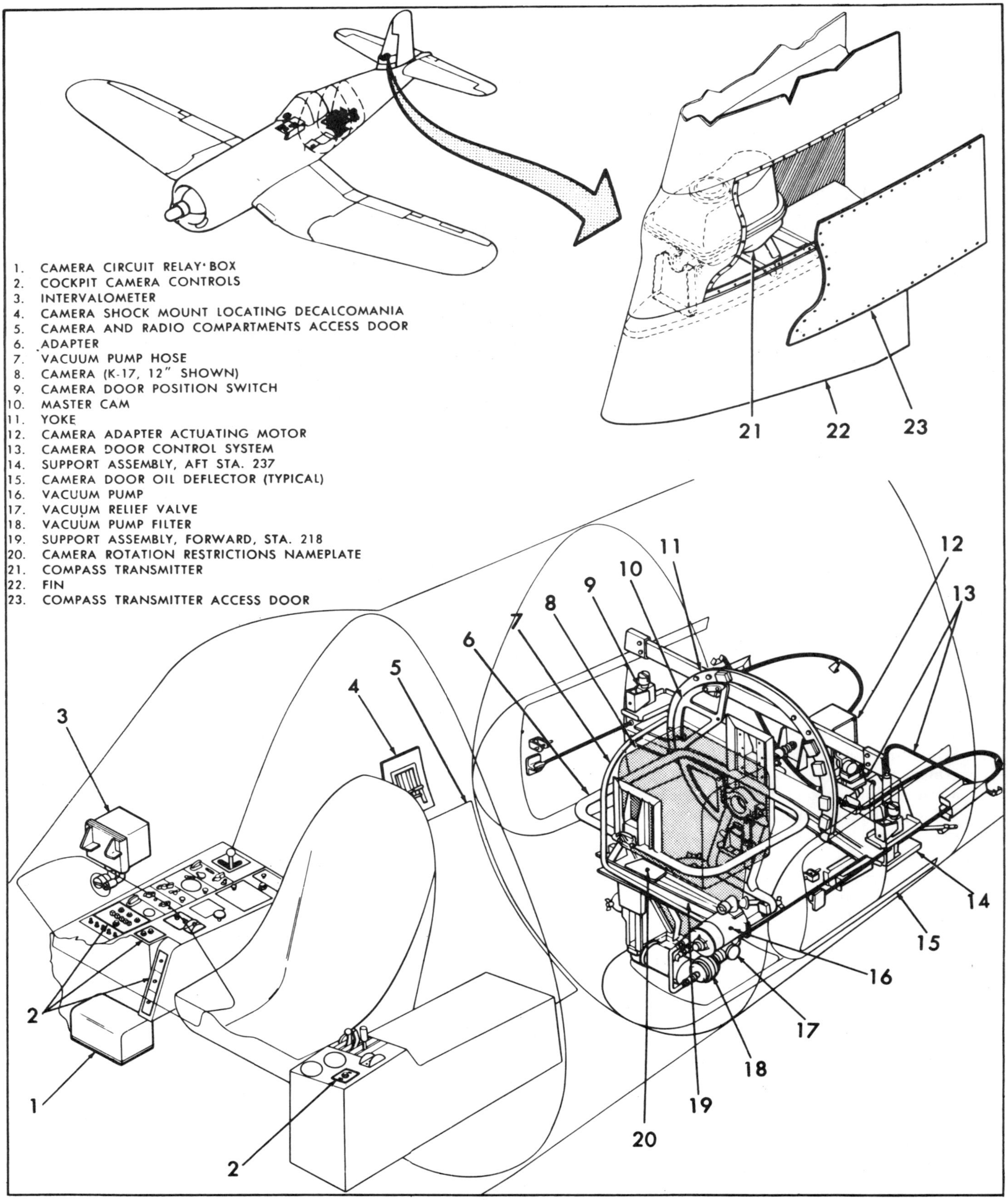

Figure C-2. Photographic Equipment

from altitude-speed charts (see figures C-8 through C-13). The interval selection is dependent upon altitude, airplane speed, focal length of the camera, and the percentage of overlap desired. The counter should be reset by depressing the reset cap and turning it clockwise. Upon reaching the area to be photographed, set the setting hand by depressing and turning the setting knob. Clockwise rotation of the knob decreases the interval time, and counter-clockwise rotation increases the interval time. To operate the intervalometer, snap the toggle switch to the "ON" position. If the intervalometer is already in operation and it is desired any instant to begin a new series of exposures, the recycle knob must be depressed. An exposure is then made immediately, and the complete cycle is started again with the set interval starting before the next exposure. If, at any time before the intervalometer starts automatic operation or during the operation of the instrument, an extra picture is desired, the operator depresses the extra-picture switch button. Pressing this button between automatically timed exposures will not alter the timing as shown on the dial. If the air speed, altitude, or any other variable entering into the determination of the proper interval changes, the time interval must be rechecked and the intervalometer reset if necessary.

C-6. "K" SERIES CAMERA CONTROL PANELS. *(See figure C-3.)* Two of the three camera control panels are located on the right hand control panel in the cockpit. One is located forward of the master switch and VHF panel and carries the five switches necessary for rotating the camera. The five switches, one for each of the five camera positions (three and fifteen degrees down from the horizontal on both the rignt and left sides and the vertical), are depressed to move the camera to the position desired. Forward of these switches is the green camera position light, which is lighted when the camera is in position and not lighted during the time the camera is in transit. Included in this panel are three amber camera door position lights which are lighted when the camera doors are fully open. Forward of the oxygen bottle and seat adjustment control is a panel containing the master camera switch, the door control switch, the manual and automatic camera operation switch, the amber intervalometer warning light and the red film breakage warning light. Circuit breakers for the camera control, vacuum pump and camera door circuits are located on the nose (see figure C-3, View A-A) of the console. The third camera control panel is located on the left hand control panel in the cockpit and contains the manual picture switch.

C-7. "K" SERIES MANUAL-AUTOMATIC SWITCH. *(See figure C-3.)* With the camera control switch, located on the right hand control panel, in the "AUTOMATIC" position, all pictures will be taken in accordance with the setting of the intervalometer, with no further attention required on the part of the pilot other than that of maintaining attitude and altitude conditions previously determined. If it is desired to take individual pictures the camera control switch should be placed in the "MANUAL" position; and the manual control push-button, located on the left hand control panel forward of the master water injection switch, depressed for each picture desired.

C-8. "K" SERIES OPERATION. *(See figure C-5)* When the master camera switch, located on the camera control panel on the right hand control panel is moved to the "ON" position, power from the airplane's electrical system is directed to the camera electrical operating system. Operation of the camera system is as follows: With the master camera switch in the "ON" position, power flows from the plus bus of the airplane's electrical system to the camera control circuit breaker, to the camera bus, through a capacitor in this circuit to the vacuum pump. In addition, power passes from the plus bus through the camera door circuit breaker to the camera door circuit. The red film feed breakage warning light circuit is closed when film breakage occurs. The amber intervalometer warning light is lighted two seconds before the intervalometer trips the camera during automatic operation. With the camera door position switch in the "OPEN" position, power flows from the camera door circuit breaker through the camera door switch to the camera door actuating motor, and the three camera doors open simultaneously. Movement of the camera door switch to the "CLOSED" position allows power to flow to the other side of the door circuit and the doors close. When the doors are fully opened they close microswitches, which are actuated by contact bolts on the doors, and allow power to flow from the camera bus to the door microswitches and then forward to three amber, door position lights located in the cockpit. When the three degree left position switch is depressed, power will flow from the camera bus through the camera control panel, aft to camera position microswitch No. 11, located on the yoke, and then to the relay in the camera adapter actuator control box. Power through this switch also energizes the normally closed green camera position indicator light circuit. This turns the light off during tne time the camera is in transit. At the same time, the relay in the camera adapter actuator control box directs power to the sway brace solenoid, retracting the solenoid from its extended position. The solenoid in retracting closes a switch, located on a bracket above the solenoid, and in doing so, causes power flow to the camera adapter actuating motor which then rotates the adapter and the camera into the selected position. When the camera has reached this position, the aluminum master cam secured to the adapter opens camera position switch No. 1 and rotation ceases. Power to the relay in the camera control panel in the cockpit stops and the camera position indicating light goes on. Power is also cut off from the camera adapter actuator relay, de-energizing the actuator motor and the solenoid sway brace. The solenoid sway brace then extends and meshes with the serrated mating pad on the fuselage structure, locking the camera in position. With the doors fully opened, power flows from the plus

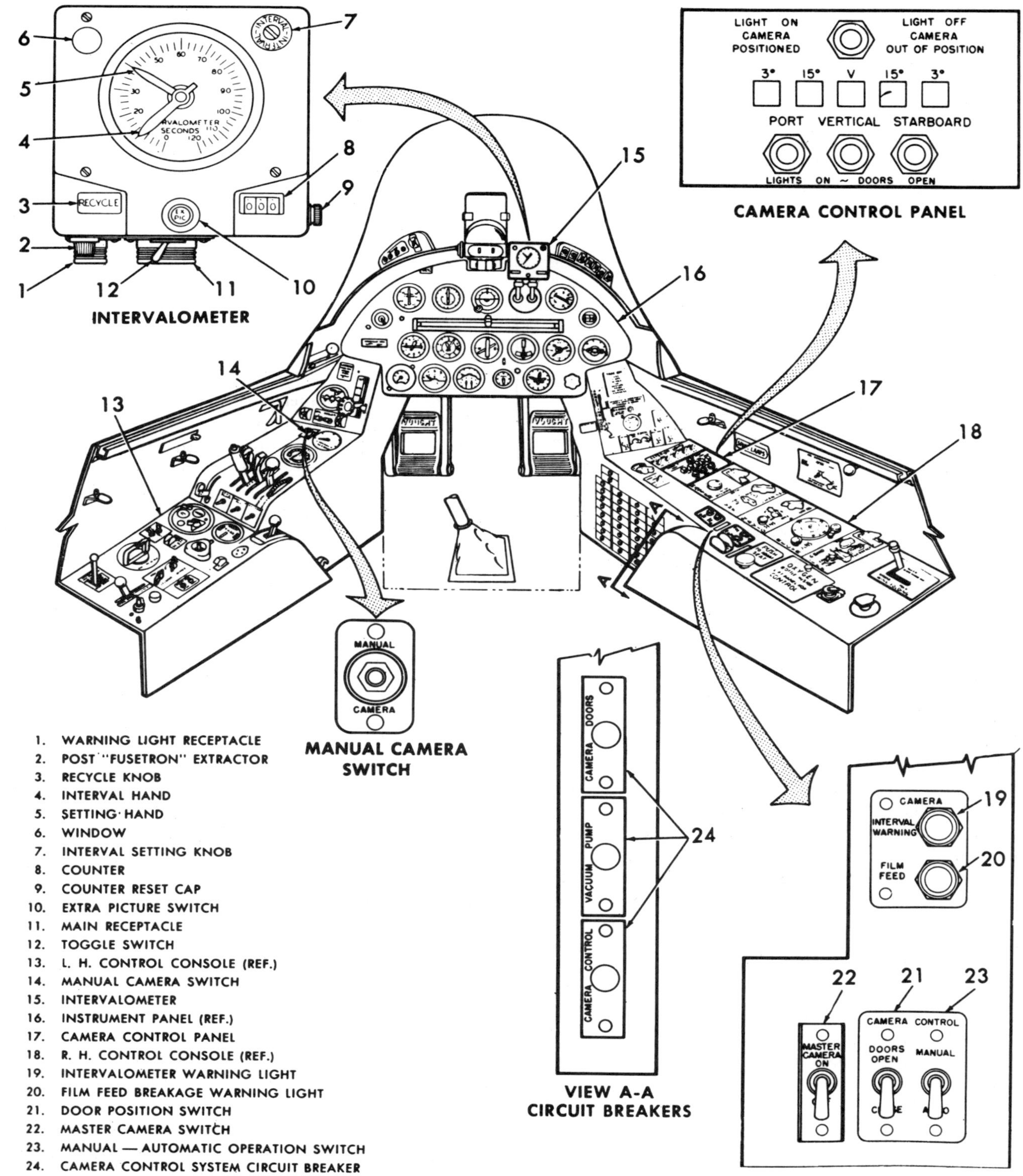

1. WARNING LIGHT RECEPTACLE
2. POST "FUSETRON" EXTRACTOR
3. RECYCLE KNOB
4. INTERVAL HAND
5. SETTING HAND
6. WINDOW
7. INTERVAL SETTING KNOB
8. COUNTER
9. COUNTER RESET CAP
10. EXTRA PICTURE SWITCH
11. MAIN RECEPTACLE
12. TOGGLE SWITCH
13. L. H. CONTROL CONSOLE (REF.)
14. MANUAL CAMERA SWITCH
15. INTERVALOMETER
16. INSTRUMENT PANEL (REF.)
17. CAMERA CONTROL PANEL
18. R. H. CONTROL CONSOLE (REF.)
19. INTERVALOMETER WARNING LIGHT
20. FILM FEED BREAKAGE WARNING LIGHT
21. DOOR POSITION SWITCH
22. MASTER CAMERA SWITCH
23. MANUAL — AUTOMATIC OPERATION SWITCH
24. CAMERA CONTROL SYSTEM CIRCUIT BREAKER

Figure C-3. Camera Cockpit Controls

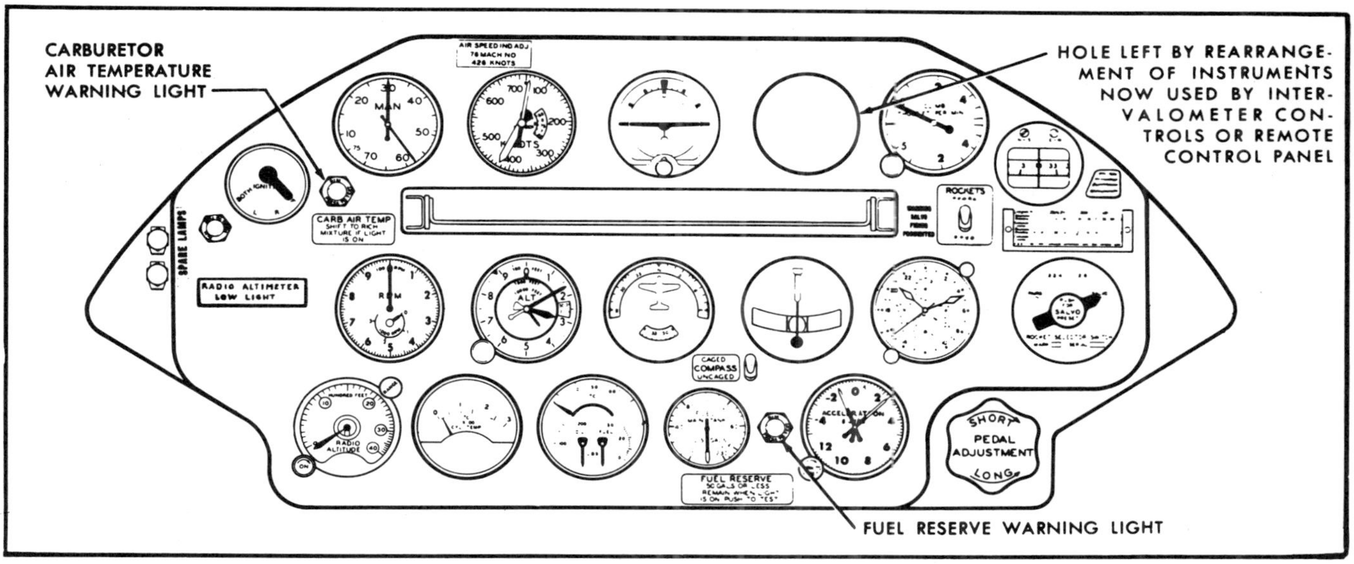

Figure C-4. F4U-5P Instrument Board

tion microswitches (No. 9-vertical, No. 10-right, and No. 11-left) completing the circuit to the camera and permitting camera operation. In the three degree left position, No. 11 switch is actuated by a phenolic cam, located on the master cam, allowing power to flow to the relay in the cockpit relay box and then to the camera, which is now ready to take pictures manually or automatically. Operation of the system when other camera positions are selected is the same with the exception that other position microswitches are brought into action.

Note

This type control system prevents camera operation and film waste when the camera doors are not open.

C-8. PREFLIGHT CHECK OF COMPLETE INSTALLATION.

C-9. PROCEDURE. After the camera and loaded magazine have been installed in the airplane, check the operation of the entire installation as follows:

a. Turn on the master camera switch.

b. Open the vertical and oblique sliding doors.

c. Check the rotation of the camera to all positions.

d. Check the door operation and position indicating lights.

e. Set intervalometer dial at nine seconds or more.

f. Place camera control switch in "AUTOMATIC."

g. Start the intervalometer and check its operation through two exposures.

h. Turn off intervalometer switch.

i. Check manual selection by depressing the manual push button for one exposure.

j. Close camera doors.

k. Turn off the master camera switch until take-off to avoid overheating the camera and intervalometer and to prevent excessive drain on the battery.

Note

It will be necessary for two men to make the above check, one to operate the switches and one to watch the camera.

WARNING

Satisfactory oblique photographs cannot be made from this airplane unless exhaust stack extensions are installed. (See figure C-1.)

C-10. PROCEDURE AT TAKE-OFF.

C-11. PROCEDURE AT TAKE-OFF. Observe the following steps at take-off:

a. Set the intervalometer counter to zero. The counter located on the side of the case should be reset by depressing the reset cap and turning it clockwise.

Note

Before proceeding with the next step, make sure the intervalometer is "OFF" and the camera doors are "CLOSED" to insure that the camera will not operate when the master camera switch is moved to the "ON" position.

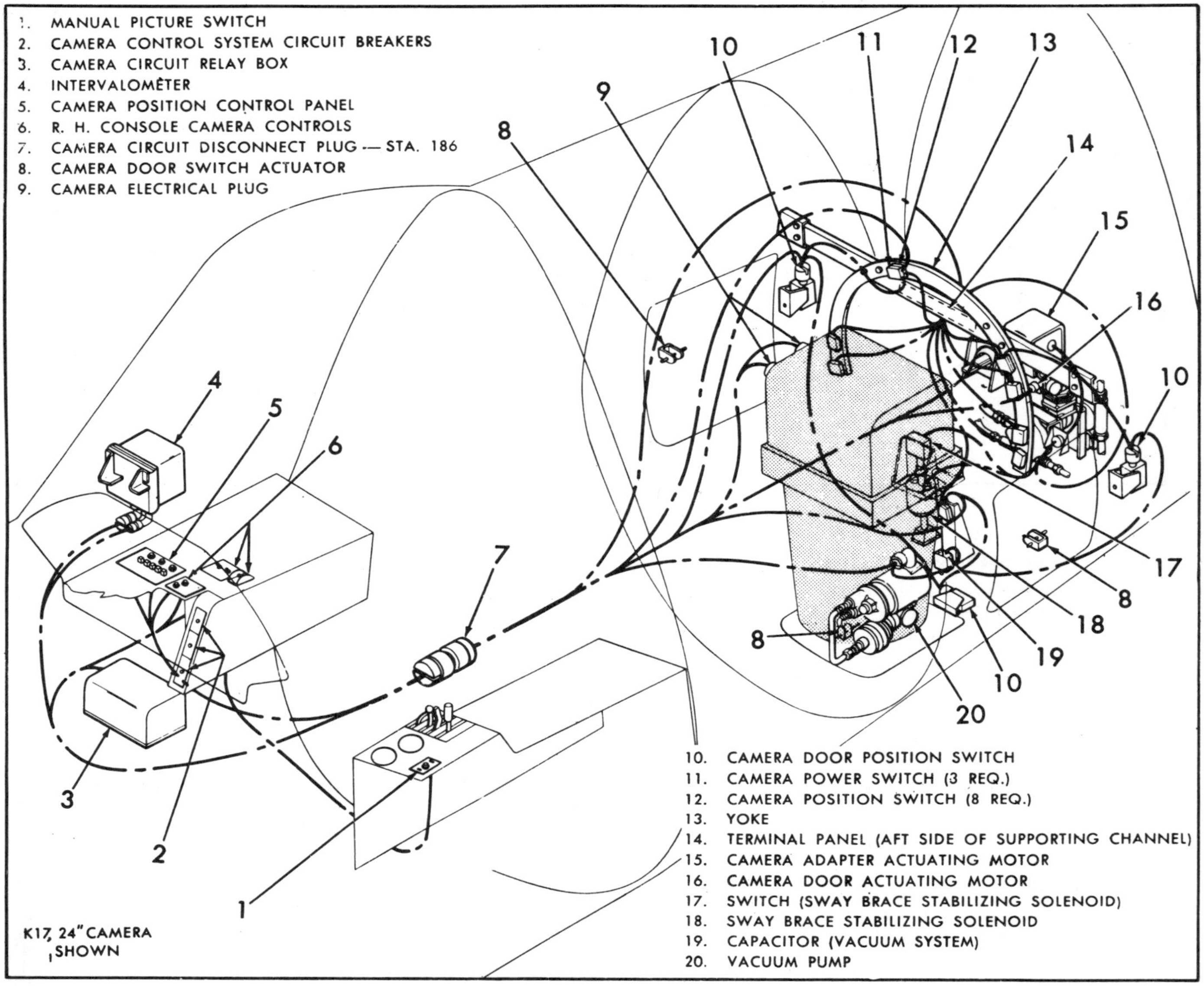

Figure C-5. Camera Electrical System

b. Turn on the master camera switch to start camera magazine heater operation.

C-12. CHECK-OFF LIST PRIOR TO CAMERA OPERATION.

C-13. PROCEDURE. To prepare the camera for operation proceed as follows:

a. Master camera switch "ON."

b. Set interval on intervalometer.

c. Select "MANUAL" or "AUTOMATIC" operation as required.

d. Open camera doors. Note door position lights. Both vertical and oblique door position lights should light to indicate doors full open.

C-14. AT TARGET AREA.

C-15. PROCEDURE. Upon reaching the area to be photographed, proceed as follows:

a. Rotate the camera to the desired position.

b. Set the setting hand on the intervalometer by depressing and turning the setting knob. Clockwise rotation of the knob decreases the interval (increases the rate) at which photographs are taken; counterclockwise rotation increases the interval (decreases the rate) at which photographs are taken. The interval hand, indicating the remaining time portion of the set interval, returns to zero in one second increments. Upon reaching zero it automatically returns to the original set position and starts again to zero. The intervalometer warning lights on the camera control panel and intervalometer will flash two seconds before exposure takes place.

Note

The required time interval may be determined from altitude-speed charts. Interval selection is dependent upon altitude, airplane speed, focal length of camera and percentage of overlap desired (see figures C-8 through C-13).

c. Open camera doors. The camera will not operate unless the doors are open.

d. Move camera control switch to desired position, "MANUAL" or "AUTOMATIC." When on "AUTOMATIC" camera will take pictures as regulated by intervalometer setting.

e. Move intervalometer toggle switch to "ON" position.

f. If intervalometer is already in operation and it is desired at any instant to start a new series of exposures, depress recycle knob. An exposure is then made immediately, and the complete cycle started again with the set interval occurring before the next exposure.

g. If, at any time before the intervalometer starts automatic operation or during the operation, an extra picture is desired, depress the extra picture switch button. Pressing this button between automatically-timed exposures will not alter the timing as shown on the dial.

Note

If the air speed, altitude, or any other variables entering into the determination of the proper interval changes, the time interval must be rechecked and the intervalometer reset if necessary.

h. To take selective pictures, move camera control switch to "MANUAL." This cuts out the automatic feature of camera system, allowing individual pictures to be taken as desired by pressing manual control switch, located on left-hand control panel.

C-17. AT COMPLETION OF PHOTOGRAPHY— "K" SERIES CAMERA.

C-18. PROCEDURE. After completion of photography, turn off intervalometer and close vertical and oblique camera doors, leaving master camera switch in the "ON" position should the equipment be required for immediate use. Turn master camera switch off before landing.

TYPE	K-17		K-18
FOCAL LENGTH	12"	24"	24"
LENS CONE ANGLE	41°	30°	42°
SHUTTER SPEEDS	1/75 1/150 1/225	1/50 1/100 1/150	1/50 1/100 1/150
DIAPHRAGM STOPS (F VALUE)	5 6.3 8 11 16 22	6 8 11 16	6 8 11 16
CYCLE OF OPERATION	3 SECONDS		5 SECONDS
TYPE MAGAZINE	A5-A	A-9	A7 OR A8
IMAGE AREA	9" x 9"		9" x 18"
FILM CAPACITY	75' - 90 EXPOSURES 150' - 180 EXPOSURES 200' - 250 EXPOSURES	390' - 485 EXPOSURES	A-7 75' - 45 EXPOSURES A-8 390' - 250 EXPOSURES
VACUUM SOURCE	OUTSIDE		OUTSIDE
CAMERA WT. LOADED	54.5 LBS.	72.0 LBS.	72.0 LBS.
CAMERA HEIGHT	22 1/2"	25 5/8"	36 7/8"
CAMERA WIDTH	16 1/2"	16 1/2"	21 5/8"
CAMERA LENGTH	14"	15"	13"

Figure C-6. Information on K-17 and K-18 Cameras

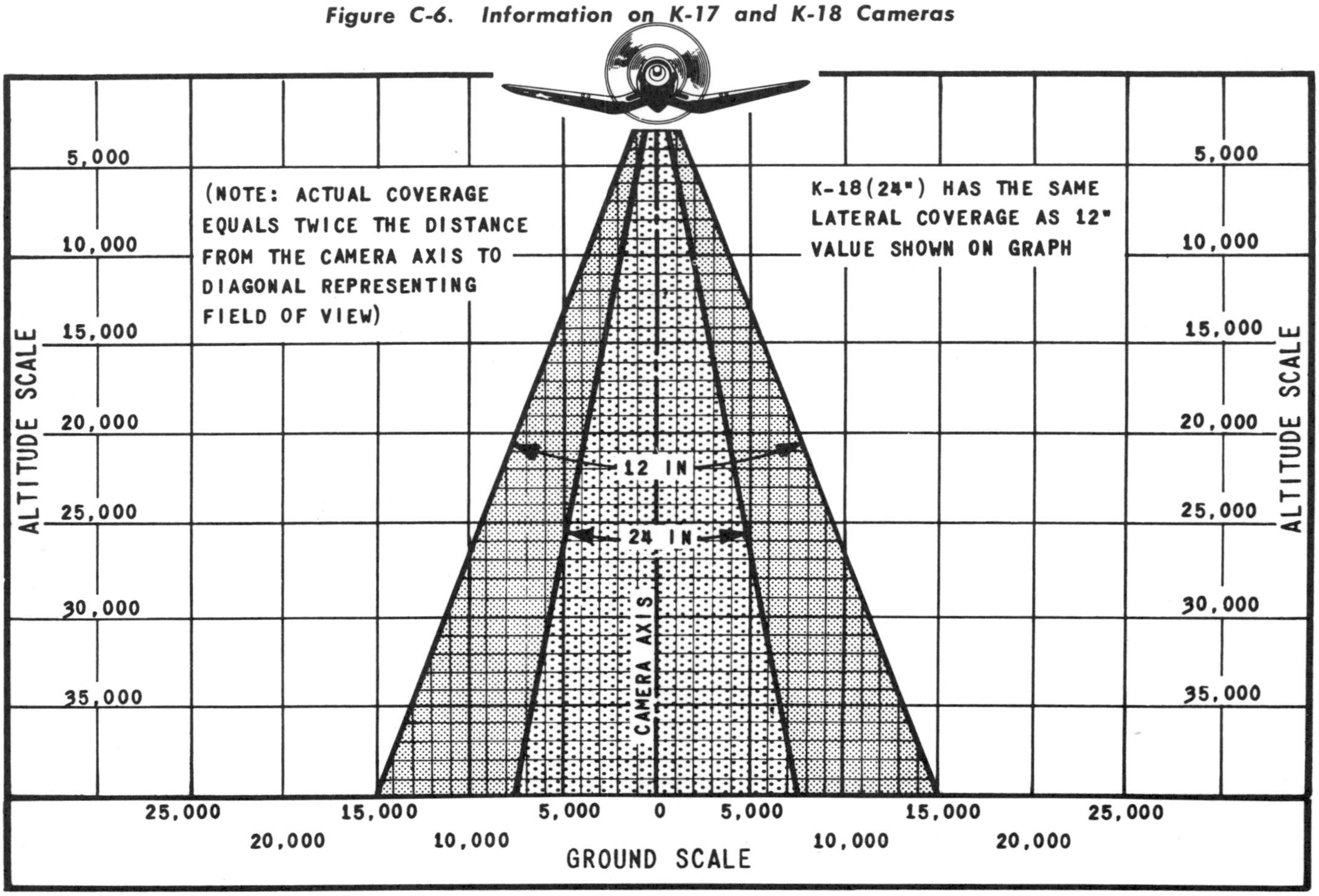

Figure C-7. Camera Coverage In Feet, K-17, 12", K-17, 24" And K-18, 24"

ALTITUDE FEET (12" FOCAL LENGTH)	KNOTS GROUND SPEED 200	220	240	260	280	300	320	340	360	380	400
1,000											
2,000											
3,000											
4,000	3	3									
5,000	4	4	3	3							
6,000	5	4	4	4	3	3	3				
7,000	6	5	5	4	4	4	3	3	3	3	
8,000	7	6	5	5	5	4	4	4	3	3	3
9,000	7	7	6	6	5	5	5	4	4	4	4
10,000	8	8	7	6	6	5	5	5	4	4	4
11,000	9	8	8	7	7	6	6	5	5	5	4
12,000	10	9	8	8	7	7	6	6	5	5	5
13,000	11	10	9	8	8	7	7	6	6	6	5
14,000	12	11	10	9	8	8	7	7	6	6	6
15,000	13	12	11	10	9	8	8	7	7	7	6
16,000	14	12	11	10	10	9	8	8	7	7	7
17,000	15	13	12	11	10	10	9	8	8	7	7
18,000	16	14	13	12	11	10	9	9	8	8	7
19,000	16	15	13	12	12	11	10	9	9	8	8
20,000	17	16	14	13	12	11	11	10	9	9	8
25,000	22	20	18	16	15	14	13	12	12	11	11
30,000	26	24	22	20	18	17	16	15	14	13	13
35,000	30	28	25	23	22	20	19	18	17	16	15
40,000	35	32	29	27	25	23	22	20	19	18	17

CAMERA WILL NOT OPERATE FASTER THAN 3 SECOND CYCLE.
60% OVERLAP WILL NOT BE OBTAINED BELOW THESE ALTITUDES.

THESE SETTINGS ARE IN SECONDS FOR 60% OVERLAP

Figure C-8. Intervalometer Settings, K-17, 12" Camera

ALTITUDE IN FEET	KNOTS GROUND SPEED 220	240	260	280	300	320	340
100	0.8	0.7	0.7	0.6	0.6	0.5	0.5
200	1.6	1.4	1.3	1.2	1.1	1.1	1.0
300	2.3	2.1	2.0	1.8	1.7	1.6	1.5
400	3.1	2.9	2.6	2.5	2.3	2.2	2.0
500	3.9	3.6	3.3	3.1	2.9	2.7	2.5

——-—— MINIMUM ALTITUDES TO STOP MOTION AT MAXIMUM SHUTTER SPEED.

-——-—- MINIMUM ALTITUDE FOR 60% OVERLAP WITH SHORTEST INTERVAL AVAILABLE (3 SECONDS).

Figure C-9. Intervalometer Setting In Seconds, K-17, 24" Camera, 3° Oblique

ALTITUDE FEET (24" FOCAL LENGTH)	KNOTS GROUND SPEED 200	220	240	260	280	300	320	340	360	380	400
1000											
2000											
3000											
4000											
5000											
6000											
7000	3										
8000	3	3									
9000	4	3	3	3							
10000	4	4	3	3	3						
11000	4	4	4	3	3	3	3				
12000	5	4	4	4	3	3	3	3			
13000	5	5	4	4	4	3	3	3	3	3	
14000	6	5	5	4	4	4	3	3	3	3	3
15000	6	6	5	5	4	4	4	3	3	3	3
16000	7	6	5	5	5	4	4	4	3	3	3
17000	7	6	6	6	5	5	4	4	4	4	3
18000	8	7	6	6	5	5	5	4	4	4	4
19000	8	7	7	6	6	5	5	4	4	4	4
20000	8	8	7	6	6	5	5	5	4	4	4
25000	11	10	9	8	7	7	6	6	6	5	5
30000	13	12	11	10	9	8	8	7	7	7	6
35000	15	14	12	11	11	10	9	9	8	8	7
40000	17	16	14	13	12	11	11	10	9	9	8

K-17 CAMERA WILL NOT OPERATE FASTER THAN 3 SECOND CYCLE.
K-18 CAMERA WILL NOT OPERATE FASTER THAN 5 SECOND CYCLE.
60% OVERLAP WILL NOT BE OBTAINED BELOW THESE ALTITUDES.

THESE SETTINGS ARE IN SECONDS FOR 60% OVERLAP

Figure C-10. Intervalometer Settings, K-17 And K-18, 24" Cameras

MINIMUM ALTITUDE PERMITTED TO OBTAIN 60% FORWARD OVERLAP AT MAXIMUM OPERATING SPEED OF CAMERA

GROUND SPEED KNOTS	200	210	220	230	240	250	260	270	280	290	300	310	320	330	340	350
K-18, 24" 5 SEC. CYCLE	11300	11900	12450	13050	13600	14150	14750	15300	15850	16450	17000	17550	18150	18700	19250	19830
K-17, 24" 3 SEC. CYCLE	6800	7140	7480	7820	8160	8500	8840	9180	9520	9860	10200	10540	10880	11220	11560	11900
K-17, 12" 3 SEC. CYCLE	3400	3570	3740	3910	4080	4250	4420	4590	4760	4930	5100	5270	5440	5610	5780	5950

MINIMUM ALTITUDE PERMITTED TO STOP MOTION AT MAXIMUM SHUTTER SPEED OF CAMERA

GROUND SPEED KNOTS	200	210	220	230	240	250	260	270	280	290	300	310	320	330	340	350
K-18, 24" LENS 1/150 SEC.	5390	5660	5930	6200	6470	6740	7010	7280	7550	7820	8090	8360	8630	8900	9170	9440
K-17, 24" LENS 1/150 SEC.	5390	5660	5930	6200	6470	6740	7010	7280	7550	7820	8090	8360	8630	8900	9170	9440
K-17, 12" LENS 1/225 SEC.	1790	1875	1960	2050	2150	2240	2330	2420	2510	2600	2695	2780	2870	2960	3045	3135

Figure C-11. Minimum Altitudes—"K" Series Camera

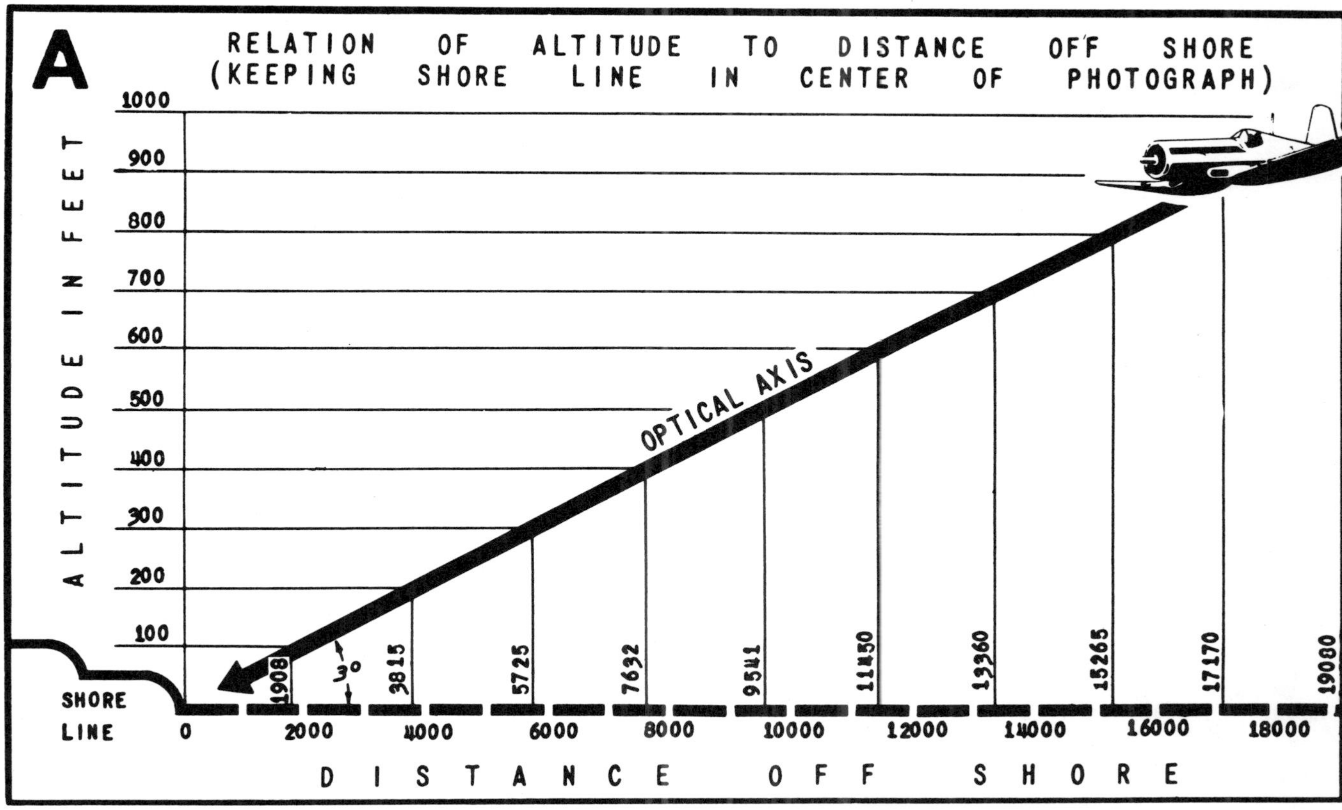

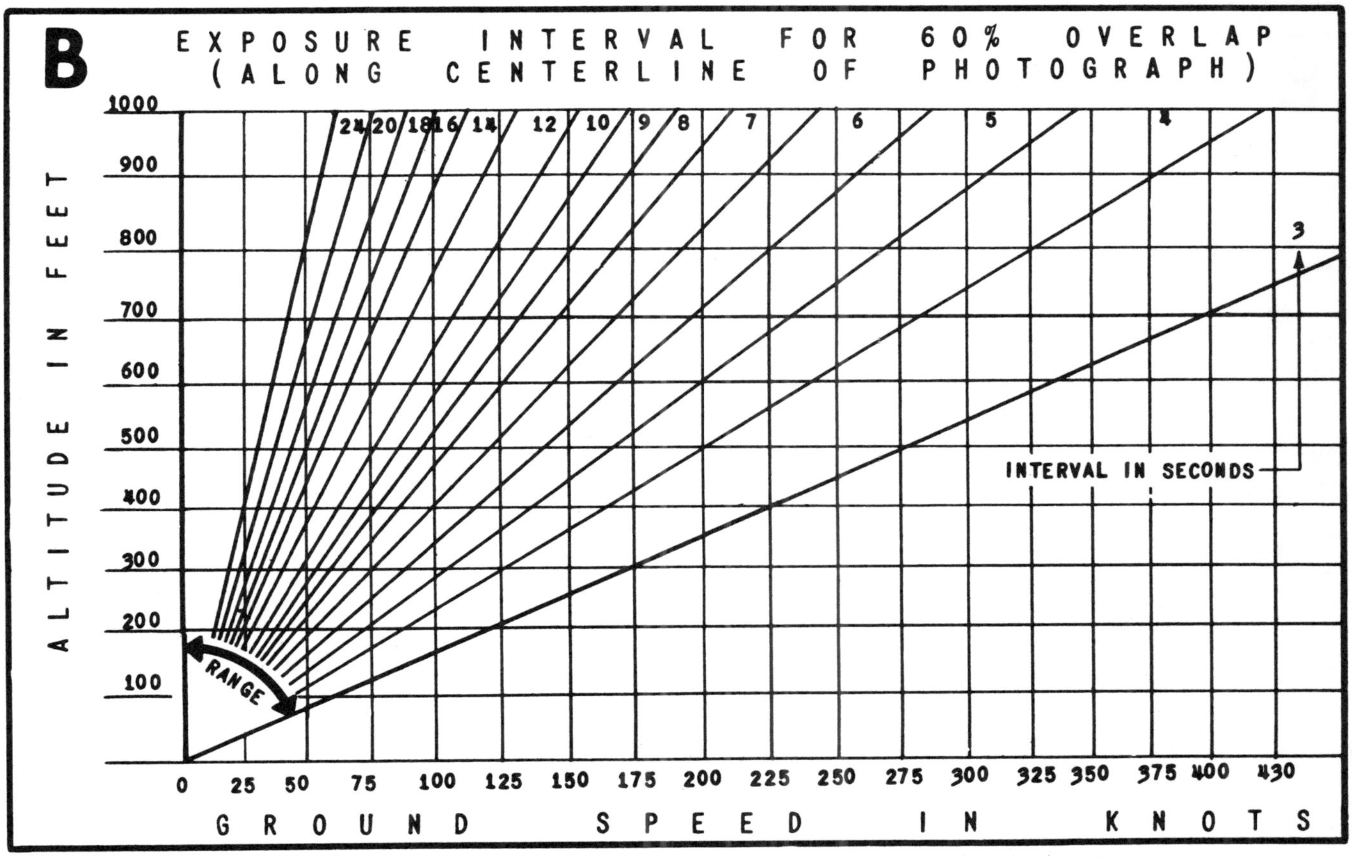

Figure C-12. Oblique K-17, 24" Camera Installation Depressed 3°

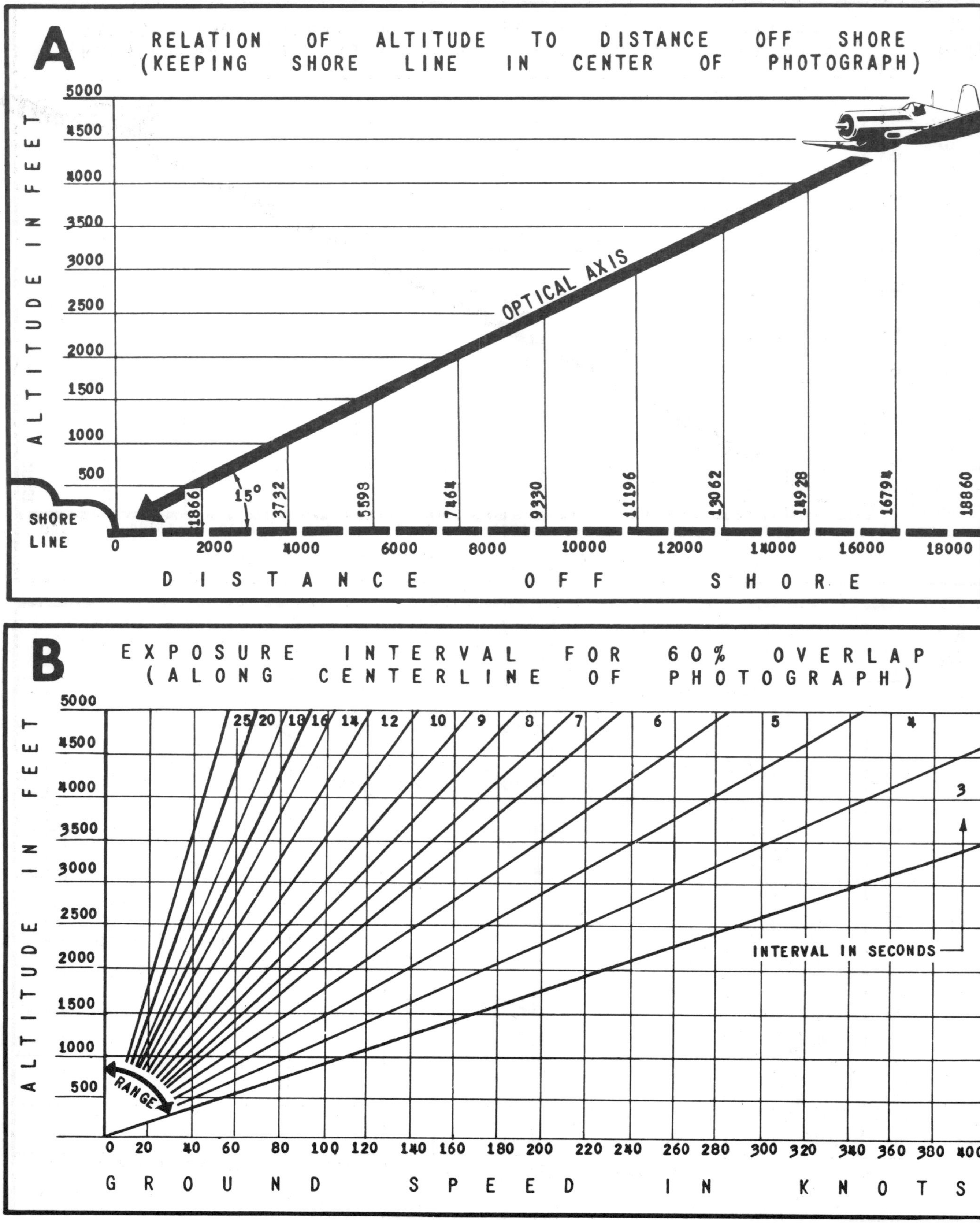

Figure C-13. Oblique K-17, 24" Camera Installation Depressed 15°

C-19. S-7S CONTINUOUS STRIP CAMERA INSTALLATION.

C-20. GENERAL. *(See figure C-14.)* The F4U-5P airplane is equipped to accommodate either the "K" series aerial cameras or the S-7S continuous strip camera. Provisions for camera installation are such that conversion from one camera installation to another can be readily accomplished in the field. Refer to paragraph C-2 for a more detailed description of these provisions. For information on the "K" series cameras, refer to paragraphs C-6 through C-18.

C-21. S-7S REMOTE CONTROL ASSEMBLY. *(See figure C-15.)* The S-7S continuous strip camera installation in the F4U-5P is controlled by means of a remote control assembly. This unit consists of a film speed indicator, a film footage indicator, a film speed light, two synchronizing lights, a camera switch, a servo power switch, an amplifier power switch, and a switch for manual synchronization of the film and image speeds. The control assembly is located at the upper right-hand side of the instrument panel, replacing the intervalometer installation used on the "K" series camera installation. Ordinarily, film speed is controlled automatically by the servo synchronizer.

Note

When the amplifier switch is placed in the "OFF" position, film speed may be preset to any value comparable to indicated airspeed by operating the spring-loaded "FAST-SLOW" switch. Once a setting is obtained (by holding the switch until the film speed dial indicates the desired setting) the film speed will remain constant until the "FAST-SLOW" switch is again deflected. To obtain the correct film speed setting when controlling the camera manually, it is suggested that the following formula be used: $S = \frac{22FV}{15H}$, where—

S = film speed; inches/second
F = lens focal length; inches
V = indicated airspeed; mph
H = absolute altitude; feet.

C-22. S-7S CIRCUIT BREAKERS. An S-7S continuous strip camera circuit breaker is located just aft of the master camera switch on the right-hand console. A radio altimeter circuit breaker is located just forward of the master camera switch. (See figure C-15.)

C-23. S-7S OPERATION. When the master camera switch, located on the right-hand control shelf, is closed, power from the plus bus flows to the camera door switch located just outboard of the master camera switch, and to the camera door position indicating lights. When the camera door switch is placed in the "OPEN" position the door actuating mechanism is energized to slide the doors open. When the doors are fully open they close master switches which light the amber door position indicating lights. The camera circuit is controlled by the switches on the remote control unit on the instrument panel. The S-7S camera motor and photo recorder are energized by closing the "CAMERA" switch. The amplifier is energized by closing the "AMPLIFIER" switch. The servo unit is energized by closing the "SERVO" switch. Power for all these switches is drawn from a plus bus and flows through the S-7S continuous strip camera circuit breaker. Electrical leads from the scanner and generator transmit electrical pulses to the amplifier. The amplifier controls the relays, located on the right-hand side of the radio deck, which cause the servo either to increase or to decrease the film speed.

C-24. PREFLIGHT CHECK—S-7S CAMERA.

C-25. PROCEDURE. After the camera has been installed and the magazine loaded, check the operation of the entire installation as follows:

Note

Before operating the S-7S continuous strip camera make sure that the vacuum pump breaker switch has been pulled out.

a. Turn on the master camera switch located on the right-hand console.

b. Open the sliding camera door by moving camera door control switch to "OPEN" position.

c. Check the door operation.

d. Turn motor on and see that feed mechanism is operating properly.

e. Open access in the bottom of the photo recorder and check to see that bulbs are on.

f. After the leader has been run off, stop the motor and set the film footage indicators, one in the cockpit and one in the camera compartment, to indicate the number of feet of unexposed film in the camera.

g. Close camera doors and turn off master camera switch.

Note

It will be necessary for two men to make the above check, one to operate the switches and one to watch the camera.

C-26. CHECK-OFF LIST PRIOR TO CAMERA OPERATION—S-7S CAMERA.

C-27. PROCEDURE. Observe the following steps prior to camera operation:

a. Master camera switch "ON."

b. Amplifier power switch should be turned on at least five minutes prior to turning on camera.

c. Open camera doors, noting door position lights. Door position lights should indicate doors full open.

1. Camera Remote Control Unit
2. Sonne Camera Circuit Breaker
3. Amplifier Electrical Plugs
4. Camera Amplifier
5. Photo Observer Camera
6. Free Air Temp Bulb
7. Flasher and Relay Assembly
8. Photo Observer
9. Photo Observer Electrical Plug
10. Photo Observer Instruments
11. Pitot and Static Lines to Photo Observer
12. Sonne Camera Generator
13. Sonne Camera Servo Unit and Power Switch
14. Sonne Camera
15. Sonne Camera Relay Unit
16. Relay and Junction Box
17. Disconnects at Station 186
18. Scanner

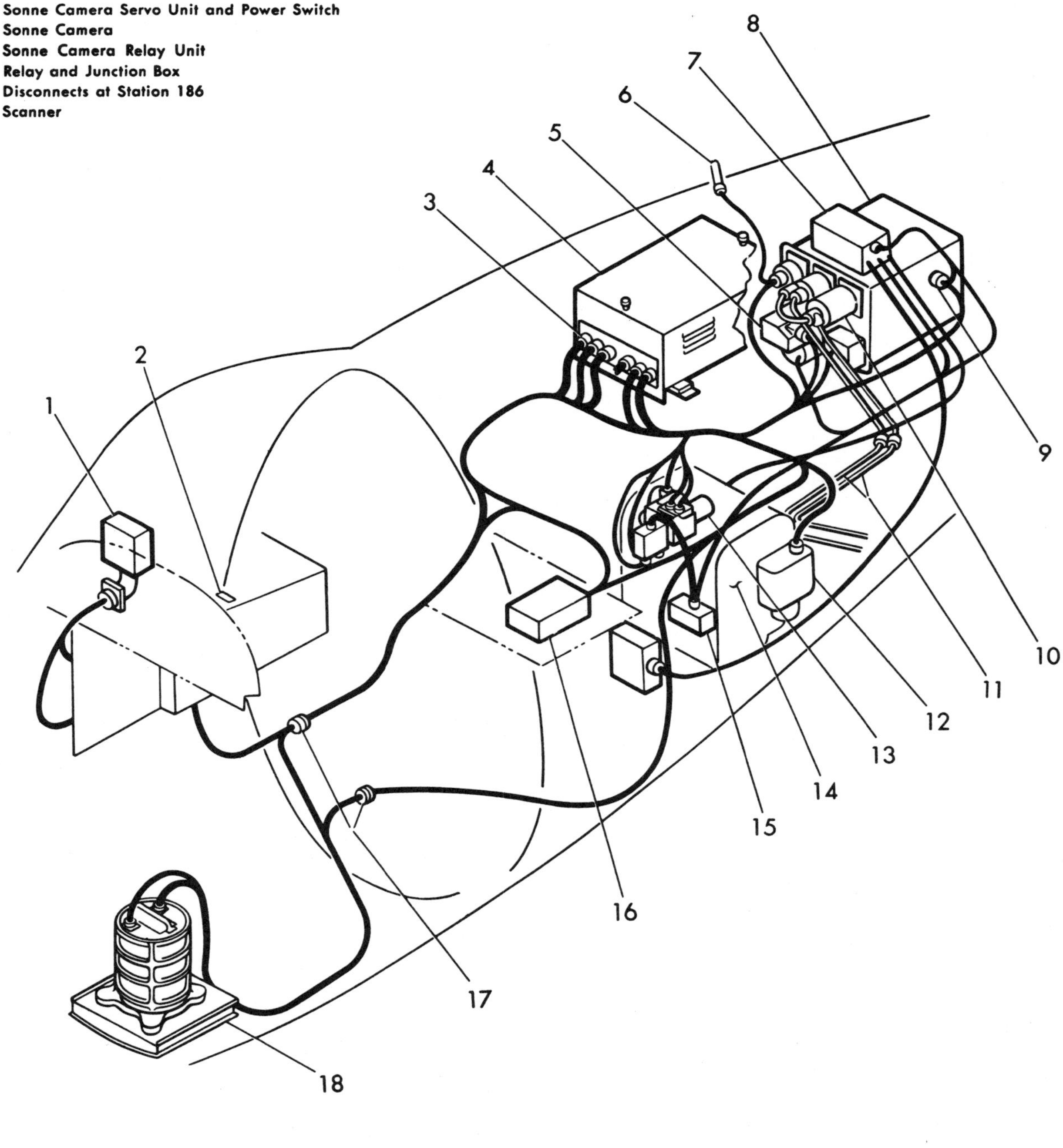

Figure C-14. S-7S Camera Installation Equipment

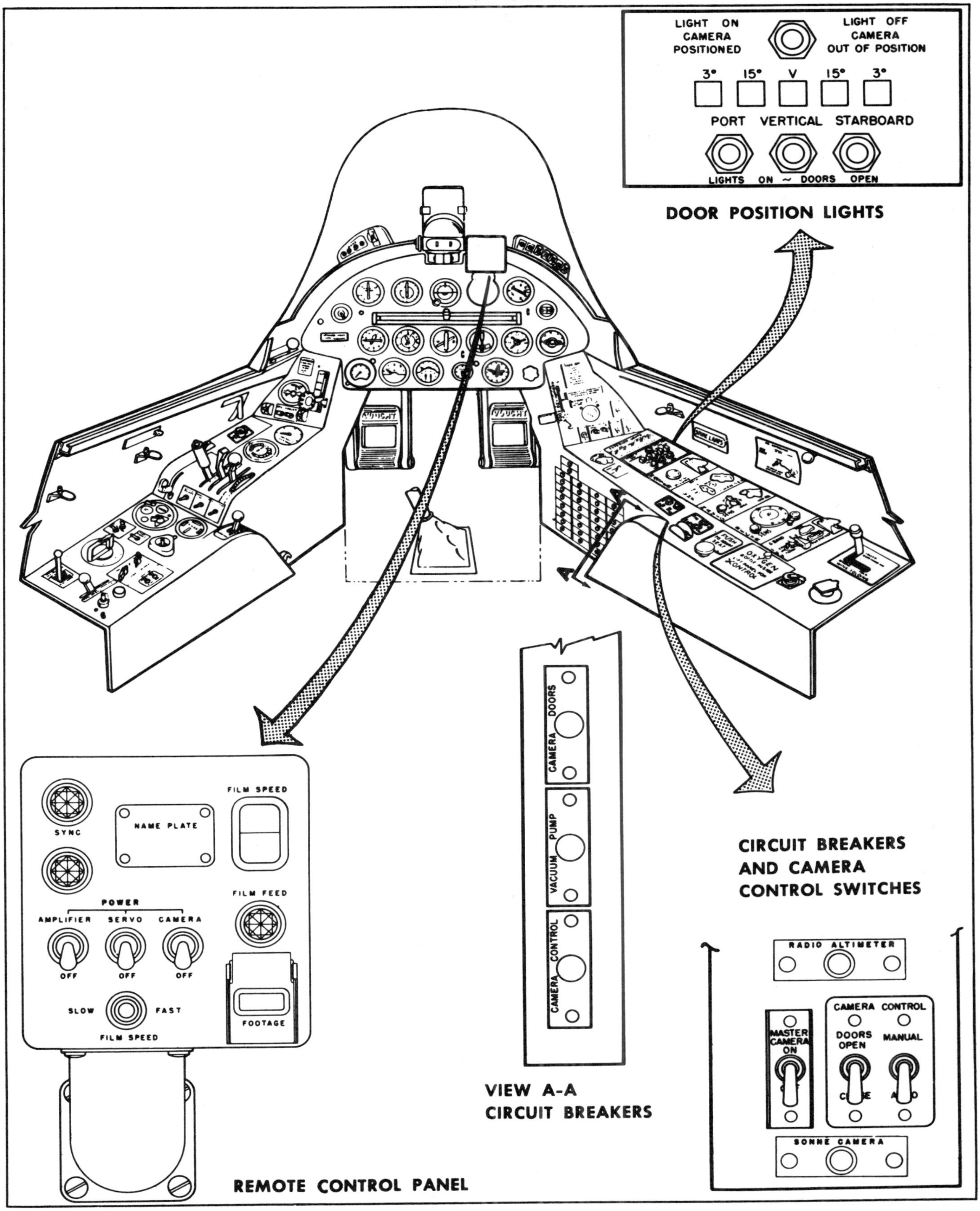

Figure C-15. S-7S Camera Cockpit Controls

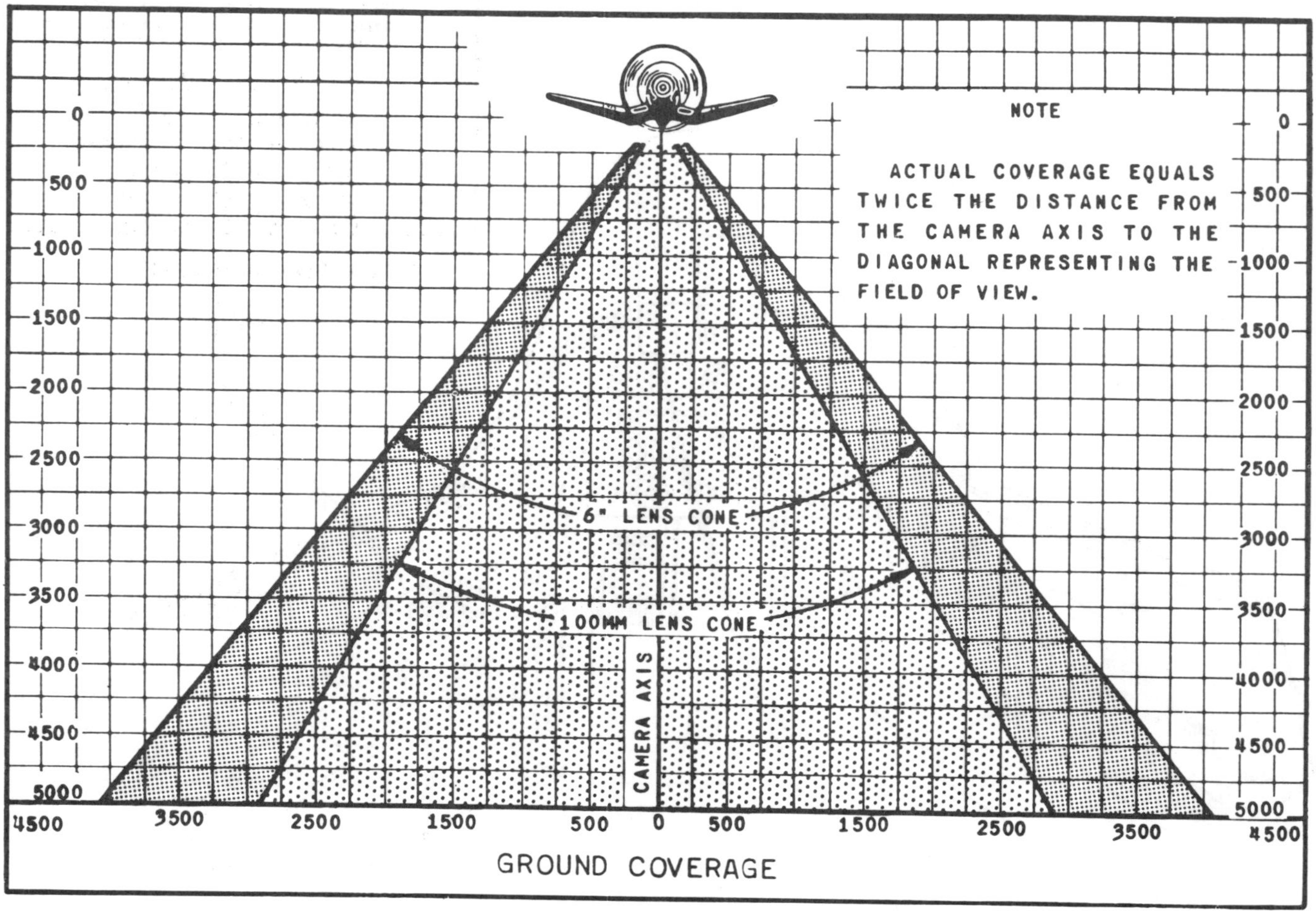

Figure C-16. S-7S Camera Ground Coverage in Feet

CAUTION

Make certain that master camera switch is on and that camera doors are open prior to closing camera switch on remote control unit. The S-7S continuous strip camera can be operated with doors closed. *DO NOT OPERATE CAMERA UNLESS DOOR POSITION LIGHTS INDICATE THAT DOORS ARE OPEN.*

C-28. AT TARGET AREA—S-7S CAMERA.

C-29. PROCEDURE. Upon reaching the area to be photographed, observe the following procedure:

a. Turn camera and servo power switch to "ON." This operation should be performed at least 15 seconds prior to reaching any specific features to be photographed.

b. Make sure that altitude corresponds to camera settings. (This information must be obtained prior to take-off.)

c. Observe indicator lights. The green light indicates that the film speed is below the image speed and is being increased by the servo unit. The red light indicates that the film speed is above the image speed and is being decreased by the servo unit. When the airplane is flying level at a uniform speed, the light should flash continuously from green to red.

d. The film footage counter registers the number of feet of unexposed film remaining. In addition to this instrument, the control unit is also equipped with a green pilot light which remains on as long as film is feeding through the camera and which goes off as soon as the film supply is exhausted or when the camera stops.

C-30. AT COMPLETION OF PHOTOGRAPHY—S-7S CAMERA.

C-31. PROCEDURE. After complete of photography, turn camera switch, servo power switch, and amplifier switch "OFF." Close camera doors and turn master camera switch to "OFF."

Appendix IV

WINTERIZATION EQUIPMENT

D–1. WINTERIZATION EQUIPMENT—GENERAL.

D–2. DESCRIPTION. The F4U-5NL is a winterized version of the F4U-5N airplane. It is basically the same as the F4U-5 airplane except that it includes provisions for both night fighter and cold weather operation. The winterized airplane is identified by the installation of deicer boots on the wings and empennage, and deicer shoes on the propeller blades. The winterization equipment can be divided into four individually controlled systems as follows: (1) Wing and empennage deicing system controlled by a switch on the left-hand console; (2) propeller deicing system controlled by a rheostat on the right-hand cowl; (3) windshield deicing system controlled by a switch on the left-hand cowl; and (4) an independent anti-blackout suit system controlled by a switch-breaker on the left-hand console.

D–3. FLIGHT CHARACTERISTICS. The flying characteristics of the F4U-5NL airplane when the boots are inoperative are basically the same as those of the F4U-5N airplane. When the boots are operative, control disturbances are negligible at airspeeds between 105 and 240 knots. With boots inflated, the airplane in the clean condition will roll to the right at airspeeds above 240 knots; at airspeeds less than 105 knots the airplane will roll to the left first and then to the right. In the landing condition, control is satisfactory down to 80 knots with power on; at speeds lower than 80 knots, control effectiveness is reduced, and rapid and large amounts of lateral stick displacement will be required to maintain the wings level. Flight at speeds lower than those specified here should be avoided when the boots are operating. Landings and dives should not be attempted with the deicer boots operating. If necessary to land with the deicer boots operating, avoid a slow approach.

D–4. MAXIMUM PERMISSIBLE INDICATED AIRSPEED AND ACCELERATIONS. The maximum permissible airspeeds and accelerations at various altitudes with deicing boots inoperative are shown on figure D–1 and with boots operative on figure D–3. These limits are for a gross weight of 12,000 pounds. For other weights, the permissible accelerations are such as to maintain a constant product of gross weight and acceleration except that 6.5 g's positive and 3.3 g's negative should not be exceeded.

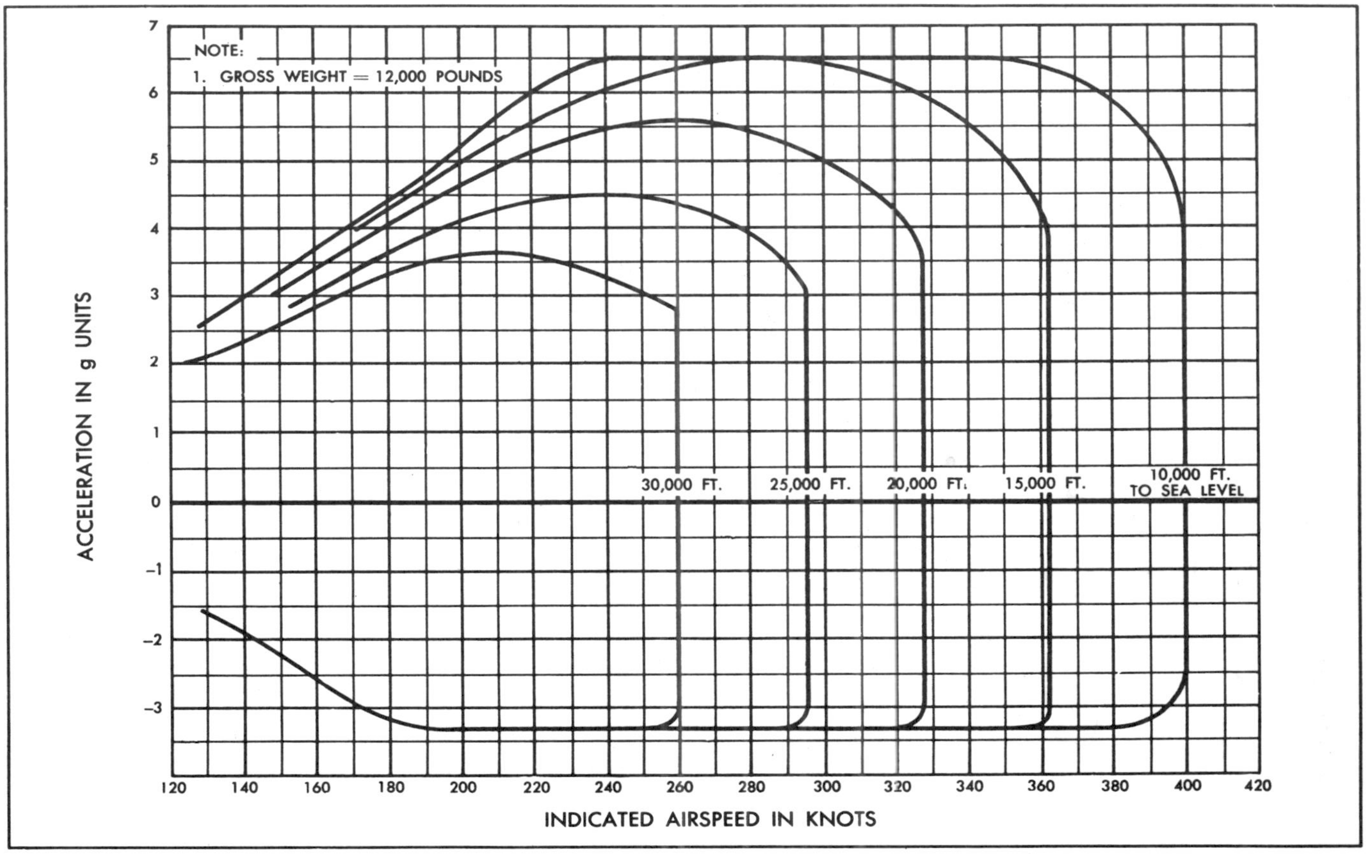

Figure D-1. Operating Flight Strength Diagram—Boots Inoperative

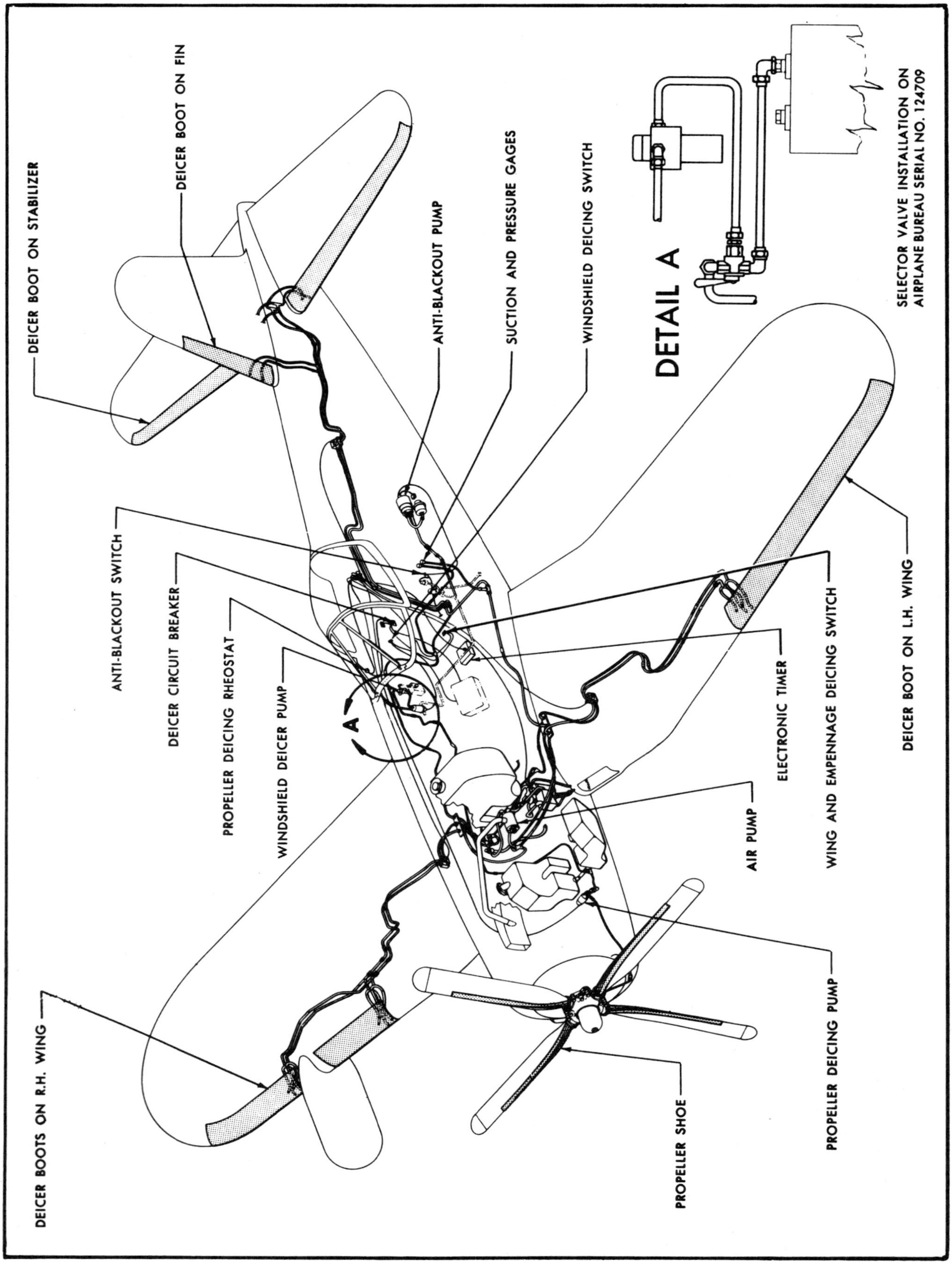

Figure D-2. F4U-5NL Winterized Airplane

D–5. WING AND EMPENNAGE DEICING SYSTEM.

D–6. DESCRIPTION. The wing and empennage deicing system consists of pneumatically operated rubber boots mounted on the leading edges of the wing and empennage. Pressure and suction for operation of the boots are provided by an engine-driven air pump. A switch located on the left-hand control panel controls the operation of the boots through an electronic timer and distributor valves. Alternate inflation and deflation of parallel tubes contained in the boots causes a rippling movement which breaks up any ice that may form on the leading edges of the wings and empennage.

D–7. DEICER CIRCUIT BREAKER. The deicer push-pull type circuit breaker completes the 28-volt power supply to all of the deicer switches when the button is pushed in or closed. The button can be pulled out or opened when there is an overheated or malfunctioning circuit. The deicer circuit breaker is located on the aft portion of the right-hand console on F4U-5NL airplanes Bureau Serial No. 124504 through 124560 and is mounted on the vertical circuit breaker panel on F4U-5NL airplanes Bureau Serial No. 124666 and subsequent.

D–8. DEICER BOOTS SWITCH. The "DEICER BOOTS" switch is located on the throttle quadrant of the left-hand control panel and is a three-position "ON–OFF–COMBAT OFF" toggle switch. A two-position "ON–OFF" switch mounted on the right-hand control panel is used on airplanes Bureau Serial No. 124504 through 124509. The deicer boots switch supplies power to the electronic timer. When the toggle is in the "ON" position, the timer operates on preset 60-to-65-second cycles after a 20-second warm-up period. The operation of this cycle is as follows:

Cycle Breakdown (seconds)	*Operating Condition*	*Cumulative Time (seconds)* *First Cycle*	*Succeeding Cycles*
20 (approx.)	Warm-up—pressure indication—0 psi	20	
5	Fill manifold—pressure indication—15 psi	25	5
10	Wing boots pulsating—pressure indication—15 psi	35	15
10	Tail boots pulsating—pressure indication—15 psi	45	25
10	Boots inoperative—pressure indication—15 psi	55	35
25-30	Boots inoperative—pressure indication—0 psi	80-85	60-65

When the toggle is moved to "OFF," the timer will finish any previously started cycle before turning off. When in the "COMBAT OFF" position, the system is stopped immediately.

Note

Use "OFF" for non-combat flying when deicing is not needed.

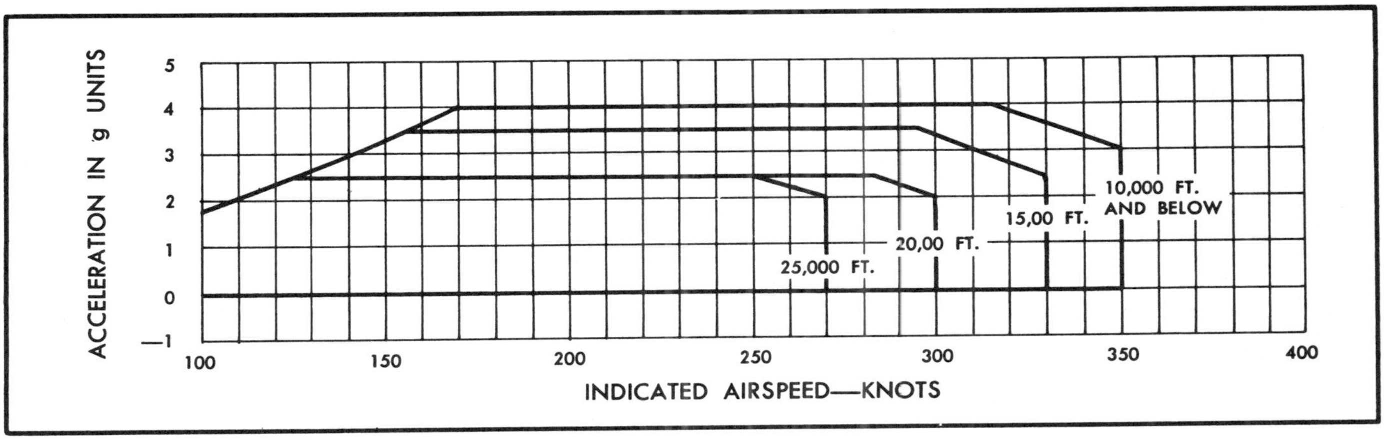

Figure D-3. Maximum Permissible Indicated Airspeed and Accelerations—Boots Operating

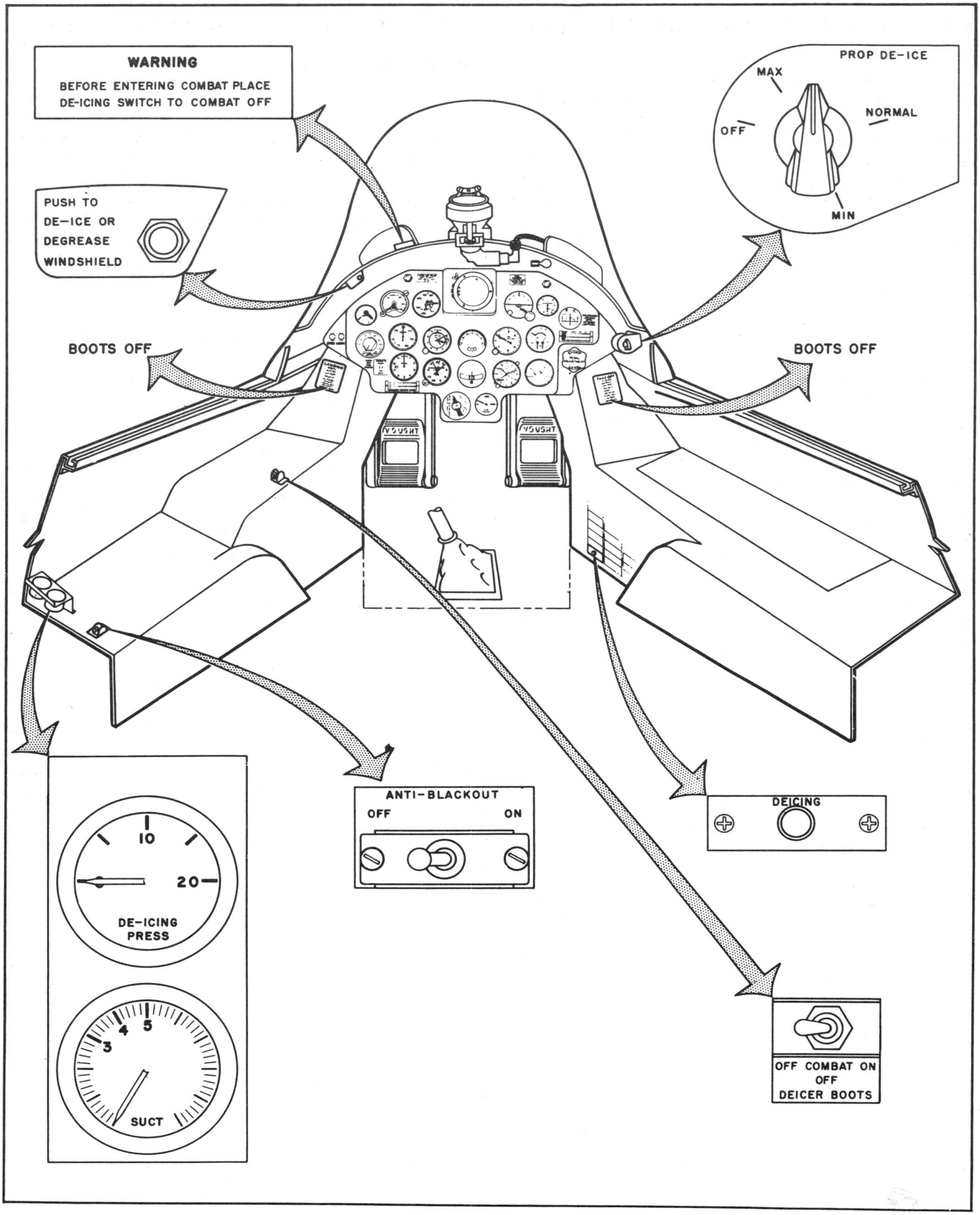

Figure D–4. Cockpit—View Looking Forward

D-9. PRESSURE AND SUCTION GAGES. Two gages mounted on the aft portion of the left-hand console indicate air pressure and suction in the wing and empennage deicing system. The pressure gage should read approximately 15 psi and should indicate pressure only when the system is operating. The suction gage should indicate 4 to 5 inches Hg. at all times when the engine is operating. However, at speeds above 180 knots (approximately), the suction may read as high as 7 inches Hg.

D-10. PROPELLER DEICING SYSTEM.

D-11. DESCRIPTION. The propeller deicing system consists of deicer shoes mounted on each propeller blade and a fluid metering pump which is controlled by a rheostat located on the right-hand cowl. The fluid metering pump draws anti-icing fluid from the water injection tanks and pumps it into a slinger ring mounted on the propeller hub. Centrifugal force carries the fluid from the slinger ring outward through ports to troughs and shoes installed on each propeller blade. The propeller shoes are grooved to hold the fluid and carry it outward over the blade surface, thereby preventing the formation of ice on the propeller blade.

D-12. OPERATION OF PROPELLER DEICING RHEOSTAT. The propeller deicing rheostat is located on the right-hand cowl. It contains a switch element for the "OFF" position. Clockwise rotation of the rheostat varies the pump speeds and controls the amount of anti-icing fluid delivered to the propeller blade. Turn the rheostat to "MAX" for 1 minute, then turn to "NORMAL."

D-13. WINDSHIELD DEICING SYSTEM.

D-14. DESCRIPTION. The windshield deicing system consists of three atomizer tubes installed on the windshield. A fluid metering pump draws anti-icing fluid from the water injection tanks and pumps it to the windshield. The pump is controlled by a "PUSH TO DEICE OR DEGREASE WINDSHIELD" switch mounted on the left-hand cowl.

D-15. OPERATION OF WINDSHIELD DEICING SYSTEM. A "PUSH TO DEICE OR DEGREASE WINDSHIELD" switch is located on the left-hand cowl. The windshield deicer pump will operate as long as this switch is held in.

D-16. ANTI-BLACKOUT SUIT SYSTEM.

D-17. The anti-blackout suit system is essentially the same as on other F4U-5 airplanes (refer to paragraph 4-49) except that the pump is electrically operated and is controlled by a switch-breaker mounted on the left-hand console.

CAUTION

The anti-blackout switch-breaker must be in the "ON" position for operation of the anti-blackout suit.